The Cooking of Vienna's Empire

TIME LIFE BOOKS ®

The Cooking of Vienna's Empire

by

Joseph Wechsberg

and the Editors of

TIME-LIFE BOOKS

photographed by Fred Lyon

TIME-LIFE BOOKS, ALEXANDRIA, VIRGINIA

THE AUTHOR: Joseph Wechsberg (above, right) has long been famous for his articles on culinary matters in such magazines as The New Yorker, Holiday, Gourmet and Esquire, and for his books, Blue Trout and Black Truffles, The Best Things in Life and Dining at the Pavillon. Mr. Wechsberg writes in four languages—Czech, German, French and English. He has been a violinist, a lawyer, a croupier in Nice and a soldier in the Czech and American armies. Among his many enthusiasms are food, good cooking and good eating.

THE PHOTOGRAPHER: Fred Lyon (above, left) also photographed The Cooking of Italy for the FOODS OF THE WORLD library. For the present book, he traveled throughout the old Austro-Hungarian Empire, then spent a month taking photographs in the FOODS OF THE WORLD kitchen.

THE CONSULTING EDITOR: The late Michael Field relinquished a career as a concert pianist to become one of America's first-rank food experts and teachers of cooking. He conducted a school in Manhattan and wrote many articles on the culinary arts for various magazines. His books include Michael Field's Cooking School and Michael Field's Culinary Classics and Improvisations.

THE CONSULTANTS: Three additional experts have advised on their specialties. Above, left to right: George Lang is president of the George Lang Corporation, former vice president of Restaurant Associates Inc. and former director of the Four Seasons Restaurant in New York. He traveled through Hungary in connection with this volume, and is also a consultant for several other books of this series. The late Paula Peck, author of The Art of Fine Baking, advised on baking. Paul Steindler, owner of two restaurants in New York, was the consultant for the Austrian, Czechoslovakian and Yugoslavian dishes.

THE COVER: The Spanische Windtorte; recipe is on pages 196 and 197.

Contents

The Recipe Booklet that accompanies this volume has been designed for use in the kitchen. It contains all of the 99 recipes printed here plus 5 more. It also has a wipe-clean cover and a spiral binding so that it can either stand up or lie flat when open.

The Marvelous Food and Cooking of the Countries along the Danube

There is an old proverb that every country gets the cuisine it deserves. When gastronomy is everybody's favorite indoor sport, the results can be spectacular. It was no accident that Demel's superb *Konditorei* (pastry shop) in Vienna reached its apogee under Franz Josef—an emperor who not only loved pastry but understood the art of making it. From the greatest to the humblest, Austrians have always been passionately interested in food and its preparation. Who but the Viennese would think up so many ways just to serve *Schlagobers* (whipped cream) with coffee?

The sprawling Austro-Hungarian Empire, which was ruled for so long by the Habsburgs, no longer exists save in the kitchens of the areas that once made up this remarkable domain. Of the culinary contributors the most important were those encompassed by present-day Austria, Hungary, Yugoslavia and Czechoslovakia.

Each section influenced the others—to the point where it is often impossible to tell which dish originated where, or who copied whom. At the same time, each little national group clung fiercely to its individual identity, jealously preserving its own characteristics.

To complicate matters further, much of today's Yugoslavia, Czechoslovakia and Rumania had been part of the ancient kingdom of Hungary from the year 1000. When the Habsburgs conquered Hungary in the 17th Century, these lands became part of the Empire.

Thus it was mainly the interplay of Austrian and Hungarian cooking that shaped the Danubian cuisine.

The powerful, affluent capital of the Austro-Hungarian Empire was Vienna. The farther east and south one went from Vienna, the poorer was the country. Naturally the Serbs, Bohemians, Moravians, Croatians, Slovenes and Hungarians had to devise economical methods of using expensive ingredients, meat or poultry, or do without them altogether.

The same dish was bound to taste quite different in Budapest or Vienna. Perhaps due to their mysterious Oriental origins Hungarians use more spices. According to one legend, Franz Josef, Emperor of Austria and King of Hungary, was enjoying chicken *paprikás* on his private train en route to Austria. When they crossed the border, he suddenly felt ill. The engineer promptly reversed the train, and no sooner had they reached Hungarian soil again than Franz Josef recovered. Chicken *paprikás* was perfect for the King of Hungary but too spicy for the Austrian Emperor!

The Empire is gone, but many of the ancient practices survive unchanged, especially in Hungary. When Fred Lyon, the photographer of this book, and I traveled through remote Hungarian villages, we saw gingerbread makers still using their great-great-grandfathers' original molds, medieval ox-roasting on feast days, a mysterious practice of foretelling the coming year from roasted onion segments, and other archaic crafts and customs. Strange anachronisms in a "People's Democracy"!

Hundreds of small, charming peasant-style *csárdas* (inns)—offering a few dishes and wines—dot the Hungarian countryside. The fishermen's *csárdas* serve a robust fish soup *(halászlé)* made from a variety of river fishes. *Csárda* originally meant a rough country inn for shepherds and highwaymen. At night the shepherds slept on the drinking-room benches, using their long, fur-lined capes for pillow and cover. Gypsies played for their supper—and sometimes for their lives. Today the gypsy still woos the guest with his fiddling, but you won't run into any highwaymen—unless the manager should try to charge you twice for your wine.

Czechoslovakia had lost much of its old culinary eminence in recent years, but at Montreal's Expo 67, the Czechs demonstrated beautifully that the talent is still there (despite man- or state-made obstacles). Hopefully the situation inside the country may improve before long.

Yugoslavia, reflecting its diverse components, makes a tastier *musaka* than does Greece, a better-textured *kačkavalj* cheese than the south Italian *caciocavallo* to which it is related, and many interesting variations on other national originals. But on the whole, the cuisine of Yugoslavia has not yet achieved a separate identity, except in the art of grilling, where the Serbians are truly masters.

The Danube, that muddy, fascinating, capricious old river, has always provided this region with fish, poetry, trade, music, transport, romance and quarrels. Both the romance and the quarrels linger. Ask where a particular dish originated, and no two Danubians will agree. An Austrian will tell you *Nockerln* are Austrian. A Hungarian will shrug and retort, What! *Nokedli* are obviously Hungarian! A Czech is equally certain that *noky* are a Czech creation, the Serbs that it is Serbian. (It happens that all these dumplings actually stem from the Italian *gnocchi*. Does it matter? As culinary cousins, they are all delicious and individual.)

Now that you are embarking on Mr. Wechsberg's engrossing journey through Danubian cuisine, you will—happily—soon be qualified to argue about, as well as enjoy this fascinating culinary repertoire. The Austro-Hungarian cuisine, in all its rich variety, is one of the last surviving glories of a vanished empire.

—*George Lang*

I

In the Days of the Old Empire

Half a century ago Austria and Hungary still formed the core of an empire that had lasted more than 600 years—from 1282 until 1918. At one time the Habsburg Empire reached from the borders of Czarist Russia to the shores of the Adriatic Sea, and consisted of more than a dozen nationalities with over 51 million people speaking 16 different languages.

In the 18th and 19th Centuries Austria-Hungary produced some of the finest literature and music the world has known. Names such as Schnitzler, Liszt, Strauss and Mahler are as familiar in America as they are in Central Europe. Yet it is for something other than those men and their particular arts that the Habsburg Empire won its special immortality. For the Old Empire, as it is often called, was the center of that marvelous Baroque splendor wherein the traditional, mannered Old World civilization reached its apogee in wine, women and song, in nostalgia and bittersweet.

Today the Old Empire is no more. Austria is a small, neutral country the size of the State of Maine, with a population matching that of New York City. It lies between the democratic West and the Communist East. Today Hungary goes under the name of Hungarian People's Republic. Czechoslovakia and Yugoslavia, once so necessary a part of the Empire, are now Communist states whose boundaries enclose the old imperial provinces of Slovakia, Bohemia, Moravia, Silesia, Slovenia, Bosnia and Herzegovina, Croatia and Dalmatia.

The Empire is ashes, yet the lilt of the waltz and gypsy fiddle remains. Vienna is no longer the capital of an empire—but her cooking rules where her political diplomacy failed. Although the Austrian arbiter of European

politics, Prince Metternich, is long gone, the *Sachertorte* created by his chef has conquered the world. Central Europe, and especially the magic city of Vienna, has given nothing more delightful to the world than its love of good food, indeed its love of the good life.

The great culinary tradition of the Habsburg Empire lives on—and it grows. It has fascinated me that nowhere else in the world can one find within so small an area such a variety of eating and cooking habits. There is no doubt that this marvelous assortment of foods is a reflection of the Empire's variety of people and tongues.

At one extreme the peasant, the gypsy, the tremendous vitality of the Hungarian people, who until recently lived a feudal life; and at the other the Austrians, almost overcivilized and never a nation in the real sense, but an agglomeration of provinces, without the fierce national spirit of the Hungarians. Austria, and especially Vienna, was like an operetta; Hungary grew from the soil. The one, cosmopolitan and cultured, looked to the West for its nourishment, to Paris and the great world capitals, the world of the salon, the logical thought, the *mot;* the other with its folklore and peasant art, its occult customs and taboos, its mysticism, faced East, fed by the ancient wisdom that a man may know deep within himself, a life based not on books but on an oral tradition handed down from father to son. Such were the great contrasts of the Habsburg Empire. From these colorful dissonances grew one of the world's notable cuisines, reaching its highest peak with the delectable pastries that are now famous all over the world.

The importance that the Old Empire gave to the pleasures of the table is illustrated by the festivities of the Congress of Vienna, assembled to stabilize Europe after the fall of Napoleon in 1815. The Congress was in fact a meeting of great historical significance since it gave Europe 99 years of relative peace, but it is often thought of as a time of eating, drinking, dancing and loving. Prince Talleyrand, France's representative at the Congress and one of the chief protagonists in its drama of power politics, was not blind to the strategic use that could be made of the weeks of feasting and merrymaking. Keenly aware that hospitality was an intrinsic part of diplomacy, he told Louis XVIII just before leaving for Vienna, "Sire, I have more need of casseroles than written instructions." The King agreed, and Talleyrand took along his gifted young chef, Marie-Antoine Carême, who later became one of the great masters of *la grande cuisine.*

The Congress of Vienna lasted nearly 10 months, and over and beyond its political achievements it marked a high point in culinary extravagance and good living; it set a style for future generations of diplomats in the uses of hospitality in international diplomacy. Emperor Franz I, the official host, put 300 gala coaches with golden wheels at the disposal of his guests. He gave lavish banquets for the rulers of Russia, Prussia, Bavaria, Denmark, Württemberg and Baden. No menus of these great state dinners have been preserved in Vienna, but it is known that they were topped off with fantastic desserts—for instance, large disks of marzipan, filled with creamy nougat. The guests expressed the greatest admiration for Vienna's bakers, whom everyone considered to be "trained sculptors" because of the fanciful decorations they created out of sugar.

It was no more than was to be expected. For centuries the great cooks of Vienna had taken advantage of the recipes and techniques of the rest of

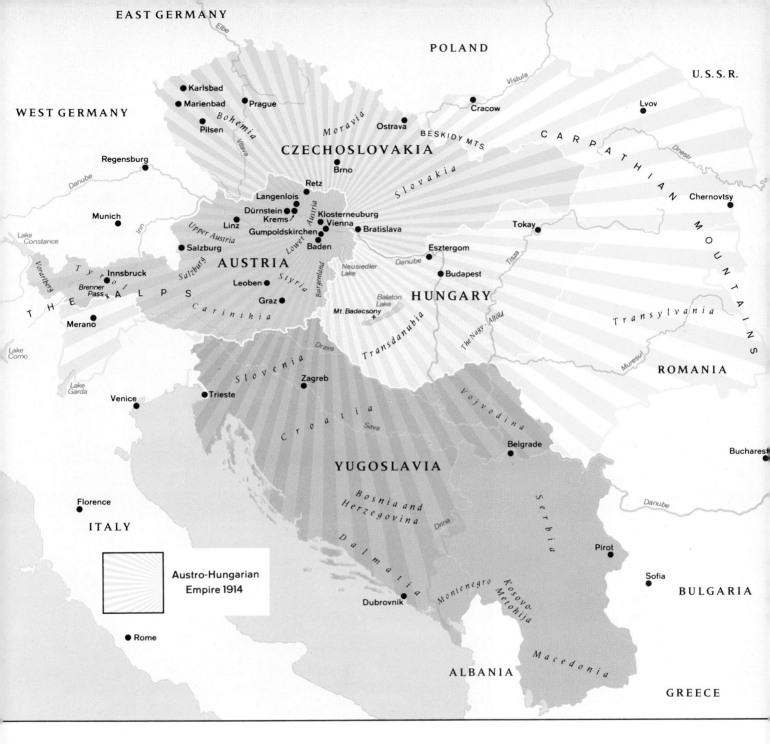

The Empire Is Dead - Long Live the Empire

Modern Austria's cooking originated in all parts of the old Austro-Hungarian Empire, whose 1914 boundaries are shown on the map above. The map has changed and the Empire is no more, but the Austro-Hungarian cuisine that excited Vienna and the world for decades is still there. The sophisticated refinement of the Viennese kitchen, which once was stimulated and nourished by its contact with the virility and variety of Hungarian, Yugoslavian and Czech cooking, is still unique. Without doubt it is one of the world's major cuisines.

The hay harvest in the Tyrol is an event conducted against a background of unbelievable beauty. These peasants, surrounded by the smell of warm hay and animals, touched by the sun on hands and neck, do their work under snowy peaks and along sweeping valleys.

the Empire; and in due course the exciting, somewhat exotic mixture known as "Viennese cooking" emerged.

Austria, and specifically Vienna, was a melting pot long before the word became a cliché. Vienna is located in a shallow basin between two mountain chains, the Alps and the Carpathians. Several centuries before the Christian era, Celtic tribes had a fishing village at the spot where later the north-south trade route from Scandinavia to Italy crossed the Danube. It was an ideal location for a "crossroads," which Vienna has remained to this day.

Around 100 B.C. the Roman legions pushed north through the Alps and along the Danube River and established a *castellum*—a settlement—exactly where Hoher Markt in Vienna's First District is today. It was called

Vindobona, from the Celtic *vindo* (white) and *bona* (field). The vineyards the Romans planted are still there today, well within Vienna's city limits.

As the Roman Empire declined, the Emperor Octavian recalled his legions. The last of them pulled out of Vindobona in 387 A.D., and during the next 500 years barbaric hordes came and went. The Visigoths, the Vandals and the Huns under Attila swept across Central Europe. They were followed by Slavs, by Avars, by Franks and Bajuvars and Burgundians. One invasion was followed by the next. But while the invaders plundered, they also left behind a great many traditions, arts and crafts, melodies and foods.

Under Austria's first ruling house, the Babenberg dynasty, founded in the 10th Century, Vienna became an important trading center. During the

Crusades homebound soldiers stopped in Vienna, bringing many spices from the East. The Viennese became familiar with muscat, pepper, ginger, cinnamon, cloves, nutmeg and sugar cane. Many historians believe that Vienna's perpetual predilection for all things sweet started with the Crusades. Two of the Babenberg rulers married Byzantine princesses—both called Theodora—who introduced a Byzantine flavor into the imperial kitchen. (This left its mark at all levels of society, and today at country fairs in Austria, children still buy "Turkish honey.")

The last Babenberg ruler, Emperor Friedrich II, was killed in battle in 1246. A generation later, after an uneasy period of intensive struggles for the throne, Count Rudolf of Habsburg marked a vital turning point in history by establishing his house as the ruling power for the next six centuries.

Slowly and methodically, the Habsburgs acquired many lands as their crown possessions, mostly through carefully arranged marriages. "Let others wage war; you, happy Austria, marry." That perceptive observation has been attributed to Matthias Corvinus, King of Hungary. At various times the Habsburg rule extended to Switzerland, Alsace, Burgundy, Artois, Franche-Comté, Spain, The Netherlands, Bohemia, Moravia, Slovakia, Silesia, the Banat, Poland, the Bukovina, Hungary, Croatia, Slovenia, Transylvania, Italy, Bosnia and Herzegovina, and even Mexico.

The golden epoch for which Vienna is so famous was the age of the Baroque, which began around 1600 and lasted until the end of the 18th Century. It was an age of exuberance originally associated with an architectural style, and the great Baroque palaces, churches and monuments built at the time still dominate Vienna's architecture. The Baroque turned into a way of life because it appealed to the Viennese love of beauty and sensuality, to their infatuation with music, drama, festivity and feasting.

The eating habits of the Baroque era were as exuberant as everything else during that epoch; and the banquets given in the palaces of Vienna's Baroque aristocrats were as splendid as those at the court of Louis XIV in Versailles. As a rule at least eight courses were served. The first course consisted of several broths, soups and purées. A potato purée soup was served alternately with a chicken purée soup. There were also a mushroom purée, an artichoke purée, and just in case somebody was still hungry for soup there were several bisques.

The second course offered various kinds of ragôuts, hams, tongues and sausages, fine pies and pâtés made of game, mostly venison, and delicious fricassees. This was followed by the third course consisting of "big" roasts: pheasant, partridge, woodcock, turkey, hare, rabbit, all garnished with lemons and oranges and olives. The fourth course offered the "small" roasts—birds like snipe, lark, ortolan, thrush. By that time one would expect to see some guests retiring from the scene, but no one seems to have left the table or been afraid of having a stroke. On went the guests to the fifth course—whole salmon, whole carp and pike, fish pies, crawfish dishes and fricassees of turtle.

The sixth course was composed of various egg dishes, jellies and blancmanges. Then came a simple seventh course—nothing but fruit, biscuits and cheese. But the final, eighth course would still be ahead, consisting of sweets, dried preserves, crystallized fruit, various marzipans and beautiful creations made of sugar in various colors.

Early in the 19th Century the Baroque era and its banquets gave way to the Biedermeier period of comfortable, relaxed living, marked by a taste for simple pleasures. The most popular dish of the day was the *Backhendl* (Viennese fried chicken). But this was also the epoch of Metternich's draconic censorship, the cholera epidemic of 1831, growing impoverishment of the working classes and unrest among university students and liberal intellectuals—all of which helped to precipitate the Revolution of 1848.

Quite a few cookbooks from the Biedermeier days still exist, containing mouth-watering and complicated recipes that no one would attempt today. I love one book that was printed in Vienna in 1846. The author starts by telling her women readers what a cook must not be: ". . . certainly not a dirty, unwashed person with fat hair and tobacco stains around her nose; not a fury who uses swear words because the poor kitchen girl broke a *Haferl* [a small cup]; not a lazy, clumsy fumbler who ruins whatever she gets into her hands; and not an arrogant, prodigal mischief-maker who spends a lot of money, achieves little, and tyrannizes the household. . . ."

The *Newest Viennese Cook Book*, published in 1834, offers recipes "for the noblest tables and very ordinary ones," for "meat-, fasting-, and mixed-dishes, also popular beverages, pastries, crèmes, gelées, and frozen things, even for people in modest circumstances, also a selection of dishes for the sick and convalescing." There are menus for every day of the year and advice on when to buy all products needed in the kitchen. A menu for Good Friday included: artichoke soup, poached eggs in mushroom sauce, potatoes with codfish, and roast pike with oysters. That gives you an idea how the Viennese ate when they were "fasting."

It was a habit of the Viennese chefs at this and later times to give gastronomic "immortality" to some of the noble families and heroes by conferring their names on certain culinary creations. Thus, the Empress Maria Theresia is glorified by a recipe for chicken breasts sautéed in butter, served with slices of ox tongue and rice and chicken meat, covered with cream sauce, a delightful way to remember her.

Admiral Tegetthoff, who defeated the Italian fleet at Lissa in 1866 (the Tegetthoff column in *Praterstern* is the Viennese equivalent of Nelson's Column in Trafalgar Square), is remembered among connoisseurs for fillets of beef Tegetthoff, served with a ragout of mussels, oysters, shrimp, *scampi*, mushrooms and truffles. The fillets are sprinkled with a few drops of port.

Metternich, who missed being immortalized through the *Sachertorte* (made by his chef, Franz Sacher), is noted only in connection with red cabbage Metternich, a garnish also including glazed potatoes and sautéed potatoes; perhaps a rather bland memorial for such an individual.

Emperor Franz Josef I is commemorated by the *Kaiserschmarrn*, often translated as the "Emperor's nothing," or the "Emperor's nonsense." (*Schmarrn* means fluff.) Actually, it does make a lot of sense. It is a pancake, made of flour, eggs, butter, milk, cream, sugar and raisins, torn with two forks into small pieces. It is served hot, with gratitude to the old gentleman who inspired it.

The Eighties and the Gay Nineties were *very* gay in Vienna, and the aristocracy and upper bourgeoisie lived especially well in the imperial city. The Black Friday of 1873 that had signaled the crash following a long, artificial boom was forgotten, and once again *joie de vivre* triumphed in Vienna.

Continued on page 18

In Sacher's Famous Hotel, Sacher's Fabulous Cake

The special glory of Austrian cooking reveals itself in the sweets. Of these noble creations the *Sachertorte,* shown at the right in all its simple luxuriousness, is the most famous. This is a chocolate-rich round spongecake *(page 186)* that is either filled or coated with apricot jam. Some cooks do both. In both cases the cake is iced with bittersweet chocolate. It was invented in 1832 by a master sugar baker named Franz Sacher to please the sweet tooth of the renowned statesman, Prince Klemens von Metternich. Sacher's descendants for many years operated Sacher's Hotel in Vienna, in whose coffeeroom this cake, with its side serving of *Schlagobers,* or whipped cream, was photographed. With it is shown a cup of coffee with more *Schlagobers,* which Viennese ladies love to take with their *Sachertorte,* and the saving glass of water needed to quench the thirst that arises when eating sweets.

A few may have sensed the inner decay of the Habsburg Empire; most people didn't want to see it and blissfully ignored the symptoms of approaching disaster. It was the time of Johann Strauss, who fascinated the Viennese with his fiddle, and of Hans Makart, who covered the walls of local palaces with his large pseudo-Venetian paintings, showing mostly naked women. His models were said to be ladies of high local society, and it was a favorite parlor game of the Viennese to speculate who might have been the well-curved models for Makart's *The Triumph of Ariadne* or *The Five Senses*. It was a time of great eating and shoddy art.

The fashionable places at the turn of the century were Demel's pastry-shop, in the Kohlmarkt; the Jockey Club, the exclusive meeting place of aristocrats; the bar of the Grand Hotel (now, alas, the headquarters of the International Atomic Energy Agency); and the fabulous Hotel Sacher.

The *chronique scandaleuse* of the Sacher has filled many books, but there were good reasons for the fame of this hotel around the turn of the century. Many of its habitués were young Habsburg archdukes and other aristocrats who served in the Imperial Guards. Their Emperor, Franz Josef I, was an ascetic, hard-working man who liked to get up early. (The Habsburgs were traditionally early risers; the Empress Maria Theresia was often issuing orders around 5 in the morning.)

Since the Kaiser was up so early, everybody around him had to get up too, which was not pleasant for the young officers who had gone to bed perhaps only a couple of hours earlier. By noon, the guard officers were starved and praying they wouldn't be asked to sit down at the Emperor's table. It must have been an ordeal to do so. Court etiquette demanded that the Emperor be served first and that no one continue eating after His Majesty had put down his fork. Unfortunately the Kaiser ate very quickly. By the time the large silver platters got to the hungry young officers, the Emperor had put down fork and knife, and the poor fellows had just one tantalizing look at the lovely dishes—or maybe even a brief taste of the excellent *Kaiserschmarrn*—before their plates were removed.

In the cold season when the Emperor stayed at the Hofburg, the imperial palace in the First District, there was always the Hotel Sacher, a couple of minutes away. As soon as the starved young men could get away from the table, they would run over to the Sacher. The food was always wonderful there. "If you don't like it, go to the Sacher!" was the refrain in all Viennese houses whenever a husband complained about the food. The secret of the Sacher cuisine was that it didn't taste like restaurant food. It had the inimitable "homey" touch, except that no one ate that well at home. The boiled beef "could be cut with the fork" and the roast made you drool. The table arrangements were wonderful, and the wine and Champagne were the best.

The ruler of this culinary Eden was Frau Anna Sacher, wife of Edouard Sacher, the son of Metternich's great chef. Frau Sacher, the friend and confidante of the mighty, was a formidable woman who always wore tailored costumes and a lace jabot and often smoked a cigar.

At night the Hotel Sacher was immensely popular for its private dining rooms, the renowned *chambres separées*. Statesmen from the nearby Ballhausplatz would meet in these secluded places for diplomatic talks. Other gentlemen would use these rooms to meet ladies who were neither their wives nor their nieces. No one knew exactly who they were. The ladies

Even in Vienna, it is the simplest food that sometimes tastes best. Witness this cabbie downing his sausage and beer with quiet satisfaction while waiting for a fare in front of St. Stephan's Cathedral.

always arrived heavily veiled, each to be cautiously taken to her tête-à-tête by one of the older waiters. The art of discretion was developed to perfection at the famous hotel. The lady's husband (or, for that matter, the gentleman's wife) might be at the hotel at the same time, in an upper-floor room, but would never know what went on in the private rooms.

But even those rich, titled Viennese who made up the Sacher's clientele had a home life, and their days followed a regular pattern. They rarely got up before 9 a.m. Breakfast was served in the bedroom—coffee with hot milk, *Kipfel* (crescent-shaped rolls), butter and jam, and perhaps a soft-boiled egg. Madame would get dressed; the manicurist might come, or the hairdresser, or the masseuse, and then it was time to go to a fitting.

The men about town meanwhile would walk on the Corso. This was the

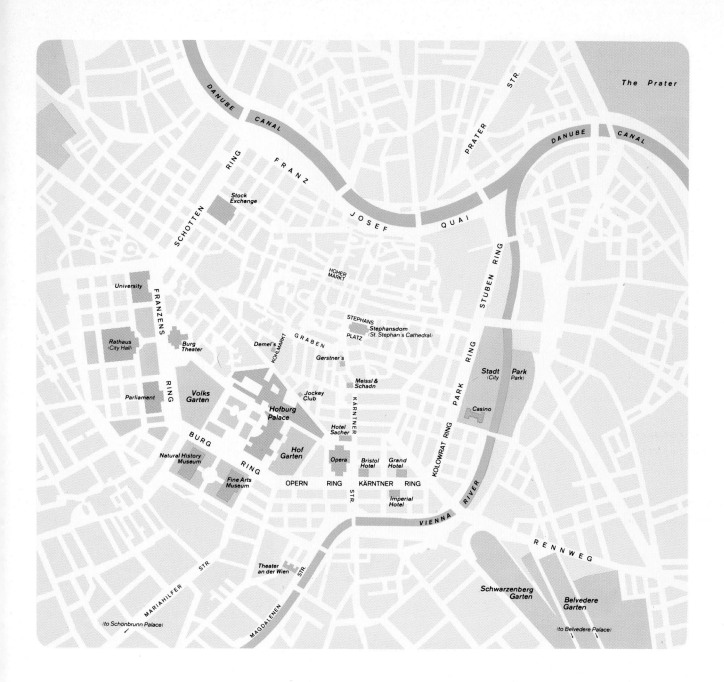

Vienna's Inner City is mapped as it was in the late 19th Century when its ring of boulevards was completed. Such famous institutions as the Jockey Club, the Grand Hotel, and Meissl and Schadn's restaurant no longer function, but the First District is still beautiful, still nostalgic with its churches, palaces—and Demel's.

promenade that extended through the fashionable streets from Demel's on the Kohlmarkt to the Graben, past the magnificent Cathedral of St. Stephan and from there to the Opera. One would always walk on the right-hand side of the street, in the shade; nothing was wrong with the other side, but one didn't walk there, except when "one didn't want to be noticed." At the Opera one crossed the Kärntnerstrasse and walked along the Ring, past the Bristol and the Grand Hotel to the Schwarzenbergplatz, and back again. An elegant man would make the long walk at least three times, watching "who greeted whom" and being careful not to greet certain people.

All this activity was hard work and one was getting hungry. One might step into Demel's or another small eating place such as Gerstner's, or Stiebitz's for a *Frühstücksgulasch* (breakfast goulash) or for a couple of *würstel* (homemade sausages). Some people preferred the bar of the Grand Hotel in midmorning.

Even after this *Gabelfrühstück* (fork breakfast) one would be hungry again by 1 o'clock, when it was time for the day's main meal, the *Mittagessen*. One usually had guests: a famous actor or musician, a retired general, an Italian countess. One would take a sherry in the salon and then the butler would open the double doors leading to the dining room. The hostess would take the arm of the guest of honor. The table was nicely set, always with white damask and flowers.

Lunch would start with a soup, and slices of bread, cut as thin as paper, were served. Then there was a *Vorspeise* (hors d'oeuvre), perhaps a timbale of fish, or crayfish tails in dill sauce. This would be followed by two meat courses, the inevitable boiled beef and then a roast or a chicken dish. During the game season there would be venison, boar, pheasant, woodcock. The sauces were not reduced (cooked down to a thicker and more concentrated consistency), as in France, but thickened by flour and cream. The vegetables were prepared with finely chopped onions. Viennese cooking was often spiced and rarely light.

The dessert alone, however, justified the fame of Austrian cooking. In the most elegant houses there was a *Mehlspeisköchin*, a woman cook specializing in warm, homemade desserts. She would be a matronly, resolute woman, probably hailing from Moravia or Bohemia, and she would create unforgettable marvels out of flour, butter, sugar, eggs, fruit, almonds and other sweet things. Her dessert was always freshly made, always warm, always eaten at once. In some houses there was a difference between summer and winter desserts. Obviously one would never serve *Topfenknödel* (cream cheese dumplings) on a hot day in July. Some women had their special, secret recipes for *Buchteln* (buns), *Kaiserschmarrn*, *Topfenpalatschinken* (cream cheese pancakes), *Griessauflauf* (farina pudding). Everybody always said that it was wonderful, and everybody took a second helping, though "one shouldn't."

By 3 o'clock, when the guests had left after coffee, brandy and cigars in the salon, the hostess was able to take off her shoes and the tight bodice with stays of whalebone and go to bed. She would tell the chambermaid to draw the curtain, and the very next minute she would be fast asleep.

An hour later she would have to get up to drive out into the Prater, the beautiful imperial gardens, in her two-wheel tonneau, with a lackey sitting behind her. She would swing her whip, decorated with a bunch of fresh violets, giving it an extra flourish when some elegant men glanced at her admiringly. Or she might have invited all her lady friends and her worst enemies around 5 p.m. for the two hours of gossip called the *Jause*. Somebody had a *Jause* almost every day, and of course one had to be there.

A large table in the salon would be beautifully set, with a samovar at one side, both for decorative effect and for serving tea; and there would be trays with sandwiches and wonderful *Torten*. "One shouldn't," but it was impossible to resist. The next morning the masseuse would have to knead off the extra flesh, but that was *her* business; after all, she was getting paid for it. But often the masseuse labored in vain. No one could work off all those *Mehlspeisen* and *Torten* and the whipped cream. Well, no one ever claimed that the Viennese women were slim. They were always called *mollert*

or *voll-schlank*, which means "full-slim" and is a somewhat polite description. And what's wrong with a little weight in the "right places" anyway?

The well-set large table at the *Jause* was quite a sight, with the lace tablecloth hanging down over the sides and little trays with delicious *Teegebäck*, dainty *petits fours* and canapés, salted or sweet. By 7 p.m., when the *dear* friends were at last going home, there was nothing left on the table. The poor women must have been starving for days; they ate up everything. If the servants were lucky, they might save (or steal) a few little things. Yet the servants never really shared their employers' food. They were told to buy tripe and calf lights and sauerkraut and other nourishing, inexpensive food, and there were always leftovers from last night's dinner.

Well, dinner. One had to go home and get dressed, and then there might be a concert in someone's house or the Opera—Vienna was a very musical city. A friend of mine remembers that his father never heard the second act of a Wagnerian opera because, finding this music interminable, he wisely slipped off to Sacher's, just across the street behind the Opera, for dinner. Meanwhile the boy, who had been among the standees in the fourth gallery, was permitted to sit in the father's parquet stall. My friend became very fond of Wagner's second acts, including that of *Die Walküre*, which (even he admits) is a terrible bore.

After the evening's music one went on to dine somewhere (if one hadn't gone for dinner during the opera), and then it was midnight, time to go.

The attention that Austrians lavished on food in the Old Empire is reflected in the organization of the royal kitchen. It consisted of the main kitchen, the large banquet kitchen, an *Olio* kitchen, a salad kitchen, two large pantries, a working room, a cold chamber, the *garde-manger* (cold buffet) kitchen, washrooms, wardrooms and offices. Seven handwagons were used to transport wood and coal. There were large grills, a special oven to make *gratins,* two large iron stoves, two brick baking ovens, two large open spits screened by large sheets of isinglass to protect the cooks from the heat. . . . Along the walls were beautiful glass-fronted cabinets with copper containers, including a giant *Gugelhupf* form (a mold). A cake baked in this form would serve 50 ladies at an imperial *Kaffeeklatsch.*

The most interesting part of the imperial kitchen was the *Olio* kitchen, where nothing but *Olio Suppe* was prepared for the annual court ball attended by about 2,000 people. The recipe for the *Olio Suppe* calls for: 20 pounds of beef, 6 pounds of ox liver, 24 pounds of veal, 16 calves feet, 20 pounds of pork, 16 pounds of mutton or lamb, 20 pounds of smoked pork, 16 pounds of venison, 5 ducks, 5 wild geese, 3 geese, 8 partridges, 8 pigeons, 10 chickens.

"With the exception of the beef all meats are roasted until brown, added to 550 liters of water and left to cook slowly. One adds 10 parsley roots, 10 carrots, 15 pieces of leek, 10 white beets, 12 pieces of celery, 16 pounds of white onions, and the following spices: 70 grams of white pepper, 100 grams of ginger, 80 grams of nutmeg, 60 grams of mace, 6 grams of cayenne pepper, 24 cloves. Six pounds of chestnuts are glazed with 200 grams of sugar and added to the soup."

Such were the joys of the good life in the irrevocably lost days of the Old Empire. It must have been a wonderful time, but it will never come again. Fortunately for us, many of the great recipes survived the Empire.

A delightful treat from Austria's rivers is the blue trout or *Forelle blau*. Three are shown resting on aspic at a country inn on the Danube *(opposite)*. The fish are killed just before they go into a pot of boiling stock, and turn blue in the cooking.

Der Kaffeesieder
Zuckerbäcker, Mandoletti Liqueur Fabr. u. Branntweinbrenner

The Coffee Conquest of Vienna

Coffee came to Austria with the Turkish army that besieged Vienna in 1683 and, although the Turks lost, the coffee won. By the 19th Century, as the lithograph above shows, the coffeehouse had become a way of life for Austrians, a sort of Everyman's Club. The coffee boiler, or proprietor, sits with his long pipe watching a chess game while his clients read newspapers or gossip. Above the central picture is his steaming coffeepot and below are the amusements and refreshments usually available in his house: a billiard rack and cues, cards, chessmen, pastries and cups of coffee. At the left is a maker of fruit cordials and at the right a distiller of brandy; both supply the coffeehouse. And in the modern coffeehouse in Salzburg *(opposite)* men read, talk and sip their *Melange* (coffee with milk), *Melange mit Schlag* (coffee with milk and whipped cream) and *Mokka* (black coffee) just as the patrons of old sipped theirs.

Social life in Budapest also revolves around coffee and the coffeehouses in which it is served. In them something of the splendor of the Old Empire survives. The elaborate porcelain *espresso* machine, above, stands in a state-owned sweetshop, once occupied by Gerbeaud's, one of the finest pastry shops in Europe. The rococo café opposite, now called the Hungaria, was the old New York, at whose tables famous authors drank coffee as they wrote their books and plays.

Vanillekipfel

VANILLA CRESCENTS

To make 36 crescents

½ pound unsalted butter, softened
½ cup sugar
2 cups sifted all-purpose flour
1¼ cups ground unblanched almonds
1 teaspoon vanilla extract
¼ teaspoon salt
Confectioners' sugar

Cream the butter and sugar together by beating them against the sides of a bowl with a wooden spoon or with an electric mixer set at medium speed until light and fluffy. Beat in the flour ½ cup at a time, then add the almonds, vanilla extract and salt, continuing to beat until the mixture becomes a slightly stiff dough. Shape the dough into a ball, wrap it in wax paper or plastic wrap and refrigerate it for about an hour. Preheat the oven to 350°. Lightly butter two 12-by-15-inch baking sheets.

Pinch off walnut-sized pieces of the chilled dough and place them on a floured board; roll each one into a strip an inch wide and ½ inch thick. This will make it about 2½ inches long. Shape each piece into a crescent by pulling it into a semicircle.

Arrange the crescents at least ½ inch apart on the baking sheets. Bake in the middle of the oven for 15 or 20 minutes, or until lightly colored. Remove the sheets from the oven and leave the crescents on them to cool for about 5 minutes, then transfer them to a cake rack. Dust with confectioners' sugar and cool about 15 minutes longer before serving.

Tascherln

VIENNESE JAM POCKETS

To make 25 pockets

1¼ cups unsalted butter, softened
⅔ cup sugar
2 hard-cooked egg yolks
1 egg yolk, lightly beaten
1 teaspoon grated orange peel
2 teaspoons vanilla extract
½ teaspoon salt
3¼ cups sifted all-purpose flour
1½ cups thick jam or preserves (apricot is suggested)
1 tablespoon water
2 egg whites

Cream the butter and sugar together by beating them against the side of a bowl with a wooden spoon or by using an electric mixer at medium speed until the mixture is light and fluffy.

Rub the hard-cooked egg yolks through a sieve with a wooden spoon, then stir them, the egg yolk, orange peel, vanilla and salt into the butter-sugar mixture. Add the flour ½ cup at a time; stir until the mixture becomes a slightly stiff dough. Shape the dough into a ball, wrap it in wax paper or plastic wrap and refrigerate it for about an hour.

On a lightly floured surface, roll the dough out into a 15-inch square about ⅛ inch thick. With a pastry wheel or sharp knife, cut the large square into 3-inch squares. Drop a teaspoon of jam onto the center of each square. Then lift a corner of each square and fold it over the opposite corner, forming a triangle. Seal the edges by pressing them firmly with the tines of a fork, then refrigerate them for 30 minutes.

Preheat the oven to 350°. With a pastry brush or paper towel lightly butter two 14-by-17-inch baking sheets, sprinkle a handful of flour over the butter, and knock out the excess flour by striking the inverted sheet against the edge of a table. Arrange the chilled triangles on the baking sheets, leaving at least ½ inch of space between them. Gently prick the center of each triangle with a fork. Mix the water and the egg whites together by beating them lightly with a fork. Then, with a pastry brush, coat each triangle lightly with the egg white mixture.

Bake the triangles on the middle shelf of the oven for 10 or 15 minutes, or until they are lightly browned. Remove them from the baking sheets with a metal spatula and cool them on a cake rack before serving.

Cookies and Cakes

Eleven delights from a sugar bakery, shown opposite, are listed below.

1 Apricot Leaves
2 Viennese Jam Pockets
3 Vanilla Crescents
4 Coffee Ring
5 Poppy Seed Roulade
6 Filbert Slices
7 Carnival Jelly Doughnuts
8 Ischl Tartlets
9 Jelly Buns
10 Golden Dumplings
11 Macaroon Jam Slices

To make about 25 slices

2 cups whole English walnuts or
   1½ cups ground
⅔ cup sugar
2 egg whites, lightly beaten
1 twelve-ounce jar apricot jam

Makronen-Schnitten

MACAROON JAM SLICES

Preheat the oven to 350°. With a pastry brush or paper towel, lightly butter a 14-by-17-inch baking sheet. Sprinkle some flour over it, tip the sheet from side to side to cover the surface evenly, then knock off the excess by inverting the sheet and striking it against the edge of a table.

Grind the walnuts by using one of the little nut graters made especially for the purpose. Or you may use packaged ground walnuts.

In a large mixing bowl, combine the ground walnuts and sugar. Add half the egg whites, and stir until the mixture forms a paste thick enough to be kneaded with the hand. Add a little more egg white if the mixture seems too dry. Shape the paste into 2 rolls about ¾ inch in diameter and 10 inches long. With the index finger make a channel about ½ inch deep down the center of each roll, leaving ¼ inch at each end of the roll. Lift the rolls with a large metal spatula, and place them, several inches apart, on the baking sheet. Bake them in the middle of the oven for 15 or 20 minutes, or until they are lightly browned.

Meanwhile, heat the jam in a saucepan until it runs easily off the spoon. Remove the rolls from the oven and fill the channels with the hot jam. Let them cool. To serve, cut the rolls into slices ¾ inch thick.

To make about 2 dozen
   salty cocktail snacks

PASTRY
8 tablespoons (1 quarter-pound stick)
   unsalted butter, softened
¼ teaspoon sugar
1⅓ cups sifted all-purpose flour
2 hard-cooked eggs
1 egg, lightly beaten
1 teaspoon salt

FILLING
½ cup whole filbert nuts
1 teaspoon coarse salt
¼ teaspoon allspice

Haselnuss-Schnitten

FILBERT SLICES

Preheat the oven to 350°. Cream the butter and sugar together by beating them against the side of a bowl with a wooden spoon or by using an electric mixer at medium speed until the mixture is light and fluffy. Then beat in the flour, ½ cup at a time. Mash the hard-cooked eggs by rubbing them through a sieve with a wooden spoon, and beat them, the lightly beaten egg and the salt into the mixture, continuing to beat until the mixture becomes a slightly stiff dough. Shape the dough into a ball, wrap it in wax paper or plastic wrap and refrigerate it for about 2 hours.

To prepare the filberts, blanch them by placing them in the oven for 10 or 15 minutes, or until the brown skin is dark in color. Cool the nuts slightly, then rub them in a towel or between the hands to remove the brown flaky skin. Pulverize them in a nut grinder.

Add the salt and the allspice to the ground nuts.

On a lightly floured surface roll the dough into a strip ¼ inch thick and 6 inches wide. It should then be about 17 inches long. Sprinkle the nut mixture evenly over it. Press the mixture into the surface of the dough by rolling it lightly with a rolling pin. Turn the pastry lengthwise in front of you and roll it, jelly-roll fashion, into a long, tubular shape. Wrap the roll in wax paper or plastic wrap and refrigerate it for about 45 minutes.

With a pastry brush or paper towel lightly butter two 12-by-15-inch baking sheets.

Slice the roll into ¾-inch slices. Arrange them side by side on the baking sheets, and bake them in the middle of the oven for about 15 minutes, or until they are a delicate golden brown. Let them cool on the baking sheets.

30

Ischler Törtchen
ISCHL TARTLETS

To make 12 tartlets

Cream the butter and sugar together by beating them against the side of a bowl with a wooden spoon or by using an electric mixer set at medium speed, until the mixture is light and fluffy. Then beat in the flour, ½-cup at a time, the almonds and cinnamon, and continue beating until the mixture becomes a slightly stiff dough. Shape the dough into a ball, wrap it in wax paper or plastic wrap and refrigerate it for about an hour.

Preheat the oven to 325°. On a lightly floured surface, roll the dough into a sheet ⅛ inch thick. With a 2½-inch cookie cutter, cut as many circles from the sheet as you can. Knead the leftover scraps of dough into a ball, and roll it out again into a ⅛-inch sheet. Cut out more circles. You should now have about 12 circles. Arrange them on an ungreased 14-by-17-inch baking sheet, leaving about an inch of space between them.

Repeat the rolling and cutting process with the other half of the dough, but before placing the second batch on a baking sheet, cut out the center of each circle with a ½-inch cookie cutter. Bake both batches in the center of the oven for 10 to 15 minutes, or until light brown.

With a metal spatula, gently ease the cookies off the baking sheets onto a cake rack. Let them cool for about 20 minutes.

Spread the tops of the solid circles with a thin coating of jam; lay a cut-out cookie on top of each, pressing the two together so that they make a sandwich. Spoon a dab of jam into the opening of each tart and sprinkle the tops with confectioners' sugar before serving.

½ pound plus 4 tablespoons (2½ quarter-pound sticks) unsalted butter, softened
⅔ cup sugar
2 cups sifted all-purpose flour
1¾ cups ground almonds
⅛ teaspoon cinnamon
5 tablespoons raspberry jam
Confectioners' sugar

Aprikosenblättergebäck
APRICOT LEAVES

To make 25 cookies

With a pastry brush or paper towel, lightly butter two 14-by-17-inch baking sheets. Sprinkle some flour over each sheet, tip it from side to side to coat the surface evenly, and knock off the excess by inverting and striking it sharply against the edge of a table. Cream the 8 tablespoons of butter and the sugar together, beating them against the side of a mixing bowl with a wooden spoon or with an electric mixer until light and fluffy. Beat in the egg yolk, then the almond paste, a tablespoonful at a time. Gradually stir in the lemon juice a teaspoonful at a time and add the lemon peel and the salt. Pour in the flour, ½ cup at a time, beating until the mixture becomes a doughy mass. Shape the dough into a ball, wrap in wax paper or plastic wrap and refrigerate for at least 1½ hours.

Preheat the oven to 375°. On a floured surface, roll the dough into a circle about ⅛ inch thick. With a 2½-inch cookie cutter—either plain or scalloped—cut out all the cookies possible. With a metal spatula, place them side by side on the baking sheets. Lightly knead the leftover scraps of dough into a ball, then roll it out again into a circle ⅛ inch thick and cut out more cookies. Repeat the process until all the dough is used.

Beat the egg white with the water to combine, then with a pastry brush, coat each cookie lightly. Bake in the middle of the oven for 10 to 12 minutes, or until the cookies are a light golden brown. Remove them from the oven and slide them onto a cake rack. Drop a dab of jam onto the center of each cookie, then sprinkle with chopped almonds.

8 tablespoons (1 quarter-pound stick) unsalted butter, softened
¼ cup sugar
1 egg yolk
½ cup almond paste
2 tablespoons fresh lemon juice
1 tablespoon grated lemon peel
½ teaspoon salt
1¼ cups sifted all-purpose flour
1 egg white
1 teaspoon water
½ cup thick apricot jam
½ cup blanched almonds, finely chopped

To make about 22 doughnuts

1 package active dry yeast
Pinch of sugar
¼ cup lukewarm water
3 cups sifted all-purpose flour
¼ teaspoon salt
2 tablespoons sugar
6 egg yolks, lightly beaten
½ cup light cream, lukewarm
1 tablespoon dark rum
1 tablespoon orange juice
1 teaspoon vanilla
3 cups apricot jam
1 cup lard (approximate)
Confectioners' sugar

Faschingskrapfen
CARNIVAL JELLY DOUGHNUTS

Sprinkle the yeast and pinch of sugar into the lukewarm water. Let stand for 2 or 3 minutes; stir it to dissolve the yeast. Set in a warm, draft-free area—such as an unlighted oven—for 2 or 3 minutes, or until the yeast has begun to bubble and has almost doubled in volume.

Sift the flour and the salt into a large mixing bowl. Make a well in the flour and pour into it the yeast solution, sugar, egg yolks, cream, rum, orange juice and vanilla. With your hands or a wooden spoon, work the flour into the other ingredients until the dough is medium-firm.

Shape the dough into a ball and put it into a large, lightly buttered bowl. Dust the top of the dough lightly with flour, cover with a kitchen towel and set it in a warm, draft-free spot (again the unlighted oven is ideal). In 45 minutes or an hour, the dough should double in bulk and leave a deep depression when pressed in the center with 2 fingers.

Punch the dough down, turn it out on a floured surface, and roll it into a circle ¼ inch thick. With a 2½-inch cookie cutter, cut the dough into as many circles as possible. Lightly shape the remaining scraps of dough into a ball and roll it again to a thickness of ¼ inch. Repeat the pro-

1 To make *Faschingskrapfen*, place the apricot jam on a circle of dough; cover with another circle.

2 Join the circles carefully with your fingertips, leaving the jam to form a little mound in the middle.

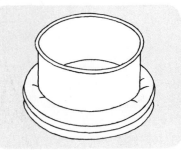

3 Seal the circles of dough completely by cutting away the outer edges with a small, circular cookie cutter.

4 Fry the doughnuts in ½ inch of hot lard until brown and crisp. Then turn over and fry the other sides.

cess until all the dough is used. Drop a teaspoon of jam onto the centers of half the circles, then sandwich each of these with one of the other circles. Press the outer edges of each pair of circles together with the fingertips. Then cut the doughnuts out again with a slightly smaller cookie cutter to trim off the edges. Place them 1 inch apart on a baking sheet lined with a clean cloth dusted with flour. Let the doughnuts rise in the unlighted oven or other draft-free area for about 20 minutes, or until they rise about ½ inch in the center and look light and puffy.

In a heavy 8- or 10-inch skillet, heat the lard over low heat until a light haze forms over it. With a metal spatula, slide 4 or 5 of the doughnuts into the hot fat. They will begin to bubble and puff up, and in about 2 minutes should be golden brown on the bottom. Turn them over with a slotted spoon and cook them a few minutes longer, or until they are brown. Remove them to a plate lined with paper towels. Proceed until all the doughnuts are done. (You may have to add more lard.)

Dust the doughnuts with confectioners' sugar before serving them.

Gugelhupf
COFFEE RING

Place the raisins in a small bowl, pour in the rum and let them soak for about 30 minutes. Then drain and squeeze the raisins dry.

Meanwhile, with a pastry brush and the 1 tablespoon of butter, lightly coat the bottom and sides of a 10-inch *Gugelhupf* form, or use any other ring mold that is about 5 inches deep and 10 inches in diameter. Sprinkle the 2 tablespoons of flour over the buttered mold, tipping the mold from side to side to spread the flour evenly. Then invert the mold and rap it sharply on a table to remove any excess flour. Arrange the almonds in a circle on the bottom of the mold and set aside.

Pour ¼ cup of the lukewarm milk into a small, shallow bowl and sprinkle the yeast and a pinch of sugar over it. Let the yeast and sugar stand for 2 or 3 minutes, then stir to dissolve them completely. Set the bowl in a warm, draft-free place, such as an unlighted oven, for about 5 minutes, or until the mixture almost doubles in volume.

Cream the 8 tablespoons of softened unsalted butter and the ½ cup of sugar together by mashing and beating them against the sides of a bowl with a large spoon until light and fluffy. Beat in the yeast mixture and the remaining ½ cup of lukewarm milk. Then add the eggs, one at a time, beating well after each addition. Beating constantly, add the sifted flour, ½ cup at a time, and continue to beat until the dough is smooth. Then beat in the finely grated orange peel, vanilla extract and salt; lightly but thoroughly stir in the cup of raisins.

Without disturbing the almonds, carefully fit the dough into the mold, spreading it out to the sides with a spatula. Cover with a kitchen towel and set in a warm, draft-free place for 1½ hours, or until the dough has risen to the top of the mold.

Preheat the oven to 350°. Bake the *Gugelhupf* in the middle of the oven for about 40 minutes, or until it is a light golden brown. Then turn it out on a cake rack to cool. Just before serving, dust lightly with confectioners' sugar. *Gugelhupf* is traditionally served with afternoon coffee.

To make 1 ten-inch ring

1 cup seedless raisins
¼ cup dark rum
1 tablespoon butter, softened
2 tablespoons flour
2 tablespoons whole blanched almonds
¾ cup lukewarm milk (105° to 115°)
1 package active dry yeast
A pinch of sugar
8 tablespoons (1 quarter-pound stick) unsalted butter, softened
½ cup sugar
2 eggs
2 cups sifted all-purpose flour
1 tablespoon finely grated orange peel
½ teaspoon vanilla extract
½ teaspoon salt
¼ cup confectioners' sugar

To make about 56 dumplings

1¼ cups milk
9 tablespoons unsalted butter (1 quarter-pound stick plus 1 tablespoon), melted
2 tablespoons sugar
3 eggs lightly beaten
2 packages active dry yeast
Pinch of sugar
¼ cup lukewarm water
4 cups sifted flour
½ teaspoon salt

FILLING
½ cup light brown sugar
¼ cup raisins
½ cup finely chopped blanched almonds

Aranygaluska
GOLDEN DUMPLINGS

Heat the milk in a small saucepan for about 3 minutes, or until little bubbles begin to form around the edge. Remove from the heat and stir in 1 tablespoon of the melted butter and the 2 tablespoons of sugar. Continue to stir until the sugar is completely dissolved. Cool the mixture to lukewarm (110° to 115°), then beat in the eggs.

Sprinkle the yeast and the pinch of sugar into the lukewarm water. Be absolutely sure the water is lukewarm (110° to 115°)—neither too hot nor too cool to the touch. (If the water is too hot it will kill the yeast; if too cold, it will not activate the yeast.) Let the mixture stand for 2 or 3 minutes, then stir it to dissolve the yeast. Set it in a warm, draft-free place—such as an unlighted oven—for 2 or 3 minutes, or until the yeast has begun to bubble and has almost doubled in volume. Combine it with the milk-egg mixture. If the solution does not bubble and increase in volume, the yeast is inactive. Discard the solution and start over with more yeast.

Sift the flour and salt into a large mixing bowl. Make a well in the center and pour the liquid mixture into it. With your hand or a wooden spoon, work it into the flour, continuing until the mixture becomes a medium-stiff dough. Put the dough in a large lightly buttered bowl and set it in a warm, draft-free spot—again the unlighted oven is ideal—for 30 to 40 minutes, or until the dough has doubled in size.

In the meanwhile, prepare the filling by combining the brown sugar and the raisins in a small mixing bowl and stirring in the chopped blanched almonds.

Remove the dough to a floured surface and knead it. Pull the dough into an oblong shape, fold it end to end, then press it down and push it forward several times with the heels of your hands. Then turn the dough slightly toward you and repeat the process—pulling, folding, pushing and pressing. Continue kneading until the dough is smooth and elastic. This will take at least 10 minutes.

Dust your hands with flour and form the dough into balls about 1 inch in diameter. Preheat the oven to 300°.

To cook the dumplings pour 8 tablespoons of the melted butter into a small bowl. Dip a ball into the butter and put it into a 10-inch springform pan. Continue until half of the balls are all arranged close together, in a circular pattern, in the pan. Sprinkle half of the filling mixture over them. Dip the rest of the balls, one by one, in the butter and put one on top of each ball in the bottom layer. Sprinkle the rest of the filling on them. With a pastry brush, drip any butter that remains onto the filling. Cover the pan with a kitchen towel and set the dumplings in a warm, draft-free place for about ½ hour, or until the dumplings have risen to ⅔ of the height of the pan.

Bake on the middle shelf of the oven for 30 minutes, then turn the oven up to 375° and bake for 15 minutes more. The dumplings should be puffy and golden brown. Remove the pan from the oven and place on a cake rack. Release the sides of the pan, and let the rolls cool for 15 minutes on the pan bottom, then transfer them to a plate. Break the dumplings apart gently to serve them.

Mákos és Diós Kalács

POPPY SEED OR ALMOND NUT ROULADE

Sprinkle the yeast and the pinch of sugar into the lukewarm water. Be absolutely sure that the water is lukewarm (110° to 115°)—neither too hot nor too cool to the touch. (If the water is too hot it will kill the yeast; if it is too cold, it will not activate the yeast.) Let the mixture stand for 2 to 3 minutes, then stir it to dissolve the yeast completely. Set in a warm, draft-free place—such as an unlighted oven—for 2 or 3 minutes, or until the yeast has begun to bubble and has almost doubled in volume.

In a mixing bowl, combine the yeast solution, the milk, vanilla extract, lemon peel, sugar and salt, then stir in the egg yolks, 1 at a time. Beat in the flour ½ cup at a time, then beat the soft butter into the dough a tablespoon at a time.

Remove the dough to a floured surface and knead it by pulling the dough into an oblong shape, folding it end to end, then pressing it down and pushing it forward several times with the heels of your hands. Turn the dough slightly toward you and repeat the process, pulling, folding, pressing and pushing. Continue to knead, sprinkling more flour on the dough and the working surface if either becomes sticky. The dough should be smooth and elastic in about 10 minutes. Put it into a large, lightly buttered bowl, dust the top of the dough lightly with flour and cover the bowl loosely with a kitchen towel. Let the dough rise in a warm, draft-free area (the unlighted oven would be ideal) for 35 to 45 minutes; it should then have doubled in size.

POPPY SEED FILLING: Cream the butter and honey by beating them together with a wooden spoon in a mixing bowl or by using an electric mixer. Add the cream a teaspoon at a time. Stir in the ground poppy seeds, nuts, raisins and orange peel.

ALMOND NUT FILLING: Cream the butter and sugar by beating them together with a wooden spoon against the side of a mixing bowl or by using an electric mixer. Beat in the egg yolk, then gradually stir in the grated almonds, orange peel, raisins and vanilla extract. Continue to stir until the ingredients are thoroughly blended. Set the filling aside.

Turn the dough out on a floured surface, knead it again for a minute, then pat it into a rectangular shape with your hands. Roll it into a rectangle about 9 inches wide and 13 inches long; it should then be about ¼ inch thick. With a pastry brush or paper towel lightly butter an 8-by-15-inch baking sheet.

With a metal spatula, spread the poppy seed or almond nut filling over the rectangle of dough in a layer about ⅛ inch thick, leaving an unspread border of ¾ inch on each side of the rectangle. Starting with a 13-inch side, roll the dough up like a long jelly roll. (Do not close the ends.) With the aid of a metal spatula if necessary, gently maneuver the roll, seam side down, onto the baking sheet. Brush the top and sides of the roulade with the egg-milk mixture. Let it rise in a warm, draft-free spot for 20 minutes, then brush it again with the mixture. Meanwhile, preheat the oven to 350°. Bake the roll in the middle of the oven for 45 minutes, or until it is a light golden brown. The rich filling may cause the pastry to crack a little, but this will in no way impair it. Cool the roulade to room temperature on a cake rack before slicing and serving.

To make 1 thirteen-inch roulade

1 package active dry yeast
Pinch of sugar
¼ cup lukewarm water
¼ cup milk, at room temperature
1 teaspoon vanilla extract
¼ teaspoon grated lemon peel
¼ cup sugar
½ teaspoon salt
3 egg yolks
2 cups all-purpose flour
4 tablespoons unsalted butter, softened
1 egg, lightly beaten with 1 tablespoon milk

POPPY SEED FILLING
8 tablespoons (1 quarter-pound stick) unsalted butter, softened
¼ cup honey
1 tablespoon heavy cream
¼ pound ground poppy seeds
¼ cup coarsely crushed walnuts
¼ cup chopped raisins
½ teaspoon grated orange peel

ALMOND NUT FILLING
4 tablespoons unsalted butter, softened
¼ cup sugar
1 egg yolk, lightly beaten
¾ cup finely grated almonds
½ teaspoon grated orange peel
¼ cup white sultana raisins
½ teaspoon vanilla extract

To make 36 buns

2 packages active dry yeast
Pinch of sugar
¼ cup lukewarm water
½ cup milk
16 tablespoons (2 quarter-pound
　　sticks) unsalted butter, melted
¼ cup sugar
3½ cups sifted flour
¼ teaspoon salt
1 egg plus 2 egg yolks, lightly beaten
　　together
½ teaspoon grated lemon peel
1 twelve-ounce jar apricot jam
Granulated sugar

Buchteln

JELLY BUNS

Sprinkle the yeast and pinch of sugar into the lukewarm water. Let the mixture stand for 2 or 3 minutes, then stir it to dissolve the yeast. Set the container in a warm, draft-free place for 2 or 3 minutes, or until the solution has begun to bubble and has almost doubled in volume.

Pour the milk into a heavy 1-quart saucepan and warm over medium heat until bubbles form around the edge. Turn heat to low and add 8 tablespoons of butter and ¼ cup of sugar. Stir constantly until the sugar dissolves. Let cool to room temperature and then combine with the yeast mixture.

Sift the flour and salt into a deep mixing bowl. Make a well in the flour and pour into it the yeast and milk mixtures, the egg, egg yolks and the lemon peel. With your hands or a large wooden spoon, work the flour into the other ingredients until they become a medium-firm dough.

Shape the dough into a ball and put it into a large, lightly buttered bowl. Dust the top of the dough lightly with flour, cover with a kitchen towel and set it in a warm, draft-free spot (an unlighted oven would be ideal). In 45 minutes to an hour, the dough should double in bulk. Preheat the oven to 350°.

Punch the dough down and knead it by pulling it into an oblong shape, folding it end to end, then pressing it down and pushing it forward several times with the heels of the hands. Turn the mass of dough slightly toward you and repeat the process. Continue to knead, sprinkling more flour on the dough and the working surface if necessary, until the dough is smooth and elastic. This takes at least 10 minutes.

On a lightly floured surface, roll the dough into a rectangle ¼ inch thick and about 2 inches longer than it is wide. Then trim the edges to straight lines and cut it into 2½- by-4½-inch rectangles.

Thin the jam by warming it in a heavy saucepan, then place a teaspoon of it in the center of each rectangle and spread it toward the edges.

Beginning with a short side, roll each rectangle up, jelly-roll fashion, dip it in the remaining butter and stand it on end in a 9-inch springform pan. Arrange the first rolls in a circle in the pan so that they barely touch each other and the side of the pan. Continue the pattern with the rest.

For jelly buns put apricot jam on dough rectangles, roll them, and place them in the pan *(right)* to bake.

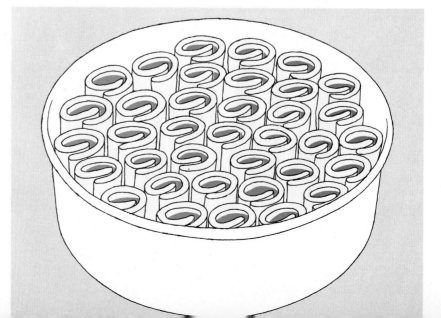

Drip any butter that is left over them. Cover the pan with a towel and let it stand in a warm, draft-free area for 15 minutes.

Bake the buns in the middle of the oven for ½ hour, or until they are golden brown, puffed up and completely fill the pan. Remove them from the oven, release the sides of the pan and sprinkle the buns with granulated sugar. Break the buns apart to serve them.

Kaiserschmarrn
EMPEROR'S PANCAKE

To serve 4 to 6

2 tablespoons raisins
4 tablespoons dark rum
4 egg yolks
3 tablespoons sugar
⅛ teaspoon salt
2 cups milk
⅛ teaspoon vanilla extract
1 cup sifted all-purpose flour
5 egg whites
4 tablespoons unsalted butter, melted
Confectioners' sugar

Soak the raisins in the rum for 30 minutes; drain and squeeze dry.

Beat the egg yolks, sugar and salt together with a whisk or rotary or electric beater until the mixture is pale yellow and thick. Stir in the milk and vanilla extract, then gradually beat in the sifted flour ½ cup at a time. Continue to beat until the mixture is smooth. Stir in the raisins.

In another bowl, preferably of unlined copper, beat the egg whites until they are stiff enough to form unwavering peaks when the beater is lifted from the bowl. Using a rubber spatula, fold the whites into the batter with an over-under cutting motion rather than a stirring motion. Continue to fold until there is no trace of the whites. Do not overfold.

In a heavy 8-inch skillet, heat 1 tablespoon of the butter over low heat. Pour in about half the batter—at least enough to cover the bottom of the skillet to a ¼-inch depth. Cook over low heat for about 4 minutes, or until the pancake has puffed up and browned slightly. (Test by lifting an edge with a spatula.) Turn the pancake out onto a plate, add another tablespoon of butter, reheat, then slide the pancake back into the skillet, uncooked side down. Cook for the same length of time. With 2 forks, pull the pancake into 6 or 8 pieces. Remove to a warm plate.

Heat another tablespoon of butter in the skillet, cook another pancake in the same way as the first, and pull it into similar pieces. Return the first batch to the skillet and cook both batches over medium heat for about 2 minutes, turning them 2 or 3 times with a spatula.

Remove the *Kaiserschmarrn* to a plate, sprinkle it with confectioners' sugar and serve with fruit syrup or a fruit compote.

Cook half of the batter for the Emperor's pancake, then pull into 6 or 8 pieces. Transfer to a warm plate.

After cooking and separating a second batch, return the first pieces to the skillet and heat together.

Now the whole pancake is placed on a plate, sprinkled liberally with sugar, and it is ready to be served.

II

Austrian Cooking Today

Boiled beef, shown opposite with pan-browned potatoes and a parsley garnish, is an Austrian specialty, usually eaten with horse-radish in vinegar, applesauce or whipped cream. Austrians are said to use 40 different cuts of meat for boiled beef. This one is from the brisket.

It used to take a lot of cooking to keep the Austrians going, and to a great extent this is still true: unlike people who get along on three meals a day, many Austrians have twice as many. They start their day with coffee and milk, *Semmeln* (breakfast rolls) and bread with butter and jam. But this is not very substantial, and so by 10 o'clock many of them need their *Gabelfrühstück*, or fork breakfast, including goulash or sometimes calf's lungs, or a pair of hot sausages, known as *Wieners* everywhere except in Vienna, where they are called *Würstel*.

By noon everybody is hungry again and most people go home for a substantial lunch of soup, meat with potatoes and vegetables, salad and, of course, dessert—usually some kind of *Mehlspeisen*, a homemade pastry. Yet, many people are hungry again in midafternoon. The *Jause* restores them. *Jause* time is still gossip time in Vienna—at home, at a pastry shop or coffeehouse—and thus is considered by some people to be the most important meal of the day, with its coffee and whipped cream, presented with a selection of sandwiches and cakes.

By 7, when it's time to leave, everybody is hungry once again. Dinner is often a simple meal—cold meat, sausage, a vegetable casserole, eggs, salad, cheese. Many Viennese like to spend an evening at a *Heuriger*, an inn where the country's young wine is drunk, but dining out in restaurants is not as common as in Western Europe and America.

After-dinner invitations are frequent all over Austria. You are asked to come around 8:30. You will be offered a glass of wine and perhaps some small sandwiches, and around 11 black coffee will be served to keep you awake. But Austrians don't often drink coffee "with nothing," as do the Americans, who invented the coffee break; so there will be a *Torte*, or perhaps a piece of *Strudel*, so you won't have to go home on an empty stomach.

Austrian cooking and eating today is certainly less ostentatious than it was in the days of the Empire, but it is nonetheless substantial. The cooking in an Austrian home—and everywhere else in Central Europe—formerly depended on the social class of the householder. The aristocracy and the upper bourgeoisie had trained cooks, plenty of other servants and lots of money. The well-to-do had the time and money to indulge their tastes, and their eating habits were quite different from those of the "lower" classes. Now the old class distinctions are a thing of the past, and even the house-wife who strives for really good cooking is also concerned with economy. Julius Eckel's popular Viennese postwar cookbook makes careful distinc-tions between economy cooking, meatless cooking, simple cooking, fine cooking and fast cooking.

In many upper-middle-income homes people are still trying to maintain the complex tradition of Viennese cooking with all its imported dishes—the soups, roasts and sausages from southern Germany; the "Venetian" special-ties (fish fried in oil, macaroni, *risotto*); and the many other foreign ingre-dients and influences that have become part of Austrian cooking. But some of the nationalities from whom the Viennese have borrowed insist that in the transmission from one cuisine to another the original dish has suffered. Hungarians living in Vienna claim that a Viennese goulash has little in com-mon with their original Hungarian *gulyás* or *pörkölt;* they think the Vien-nese variety is too mild and too mellow, perhaps too "civilized."

The Czechs, of whom there are so many in Vienna, speak in the same way about the dumplings of their homeland, of their *Streusel* cake (light sponge-cake) and *Buchteln* (jelly buns, *page 36*), their pork roast and *Marillenknödel* (sweet dumplings filled with fresh apricots and covered with brown butter, cinnamon and sugar). The Viennese, they hold, simply do not know how to cook such dishes in the authentic way. But the fact is that these dishes are often done as well in Vienna as in Budapest or Prague. At the same time, Viennese goose liver *risotto* has little in common with Italian *risotto;* and "Polish" carp or "Polish" tongue are different from the original dishes.

The Polish influence in Austrian cooking is less noticeable than other foreign touches. However, marjoram, a popular herb in Poland, is also in demand in Vienna, where it is used for cooking beef, lamb and potatoes, and stuffed Polish cabbage is also a favorite. But similar varieties of stuffed cabbage are also cooked by the Hungarians, the Yugoslavs and the Ro-manians. Certain old Viennese cookbooks also list a "Polish sauce" that is served with sliced, boiled ox tongue or with fish. Viennese cooking then is a real "melting pot," which over the years has developed its unique quality, taking the best from other countries and adding its own refinements.

In today's typical Austrian home the noon meal—the big meal of the day —always begins with a carefully prepared soup. There is a widespread and justified belief that a good cook shows her hand in the soup.

The basic Austrian soup is *Rindsuppe* (beef broth, *page 67*), of which there are two variations: the "white," really golden yellow, for which the raw vegetables are added to the pot with all the other ingredients, and the "brown," or "dark," which differs in color as a result of the vegetables' first being browned in fat with the crushed bones. Traditionally the beef was cooked in water, but today many cooks prefer to cook it in a previously prepared stock. This preserves the flavor of the beef and enriches the broth at the same time.

All clear soups are named for the garnishes that are added to them. The most popular are the various *Knödel*, such as the *Semmelknödel* (bread dumplings, *page 138*), the *Leberknödel* (liver dumplings *page 83*), and the *Speckknödel* (bacon dumplings, *page 80*). There are all sorts of variations —*Leberschöberl* (liver squares), *Leberreis* (liver rice)—and subvariations known as *Fleckerl* (with small squares of noodle dough) and *Eingetropftes* (with a pancake mixture dropped in). The substantial soups are easier to describe—potato soup, mushroom soup, fresh-pea soup, bean soup or bread soup are exactly what they are called. They are often served on Fridays and during the Lenten season, when no meat appears on the table in many homes. But of course, at such a time fish is very much in demand.

When Austria was still a large empire a great quantity and variety of fish was eaten. Sixteenth Century writers described the huge amounts of fish that were brought in from Hungary, Bohemia and Moravia. Many monasteries had their own fish ponds. The monks cooked fish in oil and stuffed it into sausages. In 1758, Empress Maria Theresia decreed that during Lent "only officers, or Protestants might be provided with meat in inns, at separate tables," but her son, Emperor Josef II, revoked the decree, so that anyone could eat meat during Lent regardless of religious affiliation. As a consequence, the eating of fish declined.

Old people in Vienna still remember the enormous varieties of fish that were sold every morning in Vienna's Naschmarkt, the central market. You could get fish and shellfish, oysters and turtles, crayfish, imported from Styria, Galicia, Bosnia and Hungary. Sea fish arrived from Germany, Holland and from Trieste. The Adriatic, then partly an Austrian sea, supplied marvelous *scampi* and oysters.

The Naschmarkt is no longer the fabulous center of aggressive bartering that it once was. Modern stores and supermarkets elsewhere in the city have drawn away much of the clientele. Some people still go there for the best fish, the finest fruit, the fresh, tender vegetables and, of course, the Naschmarkt is still a great meeting place for gossip.

Today Austria has no seacoast, and the Austrians are no longer so fish-conscious. Frozen fish fillets are imported from the North Sea, but they are in demand only on fasting days. People coat them with bread crumbs in *Wiener Schnitzel* style. There are excellent *scampi* imported by air from Turkey, Denmark and the Adriatic coast, and once in a while one can get a first-rate turbot and genuine Channel sole. From the Austrian lakes near the Hungarian border and from Hungary itself comes *Fogosch,* a delicious fish served *am Rost* (grilled). In Hungary, the fish is called *fogas* and the best, from Lake Balaton, is considered a great delicacy in Vienna. But not many can afford expensive imported fish. The best fishmonger in the Naschmarkt tells me that her customers are mostly *Ausländer*—foreigners and diplomats. The Austrians buy the less costly salmon, pike, perch, sturgeon and whatever domestic fresh-water varieties are available.

Krebse (river crayfish), of which the Viennese imported so much from

Hungary, Bohemia and Moravia during the 16th and 17th Centuries, are also expensive today. They are served in a soup, or cold with mayonnaise. The best crayfish dish is *Krebsschwänze* cooked in dill sauce and served with steamed rice. One of the most popular fish is carp (which many foreigners consider a muddy-tasting fish), and Austrian housewives give tacit agreement, for they sometimes keep a live carp in a bathtub for several days until it has lost its insipid taste and acquired a fine, fresh flavor. Fried carp is the traditional main dish for the Christmas Eve and New Year's Eve dinner. More adventurous cooks prepare carp in aspic, Polish style; or cold carp in paprika sauce, obviously a Hungarian touch; or carp baked in black sauce, which suggests the Czech influence.

The Austrians, like the Germans, enjoy eating marinated herring; it is said to perform miracles against hangovers. But they do not appreciate the great delight of fresh herring in spring, so loved in Holland, Denmark and northern Germany. Maybe someday the taste will conquer them.

The great fish contribution of the Austrian cuisine is brook trout, *Bach-forelle*. The classic preparation is *au bleu*—live trout taken out of the water, killed by a blow on the head, cleaned quickly and briefly boiled in a court bouillon with vinegar. The trout turns blue and immediately curls. It is served with melted butter and new potatoes. This is a gastronomic joy, especially when you get it in a mountain inn, where the trout is caught in a cold, clear mountain brook. It is essential that the trout be alive shortly before it is eaten; otherwise it would not turn blue (a sign of its freshness)

A baker's boy leaves Eduard Mang's 116-year-old bakery with breakfast breads. Mang's (no longer run by a Mang) bakes 14 different rolls, buns and *croissants*, six kinds of black bread and three kinds of white—the full range of Viennese breads.

and the special flavor would be lost. (If it has been kept in the icebox, it will be straight when it's served, not arched; send it back.)

If you ask an Austrian what he considers the main element in his country's cuisine he would probably say meat and poultry—boiled beef *(page 67)*, *Wiener Schnitzel (page 59)* and *Backhendl (page 64)*. There is no question of the importance of meat in the Austrian diet.

Although the Viennese confess that they like nothing better than their boiled beef or a *Wiener Schnitzel,* the statistics of Austria's meat consumption seem to contradict the favorite eating habits. Almost 60 per cent of all meat bought is pork. Beef comes next, at about 25 per cent. Veal, always expensive, accounts for less than 10 per cent. The rest is poultry and a small amount of mutton. In other words they eat less expensively than they admit.

Pork is of a high quality and is prepared in many ways. In winter the Viennese make roasts of pork flavored with caraway seeds, garlic and mustard, accompanied by red or white cabbage, sauerkraut, dried peas, lentils, potatoes or dumplings. Or they eat pork with horseradish, known locally as *Krenfleisch.* The origin of these dishes is unmistakably Bohemian.

The pork roast called *Jungschweinsbraten,* from a pig less than six months old, is a big favorite. (A roast from older animals is called *Schweinsbraten.)* *Jungschweinsbraten,* either loin or leg, boned or on the bone, is always prepared with the rind on. It is seasoned, browned, placed in the roasting pan with the rind side down. Beef stock is added, then carrots and onions, and then the sauce is thickened with cream. The crackling should be brown and crisp. Sometimes poppy seeds are added.

Much has been written about the glories of Vienna's *Tafelspitz,* the most celebrated local cut of boiled beef. During the reign of Franz Josef I everyone knew that the Emperor preferred boiled beef for lunch when he was alone. Following His Majesty's example, a great many Viennese had boiled beef for lunch almost every weekday in their lives, often eating the same cut day after day. Sunday, however, was reserved for *Wiener Schnitzel, Backhendl* or some kind of roast.

Before Allied bombs were dropped on Meissl and Schadn's, in March 1945, this most famous of Vienna's beef restaurants had been a place where the whole ritual of cooking and eating boiled beef could be seen. The restaurant's two floors catered to two pocketbooks of sharply contrasted size, and the elegance of each of the surroundings varied accordingly. But it was the formalities of eating that were so interesting. These were many and they were never questioned. Only those who didn't know any better ordered "boiled beef" pure and simple. To do so was to invite the contempt of waiters and any habitués who might be within earshot, as there were 24 varieties of beef to choose from, all for boiling and yet all different. One was expected to be precise in one's order. Each of Meissl and Schadn's famous customers from Gustav Mahler to Richard Strauss had his own particular cut and every waiter knew what it was.

The high quality of the meat was largely due to the fact that the steers were fed on sugar-beet mash and molasses, which made their meat juicy, tender and delicious. It was kept for about two weeks in large cool chambers. Never longer. Nothing but a clear consommé was considered a suitable preparation for the main beef course, and the guest was not expected to

Continued on page 47

A Colorful Landmark of Another Day

One of the most famous landmarks of old Vienna is the Naschmarkt, or Nibble Market. Although its days are nearly over (it is being forced from the center of the city by supermarkets and modern stores), it still holds joys that bring a gleam of anticipation to the eyes of the little boy entering the market with his mother, who might buy meat, fruit or any of the pickled vegetables in the jars shown below. There was a time when all Vienna considered it vital to know the latest developments in the market, such as whether the peasants of Styria, Carinthia, Lower Austria or Hungary had begun bringing in the first tomatoes and at what prices. In "the old days" the Naschmarkt was not only the best place to buy food, but the very center of the *best* gossip, the most aggressive bartering, the loudest exchanged confidences and advice. Indeed this small area of ramshackle buildings and stalls and carts throbbed with the great life of this great city.

A waiter in Figlmuller's restaurant in Vienna serves a pair of *Wiener Schnitzel* with the salads that usually accompany this famous veal dish.

allow liquor of any kind to spoil the palate. He was also expected to be on time for his dinner, as everything was cooked fresh.

It was the endless number of garnitures that gave variety to the boiled meat. The most basic of these side dishes was grated horseradish, prepared either with vinegar, applesauce or whipped cream. Or there would be at least one of the many cold sauces. The most famous were made from chives, from gherkins or from anchovies. In addition, there would be a hot sauce, which might be of dill, tomato, mushroom, onion or cucumber. Sautéed potatoes, a salad of red beets, and pickles completed the meal.

Even before Meissl and Schadn's was destroyed, much of the cult had begun to disappear. A certain laxity showed, both on the part of guest and waiter. Yet, many Viennese still prefer boiled beef to any other dish and still care deeply how it is cooked and served.

It is impossible to translate into English the names of the various cuts that are used for boiled beef in Vienna, and today's generation is not always certain about the somewhat subtle distinctions between, let us say, the *Kruspelspitz*, "located just below the *Rieddeckel*, very juicy, somewhat coarse-fibered meat of excellent taste," and the *Rieddeckel*, "a succulent meat, very popular for making stock."

"Beef," said Marie-Antoine Carême, the great master of French cuisine, "is the soul of cookery," and boiled beef can be called the soul of Viennese cooking. But while the Viennese go wild over boiled beef, it is the *Wiener Schnitzel* that is Vienna's most famous meat dish outside of Austria. A *Schnitzel* is traditionally a veal scallop, but not all *Schnitzel* are made of veal. Some economical Viennese housewives use a thin, well-flattened slice of beef to make a *Wiener Schnitzel*, and some cooks, mostly Czechs, use pork. Many Viennese cooks claim that the *Schnitzel* would burn in hot butter, and so today, for the most part, the Viennese fry their *Wiener Schnitzel* in lard, or sometimes a mixture of lard and butter. Some people even claim that the lard gives it the characteristic taste.

Some prefer the fillet of veal for *Schnitzel*, but most people who consider that cut too tender and too expensive use the leg, especially its innermost part, which Vienna's butchers know as *Kaiserteil*. It is truly an "emperor's cut." But above all, the veal should be fine-grained—young and tender, bright and juicy. The best comes from Salzburg.

Experienced "schnitzlers" plan well ahead. First they prepare the potato salad or green salad that goes with it, and the roasted or mashed potatoes. They make their own toasted bread crumbs rather than buying them readymade. They trim their veal scallops and make a few incisions all round the edges so the *Schnitzel* will not curl up while it is being fried. They have three bowls ready. One is filled with a mixture of flour and salt, the second with beaten egg and the third with the bread crumbs. The scallops are pounded lightly with a cutlet bat or meat pounder and are then seasoned with salt on both sides. Meanwhile the finest available fresh lard or butter is slowly heated in a frying pan that must not be too shallow. The melted fat should be about half an inch deep.

Now you must work fast: first, dip the scallops in flour—lightly, so that they are very thinly coated. Second, dip them into the beaten egg, again lightly; they should be only coated with egg, not soaked in it. Third, dip the scallops into the bread crumbs, again lightly. They should be evenly coated on both sides. Excess bread crumbs should be carefully shaken off.

By this time the fat should be hot enough—and the scallops are put into the frying pan. (If you leave the coated scallops on the table too long the breading may separate from the meat.) Don't crowd the scallops in the frying pan; they need space to fry properly. If you don't have a large enough pan, trim them to size.

All *Schnitzel* cooks agree that the color of a *Wiener Schnitzel* should be a light golden brown. Certain Breughel paintings and Stradivari violins have the perfect *Schnitzel* color. After the first side acquires the right hue, turn the scallop over, and continue to cook.

The perfect crust should blow up in a few places but never break away from the meat. In Vienna they say you should be able to slip a knife between the coating and the meat—but please don't try it. It doesn't always work. Take out the *Schnitzel* (after three or four minutes) and drain it well on absorbent kitchen paper. (Of course, you should have the paper ready— don't run around looking for it now.)

In my carefree days in Vienna it was said that the test of a perfect *Wiener Schnitzel* was to be able to sit down on it, for at least one full second, without leaving a fat stain on the seat of your pants. I once tried it but something must have gone wrong with that particular *Wiener Schnitzel*. It left a stain on the seat of my new, light-gray pants.

When the *Wiener Schnitzel* is ready, it must be served at once if you want to enjoy its crispness. Many people "leave it in the oven," which is a sin.

An Austrian *Ausflug* is a picnic—but an elaborate one, all dressed up and nearly formal. This one, on the grounds of the Laxenburg Palace south of Vienna, is spread on an embroidered tablecloth that has graced the family's *Ausflüge* year after year since 1905.

Connoisseurs serve nothing but a large wedge of lemon on the plate with the *Schnitzel*. But you may not want to be a connoisseur. Do as you wish.

How big should a *Wiener Schnitzel* be? The Viennese theory is that when it is served, you should not be able to see the rim of your plate. As a student I frequented a certain restaurant in the Eighth District where they had enormous *Wiener Schnitzel* twice a week. It would hang down over the large plate, and I would happily eat my way around until I began to see the plate. It was quite wonderful, but I couldn't do it today.

When the Viennese don't have a *Wiener Schnitzel*, they may eat one of the many other varieties of *Schnitzel*. There is the popular *Naturschnitzel*, dipped in flour, simple and delicious, that doctors prescribe for a light diet. The Parisian *Schnitzel* is similar to the *Wiener Schnitzel*, dipped in flour and egg but without the bread crumbs. The *Cordon Bleu Schnitzel* is a de luxe version that is said to be a Swiss invention, perhaps because it has a slice of Emmental cheese and a slice of cooked ham inside the folded *Schnitzel*. The *Prague Schnitzel* is similar to a *Cordon Bleu*, covered with chopped Prague ham and served with tomatoes and green salad, and garnished with egg. The list is almost endless.

There is also a *Sardellenschnitzel*, with an anchovy and butter paste inside the scallop. The *Parmaschnitzel* shows the Italian influence. The lightly fried scallops are covered with grated Parmesan cheese and cream and baked in a hot oven for 15 minutes. One of the popular kinds of *Paprikaschnitzel*, a variety of *Naturschnitzel*, is served with paprika sauce and finished with sour cream. Also popular is the *Rahmschnitzel*, which is a *Naturschnitzel* served in a heavy cream sauce.

But the main dish of an Austrian meal need not necessarily be beef, veal, pork or fish. Chicken has always been an Austrian delicacy eaten on special occasions by those who could afford it. The 14th Century minnesinger, Heinrich von Neustadt, reprimanded the Viennese women for "drinking a carafe of wine and eating half a fried chicken before going to Mass, so they will feel better in head and stomach." This is probably the first mention of the *Backhendl*, the Viennese version of fried chicken that, during the Biedermeier period (the first half of the 19th Century), became Austria's culinary symbol of upper-class prosperity. Unlike two other gastronomic symbols— the *Wiener Schnitzel* and boiled beef—that stood for the *petit bourgeois* way of life, the *Backhendl* was an aristocratic dish.

The *Backhendl* remains the durable symbol of gustatory happiness. In the early 19th Century it was called *Huhn im Schlafrock*, chicken in a dressing gown. It is a young spring chicken, prepared exactly as a *Wiener Schnitzel* —dipped first in flour, then in beaten egg and bread crumbs, and fried in hot lard to a golden-brown color.

Viennese cookbooks describe precisely the preparation of the *Backhendl* but rarely explain what sort of chicken should be used because they take it for granted that everybody knows. The chicken should be plump and tender, and its weight should be from one and a half to two pounds when it is ready for the frying pan. This should be enough for four people.

The chicken is cleaned and quartered; the wing tips must be cut off. Although a tough bird may be improved by marinating in lemon juice, the high quality of American poultry makes this unnecessary. Traditionally, from then on it's the *Schnitzel* procedure—season, coat the pieces three times, shake off the surplus bread crumbs, fry in smoking hot fat. It takes 12 to 15 minutes to fry the *Backhendl* to the prescribed golden-brown on both sides. However, the liver—often served separately—should be put into the fat only during the last five minutes. Drain the pieces on absorbent kitchen paper. *Backhendl* should be served at once in order to keep its delicious crispness. A wedge of lemon, sometimes fried parsley, and a salad are served with it.

Foreigners often wonder about the fascination of this dish (unless they happen to come from the southern part of the United States where the cult of fried chicken also flourishes). But the *Backhendl* itself is only part of a ritual that would not be complete without its special atmosphere. It should be eaten on a warm summer night, when one sits outside in the garden, and there should be a chilled bottle of white wine with it, a Gumpoldskirchner, perhaps. Somewhere in the background there ought to be music, possibly Johann Strauss. The garden-and-music mood belongs to the *Backhendl* as the smell of the seacoast belongs to a genuine *bouillabaisse,* or as the first autumn haze and dark fir trees belong to a dish of game.

Game somehow never became widely accepted in Austrian home cooking. A small minority loves it. There used to be seasons in game, but nowadays one gets venison (roe deer, red deer, fallow deer) all year round from the cold chambers of the game and poultry shops. Many restaurants organize *Wildbretwochen,* "game festival weeks," serving venison *(page 81),* partridge, pheasant, boar, hare and woodcock in many ways. Older cooks still marinate most game to make it tender, but a new school of game cooks claims that a marinade affects the meat's fine flavor. These cooks serve fillets of hare or venison grilled or quickly roasted. Game is served with fresh or pickled cabbage, fruit, cranberries, red currants, and various sauces and purées.

There is really no area of the national cooking in which the average Austrian housewife is not at home. This adaptability—or maybe it is a native gift —is perhaps best shown in the use of leftovers. Austrian cooks waste nothing. Almost all their cookbooks have long chapters on *Resteküche,* or leftover cooking, giving recipes for leftover vegetables, meat and fish. Boiled fish leftovers are turned into a salad. Meat leftovers are served the next day fried or baked in butter or baked with noodles. Leftovers of boiled beef are served as *Zwiebelfleisch* (beef sautéed with onions and spices, *page 85*) or as *Kroketten* (fried in bread crumbs and oil) or as cold beef salads. Leftover vegetables are used for *Gemüseschnitzel,* mixed with all sorts of other leftovers, mushrooms and spices, and fried in butter.

Minced meat is a favorite economy dish. The most popular guise for minced meat is a meat loaf made of various meats (beef, pork and veal), mixed with stale white bread soaked in milk, which makes the meat light and fluffy, and with finely minced onion and bacon, an egg, butter, parsley, salt and pepper. All this, Viennese experts tell you, should be done with wet hands, so that the mixture is well kneaded. The meat loaf is baked in a moderate oven and served with a sour-cream sauce, made with the meat juice.

The need for economy has taught the cooks of Austria to use every bit of veal. They know that a calf does not consist only of scallops. They make a very tasty dish, called *Gefüllte Kalbsbrust,* stuffed breast of veal, of a rather inexpensive cut, with a stuffing that gives the cooks a chance to create and improvise. Roast knuckle of veal, served with potatoes and green salad is a very popular dish. It may be served with onions, carrots and tomatoes that have been simmered with it, or with a stuffing of seasoned bread crumbs, onion, carrot, liver and parsley. The cheaper cuts of veal are used for *Eingemachtes*, a sort of veal ragôut with vegetables in a white sauce.

Austrian cooking has given us a variety of great dishes for almost every course of the meal: soup, fish, meat, poultry and, of course, dessert. But in the realm of vegetables, the Austrian contribution has been negligible. Despite the fact that numerous foreign techniques and dishes have been appropriated by Austrian cooks over the centuries, they have still not learned how best to treat vegetables. Minimum cooking to preserve the goodness and the sweet, fresh quality that can make any vegetable a joy is an ideal that most Austrian cooks appear to be quite unaware of. Instead of leaving them alone, the Austrians insist upon sprinkling bread crumbs fried in butter over them, or serving them in a purée, or in a light or dark *Einbrenn*, a *roux* made with flour and butter and a little beef stock.

The Austrians explain that their winters are long and severe and they must depend on "winter vegetables"—sauerkraut, carrots, cabbage, dried peas, lentils. They roast their cabbage with onions, add heavy cream and butter to their purées of peas and lentils. Many vegetables show their non-Viennese origin. Hungarian *Kürbiskraut*, for instance, has nothing to do with kraut, but is shredded marrow (a large variety of summer squash), cooked with chopped onions, diced bacon and chopped tomatoes, sugar, paprika and spices, flour and sour cream. And there is *lecsó*, a Hungarian dish of peppers and tomatoes, cooked in hot lard with onions, garlic, and possibly caraway seeds and basil.

Mushrooms are important in Austrian cooking—fried, breaded, cooked with cream, onion or lemon juice. When *Eierschwammerln* (chanterelle mushrooms) are in season, the Austrians sauté them in melted butter and serve them with scrambled eggs; or they may be sautéed with onions and used as a topping for the *Schnitzel*.

Every Viennese meal has plenty of starch. Potatoes are served in endless variations, almost as many as there are in potato-conscious Germany. The first new potatoes of the season are a treat: they are simply boiled, served hot with fresh butter, or perhaps caraway seeds or grated cheese and a tiny bit of salt. Later in the season the Viennese love their *Kipfler* potatoes (they are shaped like a *croissant*, or *Kipfel*), which are waxy and yellowish and are used to make the beloved potato salad (with vinegar, oil, sugar, salt, pepper, mustard and finely chopped onions). All year round the Austrians eat potatoes prepared in various ways—puréed, sautéed in butter and lard, cooked in goulash—and if they don't have potatoes, they have dumplings or *Nockerln* or pasta or rice.

As a contrast to all the starch, Austrians serve salad with almost every meal. In small restaurants it comes in a small glass dish, frequently with a sugar and lemon dressing, in which sliced cucumber often floats. Lettuce salad (Boston variety) is served with a little dressing and is often decorated with quartered hard-boiled eggs. There is also cauliflower salad, corn salad, lentil salad (with chopped ham and chopped onion), sliced-beet salad, tomato salad (served with chopped onion or sometimes with parsley and

Marzipan candies (made of almond paste, sugar and egg white) are favorite sweets in Austria. These, on an open street stand in a town near Vienna, have been colored and shaped to look like sausages and other meats.

chives). Other salads are sometimes made with green peppers cut into rings, celery knob, cooked French beans and cucumbers. The so-called Gypsy salad contains raw cauliflower, tomatoes, olives, gherkins and cucumbers. Mushrooms and radishes are marinated for use as hors d'oeuvre.

By now you've had so many calories in your soup, your potatoes, dumplings, or vegetables cooked in a white sauce, that you might well think you have had enough. But the climax of the meal is still to come: the dessert. There are meatless meals in Austria, because meat is expensive, but I have never heard of a dessertless meal. All Viennese cookbooks devote a large part of their contents to desserts, and usually more space is given to these than to everything else together. Gretel Beer's *Austrian Cooking*, for example, devotes 111 pages to desserts, pastries and biscuits and 94 pages to everything else, which shows us where Viennese tastes lie.

At a restaurant most Viennese first look toward the end of the menu under *Mehlspeisen*, choose their *Mehlspeise* first, and then work back to soups and the rest of the menu. An Austrian always ends his meal with a *Mehlspeise* —something that is warm or cold, but always substantial and sweet. He also knows that a *gulyás* or a *Beinfleisch* are best eaten in "his" *Stamm-Beisel*, as he calls his favorite eating place, but the *Mehlspeisen*—although often delicious in the right restaurant—really are best eaten at home.

I don't think anyone would argue with my saying that Vienna's pastry *(Chapter 7)* is the country's chief contribution to international gastronomy —often imitated, but seldom equaled. It is a delight to look at, a joy to taste and fun to make in the kitchen.

But, of course, one of the most beloved local institutions in Vienna is the *Heuriger (pages 54-57)*. This is not a restaurant, not even a place where one goes to eat, but it belongs among the few good things in life that no Viennese would want to miss. *Heuriger* literally means "this year's." To the Viennese it denotes "this year's wine," and, by extension, "the place where this year's wine is drunk." Actually, it is not this year's wine in the sense of the calendar year, but of the wine year, which begins with the autumnal harvest. The *Heuriger* that one drinks in the spring and summer is last autumn's harvest. Incidentally, one doesn't go to the *Heuriger* simply in order to drink; that would be a misconception. The *Heuriger* is to a Viennese what the pub is to an Englishman and the old-fashioned Third Avenue saloon to an old-fashioned New Yorker: a place where he is certain to find congenial companionship, where somebody is going to listen, where he can be himself among friends. The drinking is just part of it, though it often becomes an important and engrossing part.

The authentic *Heuriger* is a small place. The owner raises his own grapes, harvests them between September and November, and makes his own wine. He may have only a small vineyard, just a few acres, and produce only a few barrels of wine. When he feels that his wine has aged enough, usually a few months, he hangs a fir branch above the entrance of his house. That means it is *ausg'steckt*—there is new wine for sale—and you'd better come soon because the supply may last only a few weeks. Vienna's newspapers publish a daily list of the places that will be open that night. When the supply runs out, the decent proprietor takes down the branch and closes his place until the next harvest. He would never sell somebody else's wine. He has his group of customer-friends, experienced *Weinbeisser* (literally, "wine biters") who try the new wine in the press house.

When it gets warm outside, the friends move into the "garden," just three or four crude, unpainted wooden tables set up amid the lilac bushes and the jasmine. There is always a walnut or linden tree (just as there seems to be a horse chestnut tree in nearly every German beer garden). There are no fancy trimmings—there is plenty of *Stimmung*, the mood. Beyond the flowers and the trees one sees some lights—either the lights of the Kahlenberg above, or the lights of the city below. The owner and his wife serve the wine in plain thick water glasses that are quickly washed but not dried. The guests bring their own food wrapped in yesterday's newspaper—sausages, bacon, hard-boiled eggs, cheese—and provide their own entertainment. Sometimes the owner, when he is in the mood, may bring out his zither or harmonica, and sing some of the sentimental songs about *Wien und Wein,* and everybody cries quietly and happily into his glass. It is all absolutely delightful and Viennese.

At the Heuriger

One of the most cherished customs of spring and summertime Vienna is to go to the *Heuriger,* the place where one drinks the *Heurige,* or new wine. This usually is the garden of the man who made the wine. A straw "sun" *(above)* or a fir branch is hoisted to show that the wine is ready and that there will be different smoked meats, pickled vegetables, hard-boiled eggs and some dark bread to eat *(opposite).* Here old friends will gather to drink, eat, sing songs and stir up sentimental feelings about being Viennese.

Inside Vienna's city limits but tucked away in its hills are many rustic pockets like the one shown at the right. In them, grapes are grown, wine is made and the *Heurigen* flourish. Here wine made from last fall's grape harvest goes down pleasantly at tables set out under arbors where the grapes for this year's wine are ripening. The wine, mainly white and light, is served in plain water glasses. In the old days if you wanted something to nibble you had to bring it yourself, but in recent years many wine growers have taken to setting out simple repasts like the one shown on the previous page and above. The *Heuriger* menu varies only slightly. Above is a plateful of Liptauer cheese, some thick brown bread, radishes, an egg, green pepper, a scallion and tomatoes.

Wiener Rostbraten
VIENNESE STEAKS

Cut the sliced onions into strips ⅛ to ¼ inch wide. In a heavy 8- or 10-inch skillet over medium heat, melt the 4 tablespoons of butter, and when the foam subsides, add the onions. Stirring occasionally, cook them for 8 to 10 minutes, or until they are colored and crisp. Add more butter if necessary while the onions are frying—they must not burn. Set the onions aside, uncovered, in the skillet.

Cut the steak into 6 equal portions. In a 10- or 12-inch heavy skillet, heat the oil and 2 tablespoons of butter over medium heat. When the butter foam subsides, add the steaks. Raise the heat to moderately high and cook the steaks briskly for 2 to 4 minutes, depending upon the degree of doneness you prefer.

Arrange the steaks on a heated platter and sprinkle them with salt and a few grindings of pepper.

Reheat the onions over high heat for a minute or so to restore their crispness. Serve the steaks with a mound of the onions placed on each one.

If you prefer a light sauce, add the stock to the skillet in which the steaks were cooked, and bring it to a boil, stirring in any brown bits clinging to the pan, then pour the sauce over the steaks before you place the onions on top. *Wiener Rostbraten* may be served with chopped parsley and crumpled bacon sprinkled over the onions.

Selchfleisch
SMOKED PORK WITH PURÉED SPLIT PEAS

Using a 4- or 5-quart saucepan or soup kettle, cover the pork butt with water and bring it to a boil. Reduce the heat to low, cover the pan partially, and simmer for about 1½ hours, or until the pork shows no resistance when pierced with the tip of a sharp knife.

In a heavy 2-quart saucepan over medium heat, cook the diced bacon until it has rendered most of its fat and is lightly browned. Remove the bacon with a slotted spoon and set it aside. Add the onions to the fat remaining in the pan and, stirring occasionally, cook them for 6 to 8 minutes, or until they are lightly colored. Pour in the stock and then add the peas, the potatoes, the reserved bacon, salt and a few grindings of pepper. Bring the stock to a boil before reducing the heat to its lowest point. Cover the pan tightly and simmer for 1½ hours, or until the peas and potatoes are soft enough to be easily mashed. Then pour the entire contents of the pan into a fine sieve set over a large bowl, and purée the peas and potatoes by rubbing them through the sieve with the back of a large spoon.

Return the purée to the saucepan, add the cream, stir, then turn the heat to its lowest point. Cover the saucepan and simmer for 4 or 5 minutes. Taste for seasoning.

Carve the pork butt into ¼-inch slices and arrange it on a platter. Serve the purée separately in a sauceboat.

To serve 6

6 medium-sized onions, peeled and thinly sliced
4 tablespoons butter
3 pounds boneless beef sirloin, cut ½ inch thick, then pounded to ¼ inch thick
3 tablespoons vegetable oil
2 tablespoons butter
Salt
Freshly ground black pepper
½ cup beef stock, fresh or canned (optional)

To serve 4

A 2-pound smoked pork butt
⅓ cup diced bacon (3 slices)
½ cup finely chopped onions
3½ cups chicken stock, fresh or canned
1 pound dried green split peas, thoroughly washed and drained
2 medium-sized potatoes, peeled and diced (about 1½ cups)
½ teaspoon salt
Freshly ground black pepper
½ cup heavy cream

Zucchetti mit Dill
ZUCCHINI WITH DILL SAUCE

Sprinkle the salt over the zucchini in a mixing bowl. Let it stand for ½ hour, then spread the strips on paper towels and pat them dry.

Melt the butter in a 1½-quart saucepan. When the foam subsides, add the zucchini. Toss it about in the butter with a spoon or spatula until well coated, then cover the pan, turn the heat to low and simmer 10 minutes, or until barely tender. Don't overcook. With a wire whisk, beat the flour into the sour cream. Pour the mixture over the zucchini and, stirring gently, simmer 2 or 3 minutes, until the sauce is thick and smooth. Stir in the sugar, vinegar and dill, and taste for seasoning.

To serve 4 to 6

½ teaspoon salt
2 pounds zucchini, peeled, seeded and cut into julienne strips ⅛ inch wide and 3 inches long
2 tablespoons butter
2 tablespoons flour
1 cup sour cream
1 teaspoon sugar
2 teaspoons vinegar
1 tablespoon finely chopped fresh dill

Gebackener Fleischstrudel
MEAT FILLING FOR STRUDEL

Heat the lard in a 12-inch skillet until a light haze forms over it, then add the onions and cook for 8 to 10 minutes, until lightly colored. Add the ground meat and cook it for 3 to 4 minutes, stirring constantly. Transfer the mixture to a bowl and stir in salt, paprika, parsley and egg. In a small saucepan melt the butter. When the foam subsides, stir in the flour, continuing to stir until all the flour is absorbed. Add the stock and cook over low heat, stirring, about 5 minutes. Stir the sauce into the meat mixture. Refrigerate while you prepare the *Strudel (pages 188-189)*. To fill the *Strudel*, follow the directions given with the *Strudel* recipe.

To fill 1 *Strudel*

4 tablespoons lard
1½ cups finely chopped onions
5 cups ground boiled beef *(page 67)* or other cooked beef or veal
1 teaspoon salt
2 tablespoons sweet Hungarian paprika
2 tablespoons finely chopped parsley
2 eggs, lightly beaten
4 tablespoons butter
4 tablespoons flour
2 cups beef stock, fresh or canned

Saure Gurken Sauce
SOUR-PICKLE SAUCE

In a 1-quart saucepan, melt the butter over medium heat. When the foam subsides, add the onions and cook for about 5 minutes, or until they are lightly colored. Add the flour and cook, stirring constantly, until it is lightly browned. Add the stock, sugar and vinegar, and bring to a boil. Cook over moderate heat for about 15 minutes, or until the sauce coats the spoon lightly. Pour through a sieve, return to the saucepan and reheat. Add the pickles and stir in the cream. Simmer until the cream is hot. Taste for seasoning. Serve in a sauceboat with boiled beef *(page 67)*.

To make 2 cups sauce

2 tablespoons butter
¼ cup finely chopped onions
2 tablespoons flour
1½ cups beef stock from the boiled beef *(page 67)*, or canned beef stock
1 tablespoon sugar
1 tablespoon white vinegar
½ cup peeled chopped dill pickle
½ cup heavy cream
Salt

Wiener Schnitzel
BREADED VEAL CUTLETS

Beat the eggs with the water only long enough to combine them. Sprinkle the veal slices liberally with salt and pepper, dip them in the flour and shake off the excess; next dip them in the beaten eggs and finally in the bread crumbs. Gently shake any excess bread crumbs from the cutlets and refrigerate for at least 20 minutes.

Heat the lard in a heavy 12-inch skillet until a light haze forms over it, then add the breaded cutlets. Cook over medium heat 3 to 4 minutes on each side, or until the cutlets are brown, and use tongs to turn them. Serve the *Wiener Schnitzel* immediately, garnished with lemon wedges or anchovy butter sauce *(page 60)*.

To serve 4

2 eggs
2 tablespoons water
2 pounds leg of veal, cut into slices ¼ inch thick
Salt
Freshly ground black pepper
¼ cup flour
1 cup fine bread crumbs
1½ cups lard

To make about ¾ cup sauce

12 anchovy fillets, drained
8 tablespoons (1 quarter-pound stick)
   unsalted butter
½ teaspoon sweet paprika

Sardellensauce
ANCHOVY BUTTER SAUCE

Chop the anchovies finely with a sharp knife. Melt the butter in a saucepan over low heat. With a wooden spoon, stir in the anchovies and paprika. Simmer for 5 minutes over very low heat; the butter should not brown. Pour the hot sauce over the *Schnitzel* after they are arranged on a platter and ready to serve.

To serve 4 to 6

2 pounds veal cutlets, cut into slices
   ¼ inch thick
1 cup lemon juice
Salt
Freshly ground black pepper
Flour
4 tablespoons butter
4 tablespoons vegetable oil
1 cup fresh mushrooms, sliced
½ cup heavy cream

Rahm Schnitzel
VEAL CUTLETS WITH MUSHROOMS

In a glass, stainless-steel or enameled baking dish, marinate the cutlets in the lemon juice for 1 hour, turning them every 20 minutes or so. Remove them from the lemon juice and pat them dry with paper towels. Salt and pepper them generously, then dip them in flour and shake off the excess.

In a heavy 12-inch skillet, heat the butter and oil over high heat. When the foam subsides, add the cutlets. Cook them for 1 or 2 minutes on each side, using tongs to turn them. Then lower the heat to medium and cook for 5 to 6 minutes longer on each side. Arrange them on a heated serving platter covered loosely with aluminum foil while preparing the sauce.

Pour off all but a thin film of fat, add the mushrooms to the skillet and cook them for 3 or 4 minutes over medium heat. Pour in the cream and bring it to a boil, stirring in any brown bits that cling to the pan. Cook briskly until the cream thickens enough to coat a spoon lightly. Taste for seasoning, then pour the sauce over the cutlets and serve immediately.

To serve 4 to 6

2 pounds leg of veal, cut into slices
   ¼ inch thick
1 cup fresh lemon juice
Salt
Flour
3 tablespoons butter
3 tablespoons lard
1 cup finely chopped onions
1½ tablespoons sweet Hungarian
   paprika
½ cup chicken stock, fresh or canned
2 tablespoons flour
1 cup sour cream

Paprika Schnitzel
VEAL CUTLETS WITH PAPRIKA

In a glass, stainless-steel or enameled baking dish, marinate the cutlets in the lemon juice for 1 hour, turning them every 20 minutes or so. Pat them dry with paper towels, salt them, then dip them in flour and shake off the excess.

In a heavy 12-inch skillet, heat the lard until a light haze forms over it, then add the cutlets. Over medium heat, cook them for 3 or 4 minutes on each side, or until lightly browned, using tongs to turn them. Arrange them on a serving platter, cover lightly with foil, and set them in a 200° oven to keep them warm.

Pour off all the fat from the skillet and replace it with the butter. Melt it over medium heat, then reduce the heat to low and add the onions. Cook them for 8 to 10 minutes, or until they are lightly colored. Remove the skillet from the heat and stir in the paprika, continuing to stir until the onions are well coated. Return the skillet to medium heat and add the chicken stock. Bring it to a boil, stirring in any brown bits clinging to the bottom and sides of the pan.

In a mixing bowl, stir the 2 tablespoons of flour into the sour cream with a wire whisk. Whisking constantly, add the sour-cream mixture to the stock in the skillet. Simmer for 2 or 3 minutes, or until the sauce is well heated. Pour the sauce over the cutlets and serve.

60

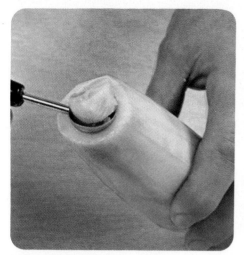

1 For stuffed cucumbers, peel one, cut off the end opposite the stem, scoop pulp and seeds from center.

2 Shake ¼ teaspoon of salt down into the hollow core to draw out the cucumber's natural liquids.

3 After cucumber has been stuffed with filling, refrigerate it for several hours. Then slice it on a slant.

Gefüllte Gurken
CUCUMBERS STUFFED WITH HAM AND SOUR PICKLES

Cut ½ inch off the tip of each cucumber, then peel the cucumbers with a vegetable scraper or sharp knife. Cut out the seeds and center pulp with a long iced-tea spoon, leaving a shell about ¼ inch thick. Pour ¼ teaspoon of salt into each cucumber, rubbing it in evenly with your forefinger, let the shells stand about 15 minutes, then dry them inside with a piece of paper towel.

In a medium-sized mixing bowl, mash the sardines to a paste with a fork or wooden spoon. Add the ham, eggs, onions, pickles, mustard and 2 tablespoons of mayonnaise. Stir the ingredients together until the mixture holds its shape in a spoon. (If it seems too dry, add more mayonnaise.) Taste for seasoning. The amount of salt needed will depend on the saltiness of the sardines and ham.

Stuff the cucumbers by standing them on end and spooning the filling in, tamping it down with a spoon as you proceed. When they are all tightly packed, wrap them separately in wax paper or aluminum foil and refrigerate them for 2 hours, or until the filling is firm.

To serve, slice the cucumbers crosswise, on a slant, in slices about ½ inch thick.

Roter Rübenkren
BEETS WITH HORSERADISH

In a deep glass, stainless-steel or enameled bowl, combine the beets and apple. Add the caraway seeds and horseradish.

In a 2-quart saucepan, combine the vinegar, sugar and salt. Stir until the sugar is completely dissolved, then simmer over low heat for 5 minutes. Pour the mixture over the beets and apple, stir gently but thoroughly, then cool to room temperature. Cover the bowl with plastic wrap and refrigerate for at least 12 hours, stirring gently from time to time.

To serve 6 to 8

2 cucumbers, 6 to 8 inches long
½ teaspoon salt
2 boneless sardines
¼ pound boiled ham, diced (¼-inch chunks)
2 hard-cooked eggs, coarsely chopped
2 teaspoons finely chopped onions
2 tablespoons minced sour pickles
1 teaspoon prepared French mustard
2 to 4 tablespoons mayonnaise, freshly made or a good commercial brand

To serve 4 to 6

2 cups thinly sliced freshly cooked or canned beets
1 small apple, peeled, cored and diced into ½-inch chunks (about ½ cup)
1 teaspoon caraway seeds
2 teaspoons grated fresh horseradish root or prepared horseradish, drained and squeezed dry
½ cup wine vinegar
1 tablespoon sugar
½ teaspoon salt

Geschmorter Schweinsbraten mit Kapern
BRAISED PORK ROAST WITH PAPRIKA, CAPERS AND CARAWAY

To serve 6

In a 4-quart casserole, heat the lard until a light haze forms over it. Add the pork and, over high heat, turning it with a fork, brown it on all sides—about 10 or 15 minutes altogether—then remove it and set it aside. Preheat the oven to 350°.

Pour off all but a thin film of the fat and add the onions. Cook them about 8 minutes over medium heat, or until they are lightly colored. Add the carrots and cook 2 or 3 minutes longer. Off the heat, stir in the paprika. Continue to stir until the vegetables are coated. Pour in the stock and bring it to a boil, stirring in any brown bits that cling to the bottom and sides of the pan. Return the pork to the pan, fat side up, salt and pepper it, and bring the liquid to a boil again. Cover tightly and braise the pork in the middle of the oven for 1½ hours, or until thoroughly cooked and tender. Baste it occasionally with the pan juices.

Transfer the pork to a heated platter. Pour the contents of the pan into a sieve set over a saucepan, pressing down hard on the vegetables before discarding them. Skim off as much of the surface fat from the pan liquid as possible and bring the sauce to a simmer on top of the stove.

With a wire whisk, beat the flour and sour cream together in a bowl, then beat the mixture into the pan. Bring the sauce to a simmer once more and add the parsley, capers and caraway seeds. Taste for seasoning.

Carve the pork into ¼- to ½-inch slices and serve with some of the sauce poured over them and the rest passed separately in a sauceboat.

4 tablespoons lard
A 3-pound boneless loin of pork (about 5 pounds with bone in)
¾ cup finely chopped onions
¾ cup diced carrots (½-inch chunks)
1 teaspoon sweet Hungarian paprika
1 cup chicken or beef stock, fresh or canned
Salt
Freshly ground black pepper
2 tablespoons flour
1 cup sour cream
1 tablespoon finely chopped parsley
1 teaspoon capers, drained, dried and chopped
1 tablespoon caraway seeds

Gesottenes Lämmernes in Majoran Sauce
BOILED LAMB IN MARJORAM SAUCE

To serve 6 to 8

Combine the lamb, onion, the cubed parsnip and carrots, and the chopped celery in a 5- or 6-quart saucepan. Pour in the water and add the salt. Bring to a boil, then lower the heat and simmer, covered, for 2½ hours, or until the lamb shows no resistance when tested with the tip of a sharp knife.

When the lamb is almost done, blanch the julienne carrots, parsnips, celery and potatoes by cooking them rapidly for 3 minutes in enough unsalted boiling water to cover them. Drain and set them aside.

Transfer the lamb to a heated platter. Pour the stock through a strainer, pressing hard on the vegetables with a wooden spoon before discarding them. Skim off the surface fat and return the stock to the pan. Boil it over high heat, uncovered, until it is reduced to about 3 cups.

Meanwhile, in another saucepan, melt the butter, stir in the flour and cook over very low heat until light brown. Add the marjoram, anchovies, lemon juice and parsley. Stir in the 3 cups of stock, continuing to whisk over low heat until the sauce is creamy and smooth.

Transfer the lamb to the large saucepan or a 4-quart casserole and pour the sauce over it. Bring it to a boil, then reduce the heat to low and add the julienne carrots, parsnips, celery and potatoes. Simmer for 10 minutes longer, or until the vegetables are tender but not mushy. Taste for seasoning. Serve the lamb on a platter with the vegetables surrounding it. Pour a few tablespoons of the sauce over the lamb and serve the rest in a sauceboat. Garnish the meat with parsley.

A 3-pound boned lamb shoulder or leg, rolled and tied
1 large onion, quartered
3 parsnips, 1 cubed, 2 scraped and cut into julienne strips (3 inches long, ½ inch wide)
5 carrots, 2 cubed, 3 scraped and cut into julienne strips (3 inches long, ½ inch wide)
3 celery stalks, 1 coarsely chopped, cut into julienne strips (3 inches long, ½ inch wide)
2 quarts water
1½ teaspoons salt
3 large potatoes (1½ to 2 pounds), peeled and sliced lengthwise into ¼-inch strips
2 tablespoons butter
2 tablespoons flour
¼ teaspoon marjoram
3 anchovy fillets, drained and finely chopped
1 tablespoon lemon juice
1 tablespoon finely chopped parsley

Lamb in marjoram sauce is an Austrian pleasure all too rarely encountered in Austria today.

A 3-pound frying chicken, cut into 4,
 6 or 8 serving pieces and skinned
1 tablespoon salt
½ cup flour
1 egg, lightly beaten
1½ cups bread crumbs
½ pound lard
Lemon wedges

Wiener Backhendl
AUSTRIAN BREADED FRIED CHICKEN

Pat the chicken pieces dry with paper towels, then salt them generously, dip them in the flour and shake off the excess. Then dip them in the egg. Roll each piece of chicken in the bread crumbs to coat it thoroughly.

If the chicken is cut into 8 pieces, no cooking after frying is necessary. If it is cut into 4 (in the Austrian tradition) or 6 pieces, preheat the oven to 250° and set a large baking dish on the middle shelf.

In a heavy 12-inch skillet, heat the lard until a light haze forms over it. (The melted fat should be about ¼ inch deep and should be kept at that depth.) Using tongs, add about half the chicken pieces. When these are a deep golden brown on one side, turn them with the tongs. If the chicken is cut into small pieces, transfer each to paper towels to drain before serving. If the pieces are larger, put each browned piece into the baking dish in the oven. In either case replace the cooked piece with an uncooked one as you fry it. Chicken cut into 6 pieces should be baked 5 to 10 minutes. One cut into 4 pieces should be baked 10 to 15 minutes.

Fry all the chicken in the same way, allowing more time for the dark meat than for the wings and breasts. The frying should take about ½ hour. Serve the chicken garnished with lemon wedges.

NOTE: To tenderize the chicken or vary the flavor, marinate it in ¼ cup of lemon juice for about 1½ hours. The pieces must be moistened thoroughly and turned occasionally.

To make 1¼ cups

1 cup sour cream
2 tablespoons lemon juice
2 teaspoons sugar
1 teaspoon salt
Freshly ground black pepper

Saure Rahmsauce für Salat
LEMON AND SOUR-CREAM SALAD DRESSING

Pour the sour cream into a mixing bowl. With a wooden spoon, stir in the lemon juice, sugar, salt and pepper. Beat until the ingredients are thoroughly blended. *Saure Rahmsauce* is used as a dressing for fresh cucumbers or delicate salad greens like Boston lettuce.

To serve 4

1 pound boiling potatoes (about 3
 large potatoes)
⅓ cup diced bacon (2 slices)
¼ cup finely chopped onions
1½ tablespoons flour
1¼ cups beef stock, fresh or canned
½ teaspoon capers, drained, dried
 and chopped
1 teaspoon grated lemon peel
⅛ teaspoon marjoram
½ teaspoon salt
Freshly ground black pepper
⅛ teaspoon thyme
1 small bay leaf
2 tablespoons finely chopped sour
 pickles
1 tablespoon white vinegar
1 teaspoon chopped parsley

Saure Erdäpfel
SOUR PICKLE AND VINEGAR POTATOES

Boil the potatoes in their skins for about 10 minutes, or until the point of a sharp knife easily penetrates them for about ½ inch. Cool them slightly. Peel them and cut them lengthwise into slices about ½ inch thick.

In a 10- or 12-inch skillet, cook the bacon for about 5 to 8 minutes over medium heat, or until it is lightly browned, then spread it on paper towels to drain. Pour off all but about 2 tablespoons of the bacon fat from the skillet. Add the onions and cook them about 8 minutes over medium heat, or until they are lightly colored. Stir in the diced bacon and flour, mixing gently until the flour is thoroughly absorbed.

Reduce the heat to low and stir in the beef stock, stirring with a whisk until the stock is slightly thickened. Add the capers, lemon peel, marjoram, salt, pepper, thyme, bay leaf and pickles. Bring the sauce to a boil, then add the potatoes and vinegar. Cover the skillet and simmer on low heat for about 25 minutes, or until tender. Remove the bay leaf and add the parsley just before serving.

Wiener Backhendl, Austrian breaded fried chicken, is accompanied here by a green salad with sour-cream dressing.

Kalbshirn in Muscheln

BROWN PURÉE OF CALF'S BRAINS IN SHELLS

Soak the brains in cold water for 2 hours, then soak for 1 hour in water to which 1 tablespoon of vinegar has been added for each quart of water. Gently pull off as much of the outside membrane as you can. Place the brains in an enameled saucepan with enough boiling water to cover; add a teaspoon of salt and a tablespoon of lemon juice for every quart of water. Partially cover and simmer for 15 or 20 minutes, then remove and drain. Chop as fine as possible. Preheat the oven to 400°. Melt the butter in an 8-inch skillet. When the foam subsides, add the brains and cook for 2 or 3 minutes, covered, stirring once or twice. Stir in the flour and cook for 2 or 3 minutes more. Add the stock and the 1½ teaspoons lemon juice, stirring constantly, and cook for 3 or 4 minutes, or until the mixture has thickened into a fairly smooth paste. Add salt and pepper to taste.

Divide the purée equally among 4 to 6 scallop shells or ramekins, and sprinkle a few bread crumbs over each. Arrange on a baking sheet and bake in the middle of the oven for 10 minutes, or until the tops are lightly browned. Sprinkle each shell with parsley. Garnish with lemon wedges.

To serve 4 to 6

2 pairs calf's brains (about 2 pounds)
White vinegar
Salt
Fresh lemon juice
2 tablespoons butter
2 tablespoons flour
⅔ cup chicken stock, fresh or canned
1½ teaspoons fresh lemon juice
Freshly ground black pepper
2 tablespoons bread crumbs
4 tablespoons finely chopped parsley
Lemon wedges

A thin sauce of stock, veal juices and vegetables is poured over a dish of *Kalbshaxe*—veal shank, served with potato dumplings.

Kalbshaxen

BRAISED VEAL SHANKS

To serve 4 to 6

4 veal shanks, about 2 pounds each,
   sawed by the butcher into 3 or 4
   pieces each
2 tablespoons butter, softened
1 cup finely chopped onions
½ cup scraped and diced parsnips
½ cup scraped and diced carrots
¼ cup coarsely chopped celery
1 bay leaf
¼ teaspoon thyme
6 peppercorns
⅛ teaspoon marjoram
⅓ cup coarsely chopped bacon
2 cups beef stock, fresh or canned
Salt

Preheat the oven to 500°. Using a pastry brush, thoroughly coat the shanks with the softened butter. Arrange them in a roasting pan. Scatter over them the onions, parsnips, carrots, celery, bay leaf, thyme, peppercorns, marjoram and bacon. Cook in the middle of the oven for about 15 minutes, or until meat and vegetables are lightly browned.

Pour the stock (first brought to a boil in a saucepan) into the pan and scrape loose the brown bits on the sides and bottom. Reduce the heat to 350°. Cover the pan and cook the veal for about 1½ hours, turning it 2 or 3 times. When the veal is tender, reduce the heat to 200°. Arrange the shanks on a platter and return to the oven to keep warm.

Strain the pan juices through a fine sieve into a saucepan, pressing down hard on the vegetables with a wooden spoon before discarding them. Skim off the surface fat with a large spoon, and taste. If the stock seems to lack intensity of flavor, reduce it to ¾ or ½ its volume by boiling it rapidly, uncovered; then taste again for seasoning. Pour the sauce over the veal shanks, or serve it separately in a sauceboat.

Veal shanks are traditionally served with potato dumplings *(page 137)*.

66

Gekochtes Rindfleisch
AUSTRIAN BOILED BEEF

In a 6- or 8-quart saucepan or soup kettle, combine the beef and chicken parts and cover them with the water. Add the salt. Bring to a boil over high heat, adding more water, if necessary, to cover. Skim off surface scum as it rises.

Meanwhile, in a heavy 12-inch skillet, heat the butter. When the foam subsides, add the chopped onions, parsnip, carrots, celery, leek and parsley. Over high heat, toss the vegetables in the hot butter for 4 or 5 minutes, or until they are lightly browned. Scrape them into the soup kettle and bring the liquid to a boil again, skim off the surface scum and add the bay leaf, peppercorns and allspice. Turn the heat to its lowest point, partially cover the pot and simmer slowly for about 2 hours, or until the beef shows no resistance when pierced with the point of a small sharp knife.

Remove the beef to a heated serving platter. Then skim the surface fat from the stock and strain the stock through a large sieve, pressing down hard on the vegetables before discarding them. Taste for seasoning. The stock may be served as a soup before the beef or on another occasion with dumplings that have been cooked in it.

To serve 4 to 6

A 3-pound boneless beef rump, bottom round, brisket or chuck roast, tied
3 pounds chicken parts (back, wings, giblets, necks)
2 quarts water
1 teaspoon salt
3 tablespoons butter
2 cups onions, quartered
1 parsnip, scraped and cut into 1-inch chunks
3 carrots, cut into 1-inch chunks
4 large celery ribs, cut into 2-inch pieces
1 leek, white part only
4 sprigs parsley
1 bay leaf
6 peppercorns
4 whole allspice

Krensauce
HORSERADISH SAUCE

Melt the butter in a heavy 8-inch skillet over medium heat. When the foam has subsided, add the onions and cook them, stirring occasionally, for 2 or 3 minutes. Stir in the flour and continue to cook for about 8 minutes longer, stirring constantly, until the onions and flour become lightly colored. Add the stock, the horseradish, salt, pepper, lemon juice and sugar. With a wire whisk stir the sauce, still over medium heat, until it becomes thick and smooth.

Turn the heat to low and stir in the cream. Simmer the sauce for about 2 minutes over very low heat. Do not boil. Taste for seasoning and serve with boiled beef.

To make 2½ cups of sauce

4 tablespoons unsalted butter
¼ cup finely chopped onions
4 tablespoons flour
2 cups beef stock, fresh or canned
4 tablespoons grated fresh horseradish root or prepared horseradish, drained and squeezed dry
¼ teaspoon salt
Freshly ground black pepper
1 tablespoon lemon juice
1 teaspoon sugar
¼ cup heavy cream

Gefüllte Melonen
MELONS STUFFED WITH CHERRIES AND WHIPPED CREAM

With a ½-inch melon-ball scoop, scoop out the balls of melon or cantaloupe, leaving a shell about ½ inch thick next to the rind. Refrigerate the melon balls and the fresh cherries together in a shallow dish, and cool the melon shells separately, for about 1 hour.

With a wire whisk or rotary beater, beat the chilled cream in a large chilled bowl until it holds its shape softly. Then gradually beat in the sugar and the vanilla extract, continuing to beat until the cream holds its shape firmly. Drain the melon balls thoroughly and with a rubber spatula, fold them, the cherries and the whipped cream together, using an over-and-under cutting motion instead of a mixing motion. Spoon the cherry, melon and whipped cream mixture into the melon shells, heaping it high. Serve Gefüllte Melonen cold—on a bed of crushed ice, if possible.

To serve 4

2 small cantaloupes or Persian melons halved and seeded
1 cup heavy cream, chilled
½ cup sugar
1 teaspoon vanilla extract
1 pound fresh, sweet cherries, pitted

III

In Austria's Provinces

Salzburg, Mozart's
birthplace and capital of the
Austrian province of the
same name, is noted as a
musical center and a tourist
resort. It is quaint, colorful
and friendly. Many houses
on the street shown at the
left date from the 16th and
17th Centuries. The
restaurant, the Wernbacher
Buffet, advertises its grilled
chicken in a unique way.

There are nine provinces in Austria, and not all of them are noted for the high quality of their cuisine. Yet, one cannot think of the best Austrian cooking without bearing in mind such areas as Styria, Burgenland, Carinthia, Lower Austria and the Tyrol. Lower Austria, largest of the provinces, and Burgenland, one of the smallest, are often called the Cinderellas of Austrian tourism. Compared to other provinces they have little to boast about; there are no high mountains, few festivals or international ski resorts, and even fewer spectacular sights. Located along the frontiers of Czechoslovakia and Hungary, these two provinces were occupied by the U.S.S.R. after World War II. While the Western Zones were enjoying their early postwar prosperity, thanks to Marshall Plan help, Lower Austria and Burgenland remained poor areas of small farms. In 1955 the Russians went home, and ever since then these provinces have been trying to catch up with the rest of the country. Although they do not match the scenic beauty of other provinces, they can nevertheless offer lovely spas (such as Baden), romantic castles (Dürnstein, Greifenstein) and magnificent old abbeys (Melk, Klosterneuburg). In a sense, it is still a region for the traveler to discover.

The food is much the same as in Vienna (which forms its own federal province inside Lower Austria), and all Viennese specialties, from liver-dumpling soup and boiled beef to *Rahmstrudel* (*Strudel* with cream) and *Palatschinken* (pancakes with a variety of fillings, *page 119*), are served. Along the Danube many restaurants serve fish, and the lakes offer carp. The Czech influence is quite strong in Lower Austria, where many of the desserts reveal their origin from beyond the border.

Lower Austria is the country's largest wine-producing area. Eighty per cent of the wines are white, made from the Riesling grape, and are drunk rather young. The best are the wines from the old monastery vineyard of Klosterneuburg, on the Danube, and from Gumpoldskirchen. They have a strong bouquet and a full, round taste. Dürnstein and Krems on the Danube, Retz near the Czech border, Langenlois in the Kamp Valley and Baden near Vienna, produce some good wines and many undistinguished ones. Of course, these are more for local consumption.

Some of the most delicious of the provincial dishes come from Burgenland, which has been called the Garden of Vienna. For more than a thousand years this "castle country" was fought over by Bavarians, Hungarians, Austrians and Turks until it became part of Hungary in 1648. It remained Hungarian until 1921, when it became an Austrian province. Its capital, Eisenstadt, is famous as the place where Joseph Haydn (born in Rohrau, Lower Austria) spent much of his life in the service of the Eszterházys, the Hungarian aristocrats who were the great musical patrons of the day. Haydn's music, with its Hungarian melodies, very much captures the spirit of old Burgenland. In the villages, geese float in the village ponds, and there are cattle and pigs roaming among the white one-story houses of the peasants. It is as romantic and pastoral as many writers have testified.

The food specialties are strongly Hungarian in flavor. Around Neusiedler Lake the people sometimes cook carp and pike in Hungarian style with paprika, or prepare boiled carp and baked pike. The local soup is a thick bean soup with small pieces of smoked bacon in it. The peasants love to eat roast goose with red cabbage, and in season there is excellent roast partridge. The best-liked desserts are the various *Palatschinken* and a yeast-dough roulade filled with raisins and poppy seeds.

The red wines from the Burgenland are the only good red wines in Austria. In Rust, the big wine-growing region on Neusiedler Lake, you may get a very solid Ruster Burgunder, or a full, round Stierblut, which comes from across the Hungarian border. These are heavy and have a stronger alcoholic content than most Austrian wines.

Some of the pleasant white wines served in Styria come from Slovenia, across the Yugoslav border. (Most of what was formerly southern Styria now belongs to Yugoslavia.) On the other hand some of the best Austrian beers, such as Gösser, which is made in Leoben, and Reininghaus and Puntigam, made in Graz, come from Styria. The province is a beautiful country, green and wild with large and dark forests, remote valleys and deep streams, and it is rich in tradition and fairy tales. The Celts and the Romans settled here, and in later centuries Styria often formed a bulwark against the Turkish invaders, who were constantly trying to enlarge their domains.

There is much game and fish in the north of Styria, while southern Styria has pork, many varieties of fruit and good white wine. Styria's great specialty is its poultry; its capons (castrated males) and poulards (sterilized females) are of the highest quality. A plump poulard, roasted in butter, with young potatoes and a crisp salad, is a gastronomic delight. The capon is often served stuffed with its own liver (with rosemary, parsley, marjoram, pepper and stale bread added) or with chestnuts.

Among the specialties of Styria are excellent soups such as *Stoss-Suppe* (made with sour milk, sour cream, potatoes and caraway seeds), *Fridattensuppe* (pancake soup) with small pancakes, rolled and cut in strips the size of a match, which one puts into hot consommé just before eating, and *Tegetthoff Suppe*, named after the Austrian admiral of Styrian origin. *Tegetthoff Suppe* is a "false" soup (a soup not made from meat stock), with mushrooms, asparagus, peas, parsnips, celery knob, carrots and small pieces of chicken.

The Styrians like to eat heartily. They are fond of heavy ragôuts such as *Steirisches Schweinernes* (pork stew) or *Steirisches Schöpsernes* (mutton stew), both made with carrots, parsley, celery, onion and spices, and served with boiled potatoes or dumplings. Game of various kinds is popular in season: roast pheasant and roast partridge, roast wild young boar and saddle of venison. In country inns all over Styria they serve *Sterz*, a sort of spoon bread made with corn; buckwheat too is part of the daily fare. An oil made from pumpkin seeds, known as *Kernöl*, is often used to prepare salads.

The southernmost Austrian province is Carinthia. The Carinthians are proud of their German past; many of the early settlers were from Bavaria. They hold old pagan beliefs that go back to the Celtic era, but there are also Slovenian customs to remind the traveler that toward the end of the Völkerwanderung, or mass migration of early times, the ancestors of the Slovenes established a state in this mountainous region. Austria's highest peak, the 12,641-foot Gross Glockner, rises in Carinthia.

It is a country of warm lakes and spas. There is much hunting (chamois, red deer, roe deer, mountain cock and black cock) and excellent fishing in the streams (trout, grayling and eel) and in the lakes (sheatfish, zander, perch). Game and fish are the local specialties. Zander, which belongs to the perch family, is grilled or fried in butter with almonds, or it may simply be boiled. Sheatfish, a large fresh-water catfish, is usually fried and served with salad. Trout, carp and golden perch are always in demand when they are available, and are prepared in a variety of ways.

In nearly all small country inns one is served the typical Carinthian dish, called *Kasnudln*. The various *Nudeln* are small, folded noodle squares, boiled in water, that contain a great variety of fillings. Some noodles, filled with ham and bacon, leftover meat, mushrooms and cottage cheese, and with melted butter poured over them, are eaten as the main dish with a green salad. Others are filled with poppy seeds or dried pears and are served as a dessert, with sugar and melted butter on top. A much loved specialty is *Kärntner Reindling*, a sort of yeast *Strudel* made with currants and cinnamon. Residents of this region drink a lot of hard country cider.

The province of Salzburg is the smallest, but one of the best-known federal provinces of Austria. The capital city of the same name is famous as the hometown of one of mankind's most astonishing creative spirits—Wolfgang Amadeus Mozart. Salzburg has much Baroque beauty—Hugo von Hofmannsthal, the great Austrian dramatist and poet, called it "the most Italian city in Austria"—and it is surrounded by the lovely Salzkammergut, an area of lakes and mountains in the eastern Alps, famous for its scenic beauty and frequent rain.

If this were a musical chronicle, I would have much to say about Salz-

Fishermen on Altaussee Lake in the Salzkammergut area of Styria's Eastern Alps set their nets for *Saibling,* a variety of trout. The pink-fleshed fish are fried in butter and served with buttered potatoes and a green salad at inviting lakeside restaurants. The little resort town of Altaussee can be seen in the background.

burg. Gastronomically, it is less significant than other Austrian locales, although there are first-class restaurants serving Viennese specialties that you might expect to find at such a center of tourism and the arts. Otherwise the home cooking, like the geographic location, is halfway between Munich to the west and Vienna to the east. The most famous local creation, *Salzburger Nockerl,* a sweet soufflé made of egg whites, beaten stiff, with sugar, butter and flour, is an impressive sight *(picture, page 79; recipe, page 85).*

For me, one of the most beautiful regions in Austria is the Tyrol. The Tyrolean Alps are different from the Alps of Bavaria, Switzerland or France. The Tyrol may lack the supreme grandeur of the Mont Blanc Massif, and there may not be the long, high valleys you find in Switzerland's Upper Engadine, but there is the simple charm that is characteristic of the Austrian countryside—a Baroque church, a dreamy old peasant village, with a Gothic statue of a saint in a picturesque square. And there is always music—church music, and the music in the night clubs that have come to the mountain resorts in the wake of tourism, and the older local songs and zither music. And, of course, the sounds of bells. All summer long one hears the cowbells from the high pastures—the *Almen*—where the cattle are grazing. In wintertime there are the jingling bells of sleds in fashionable ski resorts.

In the North Tyrol the typical dishes are strictly Austrian, but south of the Brenner Pass there is a new, fascinating mixture of Austrian and Italian cooking. One South Tyrolean cookbook has the internationalized title *Spaghetti and Speckknödel,* the latter being the bacon dumplings *(page 80)* that are a traditional Tyrolean dish.

These dumplings are made with *Bauernspeck* (peasants' bacon), the great specialty in both North and South Tyrol. The *Bergbauern* (mountain peasants) live on their isolated farms high up on lonely slopes. In the fall they slaughter pigs and keep the cured, smoked meat for the severe winter months when their houses are snowed in and they cannot get down to the valleys.

It takes patience and hard work to make a perfect piece of *Bauernspeck.* Old peasants remember that their fathers would slaughter especially well-fed pigs "just when it began to get cold." The timing was important. It still is. The bacon is left for about two months in a mild brine containing juniper and other ingredients that each family keeps secret. The meat is then hung in the *Rauchküchl* (smoke kitchen) that every peasant has in his house. The bacon must be treated only in cold smoke, slowly and carefully, until the meat becomes dark and takes on the scent of the beechwood or the stems of vines that are used to give the smoke its special aroma.

A real Tyrolean will gladly sell his birthright for a side of lean, well-

Spring in the Austrian countryside *(overleaf)* is a season of soft loveliness. This quiet village in the valley of the Inn River seems almost afloat in its apple blossoms.

Continued on page 76

smoked *Bauernspeck,* but he will not touch the products sold in many butcher shops, made quickly and artificially, with the smoking process cut to a few days. Obviously, a considerable amount of time is needed to produce a good piece of this bacon, and few peasants will spend the time today. Some of my friends in Merano have their sources, but they would rather lend you their cars or fountain pens than give you the name of a peasant high up in the mountains who still makes the genuine *Speck. Bauernspeck* is usually served between meals, as a token of local hospitality, or as an hors d'oeuvre, and it is used in cooking in various ways, especially to make the famous dumplings named after it, the *Speckknödel.* It is also eaten uncooked, in thin slices, with simply a glass of local red wine, or better, two or three glasses. Wine drinkers claim that one can never get drunk as long as one eats a slice of bacon every once in a while.

Once outside Vienna, with its near monopoly of talent and influence in matters of cooking and eating, the emphasis in the Austrian provinces is generally on hearty, wholesome food, simply prepared by age-old methods handed down from mother to daughter. Nevertheless it is possible to find instances of the revival of a more sophisticated cooking by cooks who are resurrecting some of the great old dishes of the provinces. The strong French or Italian flavor in many of these dishes reflects the diverse histories

In a mountain restaurant a Carinthian peasant shows how to eat the famous home-smoked bacon of the area along with cheese and bread. It is necessary to hold all the ingredients in the left hand, leaving the right free to slice off each with a pocketknife. When the knife is put down, a glass of beer, schnapps or wine is taken up. *Opposite:* a farmer, one of the few who still cure their bacon at home, works in his smokehouse.

of the princes, nobles and heroes who alone were in a position to bequeath such culinary splendors to posterity.

Andreas Hellrigl, a young man in his early thirties who lives at Merano in the Italian Tyrol, is just such a chef. He is helping to create a new interest in old Tyrolean cooking based upon 16th and 17th Century recipes in cookbooks that he found in monastic archives. In his adaptations he is trying to make the ancient dishes as practical and palatable as possible in the light of modern methods and tastes. Among the dishes that show a marked foreign sophistication is one for chicken legs that are partly hollowed out, filled with a delicate crayfish stuffing and then braised in butter with a little stock, a light *béchamel* sauce and Cognac.

Beef ribs Margarethe Maultasch is another old dish with colorful associations. It was named after Margarethe, the daughter of King Henry of Tyrol. Margarethe was the last descendant of the dynasty of Goerz-Tyrol, and upon her abdication in 1363, the Tyrol passed to the fortunate Habsburgs. Her ugliness was legendary, and when Sir John Tenniel was looking for a model for his illustration of the Ugly Duchess in *Alice in Wonderland,* he used the forbidding countenance that had earned Margarethe the nickname of Pocket-Mouthed Meg. This noble lady resided at a castle that overlooked Merano and the valley of the upper Etsch, and there she carried on the nu-

merous love affairs that scandalized not only the Pope but also the free-living princes of Europe. The beef ribs named after her are trimmed and boned, filled with a ragôut of white Piedmont truffles and served with a light cream sauce: a suitably frivolous and delectable epitaph.

One of the most popular dishes in the homes of the South Tyrol is *Speck-knödel* soup, a strong consommé with the famous bacon dumplings in it. Traditionally, these demand a woman's touch for the best results, as do all dumplings, and they may be made with either Tyrolean *Bauernspeck* or with the milder Hamburg bacon.

Zwiebelrostbraten (fried steak slices with onions) is another typically Tyrolean dish. Many versions exist, depending on the quality of the meat, but the best cooks use ribs or sirloin and fry the meat in lard in a deep frying pan. The meat is taken out and placed on a hot serving dish, and the onions are then sautéed in the frying pan until they take on a lovely golden color, but are still firm. The lard is drained off, some butter and a little stock are added, and the finished sauce, with the onions, is poured over the meat.

Onions are much loved in the Tyrol and are available all year round. Fried onion rings are the trademark of many Tyrolean dishes. The Tyroleans often put onions even on mashed potatoes and other vegetables, such as beans, cabbage and cauliflower.

Fried onions give the specific taste to the various kinds of Tyrolean *G'röstl* (the word means "roasted") dishes, for which housewives use various meat leftovers. The best version is called *Herreng'röstl* (roast things for gentlemen) —veal scallops finely chopped and sautéed with chopped onions, served with sliced potatoes sautéed separately in butter. It is garnished with chopped parsley. A dish of *G'röstl* immediately conjures up the vision of a large family sitting around an old wooden table laden with food and wine in the kitchen of a snug Tyrolean house, while outside the snow falls in large, lacy flakes.

Calf's liver *(page 84)* is a favored dish in the Tyrol, as it is in Vienna. It is sliced, dusted with flour and fried in lard or butter. It may be eaten with dumplings or *Nockerln* (not to be confused with the *Salzburger Nockerl* with which they have nothing in common), an Austro-Hungarian version of the Italian *gnocchi*. Since the links with Italy are so strong, the influence on the food and cooking of some of the provinces is not surprising.

These *Nockerln* are small dumplings made by dripping teaspoonfuls of dough into boiling salted water, and cooking for a couple of minutes. The dumplings are then drained in a colander, rinsed under a cold faucet, shaken dry and heated in a little melted butter, but carefully so they won't get brown. The Tyroleans, like the Hungarians, serve *Nockerln* with various kinds of goulash and other stews. One makes *Eiernockerln* by putting three lightly whisked and seasoned eggs on top of ordinary *Nockerln* in a frying pan and stirring as if scrambling eggs. This is a fine lunch dish for hot summer days, served with a crisp green salad.

The Tyroleans claim that they invented *Bauernschmaus* (peasants' feast) —a claim indignantly rejected by many Viennese. And in fact, the dish is to be found all over the country. *Bauernschmaus* might be defined as the Austrian version of an Alsatian *choucroute garnie* or a Swiss *Berner Platte*, and it is also eaten in Bavaria. It consists of several kinds of pork—smoked loin *(G'selchtes)*, fresh pork shoulder and the best available pork sausages—cooked with sauerkraut and served with dumplings. In Vienna they use bread dumplings, while in the Tyrol they prefer Tyrolean bacon dumplings.

The *G'selchtes* (smoked pork) is simmered with sauerkraut and its juice until the meat is half cooked. Then fresh pork shoulder, cut in cubes and browned in butter, is added, and the whole mixture is left simmering for another hour. Toward the end, the pork sausages, already heated or grilled, are added; they must not be split.

The presentation of this excellent dish is traditional. The *Bauernschmaus* should be served on a large platter with the various meats arranged on a bed of sauerkraut and the sausages on top, surrounded by dumplings. Every old inn has its own version, usually for at least four people, and the platter is always an impressive sight—an exhibition of Rabelaisian gourmandism that conveys the essential character of provincial cooking.

One must not forget, of course, that the cooking of the provinces of Austria, while it clearly springs from its own locales and is therefore appreciated as being "regional," is in another sense part of the foundation of what is best in the Viennese cuisine. Some people even consider it superior to Viennese cooking, though certainly it is neither as sophisticated nor as well known. After all, one can find some of the great Viennese dishes in other parts of Europe and in America, but one has to go to Austria (or cook them oneself) to taste the provincial specialties.

For dessert in the Red Room of Salzburg's Goldener Hirsch Hotel a *Salzburger Nockerl* is served. This delightful dish is a fluffy, sweet soufflé; the recipe is on page 85.

To make about 16 dumplings

½ cup finely diced bacon (about 6 strips)
2 cups ½-inch bread cubes, made from day-old bread
2 tablespoons finely chopped onions
¼ cup milk
2 tablespoons finely chopped parsley
½ cup flour
Salt

Speckknödel
BACON DUMPLINGS

In a heavy skillet over medium heat, cook the bacon until it is lightly browned, then, with a slotted spoon, transfer it to a paper towel to drain. Pour off the fat and reserve. Return 4 tablespoons of it to the skillet. Reheat the fat over medium heat until a light haze forms over it, then add the bread cubes. Toss them about in the fat until they are brown on all sides, then transfer them to a large mixing bowl.

Add 2 more tablespoons of the bacon fat to the skillet and heat it again. Add the onions and, stirring occasionally, cook them for 8 to 10 minutes, or until they are lightly colored, then scrape them into the mixing bowl with the bread cubes. Add the milk and parsley, then stir in the flour. Taste for seasoning.

Let the mixture stand for about 10 minutes, or until the croutons are thoroughly moistened. Then gently mix in the reserved bacon. Dampen your hands and form the mixture into balls about 1½ inches in diameter.

To serve with beef broth (recipe, *page* 67), bring the broth to a bubbling boil, drop the dumplings in, turn the heat to medium, and cook them, uncovered, for 12 to 14 minutes, or until they are firm to the touch.

To serve the dumplings with meat and gravy, cook them in slightly salted water, drain them, then serve them masked with the gravy.

In Austria, *Speckknödel*, topped with sauerkraut and crisply fried onions, are frequently served as a main dish.

To serve 4

½ pound broad egg noodles
8 tablespoons (1 quarter-pound stick) butter
¼ cup finely chopped onions
½ cup sour cream
3 eggs, lightly beaten
1 cup diced cooked ham (about ¼ pound)
Freshly ground black pepper
Salt
¼ cup bread crumbs

Schinkenfleckerln
LITTLE HAM AND NOODLE PATCHES

Preheat the oven to 350°. Drop the noodles into about 2 quarts of boiling salted water. Boil for 10 minutes, or until barely tender. Strain them through a colander or strainer, rinse them thoroughly with cold water, then drain. Spread the noodles out on a board and cut them into pieces as long as they are wide, making squares of about 1 inch.

Melt half the butter in an 8-inch skillet. When the foam subsides, add the onions. Cook them for 4 or 5 minutes, or until they are translucent. Add the noodle squares and the rest of the butter and toss them about until they are well coated. Cook over moderate heat for about 5 minutes.

With a wire whisk, beat the sour cream and eggs together in a large mixing bowl. Stir in the ham, a generous grinding of pepper, salt and the contents of the skillet. Butter a 2-quart casserole, scatter the bread crumbs over the butter, tip the casserole from side to side to spread them evenly, then fill the casserole with the noodle-and-ham mixture. Bake, uncovered, in the middle of the oven for 45 minutes, or until the mixture is firm.

To unmold, run a sharp thin knife around the inside of the casserole, place a warm platter over the top of it and, grasping the casserole and the platter together, turn them over. Serve with the bottom side up.

Schinkenfleckerln is usually served for a light lunch or supper, preceded by soup and accompanied by a salad.

Kalbsreisfleisch
BRAISED VEAL AND RICE

Preheat the oven to 350°. In a heavy 10-inch skillet, heat the lard over high heat until a light haze forms over it, then add the salt pork. When the pork has browned on all sides, remove it with a slotted spoon to drain on a double thickness of paper towels.

Pat the veal cubes dry with paper towels and brown them in the skillet over medium heat, adding more lard as needed. As the veal cubes brown, transfer them with a slotted spoon into a 3-quart casserole. Sprinkle them with salt and pepper.

Pour off the fat from the skillet, leaving only a thin film. Add the onions and cook them, stirring frequently, for 8 to 10 minutes, or until they are lightly colored. Off the heat, stir in the paprika, continuing to stir until the onions are well coated. Return the skillet to the heat and add the chicken stock. Bring it to a boil, stirring in any brown bits that cling to the bottom and sides of the skillet. Pour the onions and stock over the veal and stir in the diced salt pork.

Bring the casserole to a boil on top of the stove, cover it tightly and bake in the middle of the oven for about 50 minutes, or until the veal shows only slight resistance when tested with the point of a sharp knife.

At this point, stir in the rice, cover the casserole again and bake for about 25 to 30 minutes more, or until the rice is tender and has absorbed all the liquid in the pan. Stir with a fork once or twice during the cooking period and add 1 or 2 tablespoons of stock or water if necessary.

Remove from the oven, stir in the cheese if you wish, and serve.

To serve 4 to 6

2 tablespoons lard
½ cup diced salt pork, ¼-inch dice (⅛ pound)
2 pounds boneless veal shoulder or boneless neck or breast, cut into 1½-inch cubes
1 teaspoon salt
Freshly ground black pepper
1 cup finely chopped onions
½ teaspoon sweet Hungarian paprika
1 cup chicken stock, fresh or canned
1 cup uncooked rice
2 tablespoons grated Parmesan cheese (optional)

Wildbret-Koteletten
PAN-FRIED VENISON CUTLETS WITH CREAM SAUCE

THE MARINADE: In a large shallow glass, stainless-steel or enameled baking dish, combine the wine, water, juniper berries, thyme, bay leaves, onions, garlic and pepper. Add the cutlets and moisten them thoroughly with the marinade. Marinate the cutlets for 2 hours at room temperature or 4 hours in the refrigerator. Remove the cutlets, and strain and reserve the marinade.

THE CUTLETS: Pat the cutlets dry with paper towels and sprinkle them with salt and a few grindings of pepper. Dip them in flour and vigorously shake off the excess. In a heavy 10- or 12-inch skillet, heat the butter and lard over medium heat. When the foam subsides, add the cutlets—a few at a time—cooking them over high heat for 2 or 3 minutes on each side, or until they are well browned. Arrange them on a heated platter, and pour off all but a thin film of fat from the skillet.

THE SAUCE: Pour ¾ cup of the marinade through a strainer into the skillet. Bring it to a boil and boil about half of it away while scraping in any brown bits that cling to the bottom and sides of the skillet. Return the cutlets to the skillet and simmer them on low heat for 5 minutes, basting them every 2 or 3 minutes, then arrange them on a heated serving platter. Stir the cream, currant jelly and lemon juice into the skillet. Simmer until the jelly dissolves, stirring almost constantly. Taste the sauce for seasoning, then pour it over the cutlets and serve.

To serve 4 to 6

THE MARINADE
1 cup dry red wine
2 cups water
5 crushed juniper berries
¼ teaspoon thyme
2 bay leaves
1 cup coarsely chopped onions
½ teaspoon finely chopped garlic
½ teaspoon freshly ground black pepper

THE CUTLETS
12 four-ounce cutlets, about ⅜ inch thick, cut from a boned saddle of venison
½ teaspoon salt
Freshly ground black pepper
Flour
3 tablespoons butter
2 tablespoons lard

THE SAUCE
1 cup heavy cream
2 tablespoons red currant jelly
½ teaspoon fresh lemon juice
Salt

Hühner Ragout Suppe, chicken ragôut soup, with liver dumplings, often appears at lunch time in the Austrian provinces.

Hühner Ragout Suppe

CHICKEN RAGÔUT SOUP

In a 4- or 5-quart casserole or soup kettle, combine the chicken parts, veal knuckle, peppercorns, salt and stock and/or water. Add more stock or water, if necessary, to cover by an inch. Bring the liquid to a boil over high heat, skimming the scum from the surface as it rises. Then partially cover the pan and reduce the heat to its lowest point; bubbles should barely break on the surface. Simmer slowly for 1½ to 2 hours.

Meanwhile, in a 10- or 12-inch skillet, melt the butter. When the foam subsides, add the onions and cook over moderate heat for 2 or 3 minutes, then add the diced carrots, celery and parsnips. Stir them to coat them with the butter. Cover the skillet tightly and cook the vegetables over the lowest possible heat for 15 to 20 minutes, or until they are barely tender. Check the pan occasionally and add a tablespoon of the chicken stock from the casserole if necessary to keep the vegetables from browning.

Pour the soup through a large sieve into a large bowl. Remove all the edible parts of the chicken and dice them coarsely. Discard the skin, bones, veal knuckle and the peppercorns. Return the stock to the large casserole, skim off as much surface fat as you can, and bring it to a simmer again.

Now, off the heat, sprinkle the flour over the vegetables in the skillet. Stir together until the flour is thoroughly absorbed. Still off the heat, gently stir in 2 cups of the simmering stock, then return the skillet to the heat and, stirring constantly, cook for 5 to 10 minutes, or until the stock is smooth and thick. Pour the entire contents of the skillet into the simmering soup stock, whisking all the while. Add the diced chicken and bring the soup almost to a boil, then reduce the heat and simmer, partially covered, for 5 to 10 minutes longer. Taste for seasoning; it may need more salt. Pour the soup into a tureen and add the parsley.

Austrians traditionally serve dumplings with this soup and usually cook them in it. Liver dumplings *(below)* are a favorite.

1 to 1½ pounds chicken parts (necks, wings, backs, giblets)
1 small veal knuckle (about ½ pound)
8 peppercorns
1 teaspoon salt
2½ quarts chicken stock, fresh or canned, or water, or part chicken stock and part water
4 tablespoons butter
½ cup finely chopped onions
½ cup diced carrots (¼-inch chunks)
½ cup diced celery (¼-inch chunks)
½ cup diced parsnips (¼-inch chunks)
2 tablespoons flour
3 tablespoons finely chopped parsley

Leberknödel

LIVER DUMPLINGS

Soak the bread slices in the milk for about 5 minutes, then squeeze them dry. Run the bread and chicken livers together through a meat grinder into a mixing bowl, or chop them together finely with a sharp knife.

In a heavy 10- or 12-inch skillet, melt the butter. When the foam subsides, add the onions. Cook them for about 8 minutes, or until they are lightly colored, then add them to the bread-and-liver mixture. Stir in the egg whites, salt, a few grindings of pepper and the parsley. Add ½ cup bread crumbs, mix, then form 1 tablespoon of the mixture into a ball. If it is too soft to hold together firmly, add more bread crumbs by the tablespoon. Dust your hands lightly with flour and form all the mixture into balls about 1 inch in diameter. Bring to a boil the soup *(recipe, above)* in which the dumplings are to be cooked, reduce the heat to medium and drop in the dumplings. Boil, uncovered, until the dumplings rise to the surface. Reduce the heat to low and simmer for 2 or 3 minutes longer.

Serve *Leberknödel* in the soup they were cooked in, 5 to a portion.

To make 30 to 35 small dumplings

2 slices stale white bread (including crusts)
¼ cup milk
¼ pound chicken livers
1 tablespoon unsalted butter
¼ cup finely chopped red onion
2 egg whites, lightly beaten
½ teaspoon salt
Freshly ground black pepper
1 teaspoon finely chopped parsley
½ to 1 cup dry bread crumbs

To serve 4

A 4½- to 5-pound roasting chicken
1 teaspoon salt
½ teaspoon dried marjoram

THE STUFFING
8 slices day-old white bread
1 cup heavy cream
12 tablespoons (1½ quarter-pound
   sticks) unsalted butter, melted
2 egg yolks
8 large shrimp, cooked, shelled and
   coarsely chopped
4 large shrimp, uncooked, shelled and
   finely chopped or puréed in a
   blender
¼ cup finely chopped parsley
¼ cup cooked green peas, fresh,
   frozen or canned
½ teaspoon salt
Freshly ground black pepper
2 egg whites
½ cup chicken stock, fresh or
   canned (optional)

Gefüllte Hühner mit Krabben
ROAST CHICKEN STUFFED WITH SHRIMP

Preheat the oven to 350°. Wash the chicken quickly under cold running water, pat it dry with paper towels, then rub the inside of it with a mixture of the salt and the marjoram.

Toast the bread in the upper third of the oven for 5 to 8 minutes, or until it is dry but not brown. Crumble it and soak it in the cream in a mixing bowl for about 5 minutes.

In an 8-inch saucepan, combine the bread-and-cream mixture with 4 tablespoons of the melted butter, then, stirring constantly, simmer over low heat until the mixture is pasty and smooth, somewhat resembling a soft dough. Remove it from the heat, let it cool for about 10 minutes, then beat in the egg yolks, one at a time, thoroughly incorporating one before adding the other. Beat in the cooked shrimp, the raw shrimp purée, the parsley and the peas. Add the salt and a grinding of pepper.

With a wire whisk or rotary or electric beater, beat the egg whites, preferably in an unlined copper bowl, until they form stiff, unwavering peaks when the beater is lifted from the bowl. With a rubber spatula, fold the egg whites into the stuffing, using an under-and-over cutting motion rather than a mixing motion, until no trace of them remains. Fill the breast cavity of the chicken, but don't pack it tightly—the stuffing will expand as it cooks. Fold the neck skin under the chicken and secure it with several stitches of strong thread. Stuff the body cavity loosely—no more than ¾ full—and close it with trussing pins or with a needle and thread. Brush the chicken all over with some of the melted butter and place it on a rack in a roasting pan just large enough to hold it. Pour the rest of the butter over the breast. Roast the chicken in the middle of the oven for about 1½ hours, basting it frequently with the pan juices. Test for doneness by piercing a thigh with the point of a small sharp knife. If the juice that spurts out is yellow, the chicken is done. If it is pink, roast a few minutes longer and test again.

Remove the chicken to a heated serving platter and let it stand for about 10 minutes before carving it. Serve it, if you like, with the pan juices diluted with ½ cup of chicken stock that has been brought to a boil in the drippings.

To serve 4 to 6

Salt
Freshly ground black pepper
6 slices calf's liver, ½ inch thick
   (about 1½ pounds)
Flour
3 tablespoons lard
½ cup finely chopped onions
2 tablespoons white vinegar
½ cup chicken stock, fresh or canned
1 tablespoon flour
½ cup sour cream
1 teaspoon capers, drained and finely
   chopped

Tiroler Kalbsleber
CALF'S LIVER TYROLIAN STYLE

Salt and pepper the liver slices, then dip them in flour and vigorously shake off the excess.

Heat the lard in a heavy 12-inch skillet over high heat until a light haze forms over it, then add the liver slices. Cook them on high heat for 2 or 3 minutes on each side, turning them with tongs. Do not overcook; the liver should be slightly pink on the inside. Remove the liver to a platter, cover it loosely with foil, and keep it warm in a 200° oven while you make the sauce.

Pour off all but a thin film of the lard from the skillet and add the onions. Stirring occasionally, cook them for 2 or 3 minutes, or until they are slightly translucent. Pour in the vinegar, raise the heat to high and boil the vinegar almost completely away. Add the chicken stock and bring it to a boil, scraping loose and stirring in any brown bits that cling to the bottom and sides of the pan. Turn the heat to low and let the stock simmer for 2 or 3 minutes.

Meanwhile, with a wire whisk, beat the 1 tablespoon of flour into the sour cream in a small mixing bowl, then beat it into the mixture in the skillet. Add the capers and simmer on low heat a minute longer. Pour the sauce over the liver and serve at once.

Zwiebelfleisch
BEEFSTEAK AND ONIONS WITH CARAWAY SEEDS

In a heavy 10- or 12-inch skillet, heat the oil and butter. When the foam subsides, add the meat and brown it on both sides—about 5 minutes in all. Remove it to a platter.

Pour off most of the fat, leaving only a thin film on the bottom of the skillet. Add the onions and cook them, stirring occasionally, for 8 to 10 minutes, or until they are lightly colored, then add the garlic and cook for about 3 minutes longer.

Stir in the caraway seeds, the marjoram and a generous grinding of pepper. Add the vinegar and boil for 1 minute. Pour in the stock and bring to a boil, stirring in any brown bits that cling to the bottom and sides of the pan.

Return the meat to the pan and bring the beef stock to a boil again. Turn the heat to low and simmer the meat for 15 minutes or longer until it is tender.

THE SAUCE (optional): In the meanwhile, with a wire whisk, beat the flour into the sour cream in a small mixing bowl. Whisk the mixture into the skillet, then turn the heat to its lowest point and simmer for 10 minutes longer without letting the sauce reach the boiling point. Mask the steak with some of the sauce and serve the rest in a sauceboat.

To serve 4 to 6

2 tablespoons vegetable oil
2 tablespoons butter
2 pounds beef tenderloin or other tender cut of beefsteak, cut into strips 2 inches long, 1 inch wide and 1/4 inch thick
1 1/4 cups finely chopped onions
1/2 teaspoon finely chopped garlic
1/2 teaspoon caraway seeds
1/8 teaspoon marjoram
Freshly ground black pepper
2 tablespoons white vinegar
1 cup beef stock, fresh or canned

THE SAUCE (optional)
1 tablespoon flour
1 cup sour cream

Salzburger Nockerl
SALZBURG SOUFFLÉ

Preheat the oven to 350°. In a medium-sized mixing bowl, break the egg yolks up with a fork and stir in the vanilla and lemon peel. Sprinkle the flour over the yolk mixture.

In another bowl, using a wire whisk or rotary or electric beater, beat the egg whites with a pinch of salt until they cling to the beater. Add the sugar and beat until the whites form stiff, unwavering peaks. With a rubber spatula, stir an overflowing tablespoon of the whites into the yolk-and-flour mixture, then reverse the process and fold the yolk mixture into the rest of the egg whites, using an over-under cutting motion instead of a mixing motion. Don't overfold.

Generously butter an oval or oblong 8-by-10-by-2-inch baking dish attractive enough to serve from. Using the rubber spatula, make 3 mounds of the mixture in the dish. Bake the *Nockerl* in the middle of the oven 10 to 12 minutes, or until it is lightly brown on the outside but still soft on the inside. Sprinkle with confectioners' sugar and serve immediately.

To serve 6

2 egg yolks
1 teaspoon vanilla extract
1/2 teaspoon grated lemon peel
1 tablespoon flour
4 egg whites
Pinch of salt
2 tablespoons sugar
Confectioners' sugar

IV

The Food of Hungary

The famed Hungarian *gulyás* keeps warm in its traditional *bogrács*, or kettle. In this form it is called *bogrács gulyás (recipe, page 110)*. Shown against the painting of a rural religious procession, this national dish is a reminder that the Hungarians still remember their ancient past.

It takes only 45 minutes to fly from Vienna's Schwechat Airport to Budapest, the capital of Hungary. But I advise you to go by train or car—or for an even lovelier journey, take the hydrofoil and skim down the Danube—to appreciate the remarkable transition between these neighboring yet totally different cities.

As you travel south and east, the mountains and Alpine meadows give way to the lowlands on both sides of the Danube—the wide, flat plains that are so typical of Hungary. There is, of course, the Great Plain, called in Hungary the Nagy-Alföld, and if you detour into Transdanubia, beautiful Lake Balaton, Central Europe's largest lake, where swims the *fogas*, a pike-perch deservedly famous for its pale skin and tender flesh. Instead of heavy Austrian lederhosen and decorative Styrian hats there are the colorful scarves that Hungarian peasant women wrap around their heads. The lilting Schubert and Strauss waltzes give way to sad and haunting old folk songs, almost forgotten until Bartók and Kodály gave the music new life in their compositions. A lot of Austrians drink beer; most Hungarians drink wine. In place of *Gemütlichkeit* there is vitality. Austrians who live outside of Vienna have little love for their capital, but 10 million Hungarians all over their nation cherish a romantic passion for Budapest, the capital where every fifth one of them lives, and for the Danube.

Though in Vienna the Danube flows discreetly around the city, barely touching the outer suburbs, in Budapest it is very much part of the city, flowing right through it, a silvery band inseparable from the local scene. Standing on Fishermen's Bastion or on the top of Gellért Hill one enjoys the wonderful view of the city (of which the natives of Budapest never get tired) and becomes aware of the vital part that the river plays in the life of the people. Its bridges are almost like human beings to the people of Budapest, important elements of their cityscape. Lovers love to walk hand in hand along the quays; people go there to fish or to read or just to gaze out at the river and the bridges. On a beautiful Sunday afternoon the whole populace seems to be near the river, in one of the many baths and swimming pools—Budapest, a big-city health resort, has 123 warm springs—or walking in Margaret Island, with its old trees, new cafés, music bands and children's playgrounds.

The river actually separates Buda from Pest, originally two separate towns: Buda was traditionally the seat of government, and Pest was a commercial center. They do not show it today, but they are among the most-often-destroyed cities in the world. The Magyars settled them in the Ninth Century; the Mongolians under Genghis Khan captured Pest in 1241; the Turks drove the Habsburgs out of Buda 300 years later; and when the Austrians retook it a century and a half after that, the place was left a shambles. Just to make sure that the "liberated" townspeople would not get any disturbing ideas, the Austrians razed all Hungarian fortresses and castles. Lately there have been other invaders; at the end of World War II not one bridge between Buda and Pest was left intact. But the Budapest spirit, both tough and romantic, seems indestructible—and as for the cuisine, every wave of conquerors has left a mark on it.

In Hungary even more than in Austria, food and music are indissolubly linked, largely because of the strong gypsy influence on Hungarian culture. Even people who have never visited the country find it hard to think of a national dish like *gulyás* without the emotional accompaniment of a gypsy orchestra and the bone-vibrating rhythms of the zimbalon, the strange oblong instrument whose strings the musician strikes madly with little hammers. In any good café the violinist, drifting from table to table and lady to lady without need for rest or food until far into the night, responds to his tearful listeners with the exquisite anguish of the *csárdás* (originally from the Hungarian word *csárda,* a country inn where this poignant gypsy dance was performed).

Today few of the musicians are authentic gypsies, but that does not matter: Their sounds still evoke the ancient, occult, semi-barbarous infusion of gypsy ways among the Hungarians and their land. The origins of all this are lost in legend. Gypsies once were supposed to have come from Egypt, hence their name; they probably set out on their wanderings from India, and their language, Romany, is related to some Indian dialects. Taking along their curious taboos, superstitions and art forms, their caravans rolled into Italy and Spain, into Poland and Romania and—in some force —into Hungary. The first recorded indication of their presence there tells that gypsies played music to console the defeated Hungarians after the Turkish victory in the battle of Mohács in 1526. But well before that, the gypsies had introduced an element of mystery into the peasant life of the country. The mystique of fortunetelling with allegorical tarot cards (admittedly the fortunes are not to be believed) is but one of the more exotic of the arts that the gypsies have preserved in Hungary. There is nothing quite like this subtle, Oriental influence in Austria.

The gypsy contribution to Hungarian cuisine is uncertain because not much is known of what the early Hungarians ate. (Also uncertain, but not unlikely, is the gypsy origin of an omelet recipe: "First, steal three eggs. . . .") There is no doubt, however, that the marvelously hot, spicy meat stew—the *gulyás*—was developed by the Magyar tribes that roamed Central Europe long before Hungary was a state. The simple food that the Magyars brought along from their ancestral home in the Caucasian Mountains also included cabbage leaves and vine leaves stuffed with meat. Sometimes the meat was ground and mixed with rice. From the Hungarians and Turks the tribes learned to make a cereal accompaniment for *gulyás* called *tarhonya*, a flour-and-egg dough, which is pressed through a sieve to form barley-sized pellets, to be dried and roasted in lard with minced onions and parsley.

The nomads began to settle down into an organized pattern of life after the establishment of a state, around 1000 A.D. In the reign of King Stephen (1001-1038) royal decrees were issued regulating innkeepers' rates and hours in the town of Esztergom, then the Hungarian capital. However, the earliest surviving documents dealing with food date from the time of King Matthias Corvinus (1458-1490). His biographers report that the dishes served at his royal table were "varied and plentiful." It was said that the Czech nobles at his court spent most of their money on clothes, while the Hungarian grandees spent most of theirs on food. The Hungarians are still such enthusiastic eaters that their daily average calorie intake is the highest in Europe, and their annual consumption of 40 pounds of lard and 30 pounds of poultry per person is matched hardly anywhere. Their basic foodstuffs—bread, milk, pork—are inexpensive and so available to all.

Genuine Hungarian cooking began with King Matthias' wife, Beatrice d'Este, who was sufficiently a gourmet to have her cheese, onions and garlic imported from Italy. Under her influence the landowners and nobles began to cook dishes in the Italian style, often with strongly spiced sauces. The influence of Austrian and French cooking was first felt during the second half of the 17th Century. The Habsburgs and their armies threw the Turks out of Buda in 1686, and stayed on. In the Habsburg capital of Vienna, the court cuisine was mainly French and thus affected the cooking of the Czech, Polish and Hungarian aristocrats living at the Habsburg court. Reflecting this, cookbooks used in Pest in the early 18th Century mention such French dishes as consommé, braised meats, ragôuts and pâtés. Even as late as a century ago, the hot and spicy dishes for which the Hungarian cuisine is famous today were considered by the ruling class to be the food of the peasants. Traveling all over Europe during the golden era of *la grande cuisine,* the nobles and landowners sampled the exquisite creations of such superb chefs as Auguste Escoffier, acquired sophisticated tastes and brought home French cooks. Catering to their new tastes, the better restaurants in Budapest developed a cuisine that was adapted to all the nuances of French cooking.

But the basic cooking of the ordinary people did not follow suit. Most Hungarian cooks, never slavish imitators of foreign cooking, simply adapted French, German, Italian and Polish dishes to their own Hungarian taste, making some imaginative changes and often improving on the origi-

Heedless of a little girl on her way to school, a gaggle of geese in Kristóf Tanya hurry toward their destiny as liver pâté, a great delicacy in Hungary. Starting when they are 11 weeks old, the geese are force fed on corn soaked in milk to fatten their livers. At 15 weeks they are slaughtered. Besides making pâté the liver can be served in many ways. The goose meat is prized as a roast.

nal. Péter Apor of Altorja, describing the close of the 17th and opening of the 18th Centuries in *Metamorphosis Transylvaniae*, mentions the following Hungarian foods: "leg of pork with horseradish, cabbage with beef, beef with rice, stewed chicken with garlic, beef or pork with a sharp sauce well peppered." All these dishes are still popular in Hungary. (Apor did not include paprika, the hot carmine spice that characterizes the cuisine today, because it was not yet known.)

The foundation of modern Hungarian cooking is the use of lard, onions and paprika. And the favorite ingredient is rich sour cream. It is used in many soups, sauces, vegetables, stewed meats, sweets and pastries. Often sour cream is also placed on the table, in case anybody wants to put more of it into a dish already prepared with sour cream—rather in the way some Viennese will put *Schlagobers*, the whipped sweet cream, even on top of *Schlagobers*.

Hungarians use butter only occasionally for lighter cooking. Vegetable oil or butter is sometimes used for cooking fish, but the best Hungarian cooks prefer to render fresh pork fat rather than use oil, butter or compressed, processed lard. Housewives often use a mixture of lard and bacon. It is the combination of lard and spices that gives many dishes their special "Hungarian" flavor.

Traditionally, many dishes are cooked with a *roux* prepared from flour rich in an elastic protein, called gluten, that is needed to make good bread; the flour is slowly browned in hot lard and various spices and flavorings are added—onions, dill and garlic, for example.

Perhaps the most critical thing in Hungarian cooking, according to experienced cooks I have talked with, is the frying of onions. On this process depends the subtlety of color and flavor that lovers of such food expect. The onions are fried in lard—slowly and with great care. Sometimes they are fried lightly to a golden color, but for some dishes they may be done to a shade of dark brown. In between there are many variations. I have asked a number of Hungarian cooks why they forego butter, which is *de rigueur* in fine French cooking. They explained unanimously that it is a matter of taste and color: "Onions fried in butter do not yield the full aroma that you get from an onion fried in hot lard. The color also suffers. Just try to make a paprika dish with hot butter. You will find that it invariably turns out too pale."

Ah, paprika. Hungarian cooking is famous for it—but it is nonsense to believe that any dish containing a handful of this strong red spice is good Hungarian food. Good cooks agree that it should be used sparingly. And master cooks know how to treat paprika and other spices in such a

A wine steward fills pitchers from a "wine thief," the instrument used to take wine from barrels. The wine is *kéknyelü,* made from grapes grown on the slopes above Lake Balaton. The candles, here the sole illumination for this cellar of a country inn, are in holders cut from cherry wood.

way that they bring out the aroma and flavor of certain dishes and color them beautifully. The cooks are not afraid to try blends of paprika, marjoram, black pepper, savory, thyme, caraway seeds, dill, celery tops and parsley, and experiment endlessly to find pleasing combinations. But the spices must never conceal the authentic flavor of a dish. Clearly, paprika is an ingredient that has to be well understood for best results.

The irony is that with all the association in everyone's mind between paprika and Hungarian cookery, the fiery plant is not native to Hungary at all. Its origin and early history have been clouded in dissension and—if I may be permitted the word—spiced with rumor. It is doubtful if anyone really knows. Some authorities believe the invading Turks brought in paprika along with other Oriental spices; and it is true that for a long time the product was called Indian pepper. Several noted explorers, among them Livingstone, reported that paprika had been growing wild "since ancient times in East India, Abyssinia and Central Africa." The great Hungarian restaurateur Károly Gundel believed that paprika was brought to Europe from America, and George Lang, an expert's expert, writes, "We are sure of only one thing—before Columbus' voyages, paprika was unknown in Europe."

The subject of the controversy is *Capsicum annuum,* a relative of the tomato and potato (both of which did indeed come from America), an annual, branchy shrub that grows to two feet in height, bearing fruit with a cone-shaped pod three to five inches long and about an inch wide. At the end of summer the pods turn red, are picked, dried, and ground into the powder called paprika. In Hungary the coincidence of climate and handed-down agricultural expertise has created a fascinating paprika industry. Around the southern towns of Szeged and Kalocsa the hot, dry summers, the gentle spring rains and the light, fertile soil provide just what the plant needs to flourish, and "paprika families" like the Palffys and the Horvaths have developed the cultivation and processing of paprika into an art. Today in the state-owned factories the ripened plants go through electric drying machines, and the chopping and grinding are completely mechanized. But at farmhouses here and there you can still see bristling red masses of drying paprikas threaded on long strings and hung from the eaves, and the use of the ancient paprika-crushing implement called the *külü* is not yet forgotten.

Károly Gundel once told me that the very finest paprika, called "sweet," or "rose," should be mild, with a piquant, never a sharp, aftertaste. "It should intrigue the eye, stimulate the palate, never upset the stomach." Fine paprika should be milder than its relative, cayenne pepper, and should contain a certain amount of sugar. The sugar content is the reason paprika should be mixed into other ingredients with the cooking pan off the heat; if overheated the sugar turns to caramel, which spoils the color and flavor. Incidentally and for what it may be worth to paprikaphiles, Albert Szent-Györgyi, the Hungarian-American winner of a Nobel Prize in chemistry, proved that paprika is the plant world's richest source of Vitamin C.

Hungarians divide their paprika dishes into four categories—*gulyás, pörkölt, paprikás* and *tokány.* All four are varieties of hot, spicy stew. *Gulyás,* which has become the country's most famous export, has lost much of its original identity on its triumphal procession around the world, probably because its name has come to be applied indiscriminately to any paprika-laced stew. International success has not improved the taste of *gulyás.* Many Hungarians are horrified by this adverse effect of fame, and often they are unable to recognize their great dish. In the U.S. *gulyás* has become goulash, in Czechoslovakia *guláš,* and in Vienna it is known as *Gulasch,* usually with a prefix to denote some particular variety. Pseudo knowledge is widespread and increases with the distance from Budapest.

To sort out fact from fiction about *gulyás* is almost impossible. Everybody agrees that *gulyás* is a folk dish, a belly-warming shepherds' stew that has been traced back to the Ninth Century. It was invented for the same reason as other stews, ragôuts, hashes and thick soups: It was nourishing and inexpensive and it had a good taste. But most important to men who had to wander far from home, it could be prepared from previously dried ingredients that could be transported easily—a kind of ancient survival ration.

Before setting out with their herds, the Magyar shepherds cut meat into cubes and cooked it with onion in a *bogrács,* a heavy iron kettle hung over an open fire out on the *puszta* (prairie). They stewed the meat slowly until the liquid was gone, dried the remnants in the sun and put

Continued on page 96

The man opposite, wearing a traditional peasant costume, roasts bacon over an open fire. The bacon is cut in coxcomb shape and will be served in an open sandwich or as the central piece in a mixed grill. The picture at left shows how the bacon is held right over the fire.

The Country Csárda of Hungary

The *csárda*, or highway inn, was once a place where Hungarian cowboys and shepherds would eat and drink and maybe spend the night. Highwaymen also used to stop there. Today the food is still simple, usually cooked outdoors in a traditional white-painted kiln such as the one opposite, although sometimes an open fire is also used, as above. Only the highwaymen are gone.

them into a bag made from a sheep's stomach. There was nothing new about this method: Nomads had cooked similar stews since remote times. When they were hungry they took a piece of the dried food, added water and reheated it in their kettle. Depending on whether they added little or much water, it became *gulyás* meat or *gulyás* soup. The typical Hungarian touch—the paprika—probably was not added until sometime during the 18th Century.

Over the years everybody developed his own version of the national dish, basing it on one cut of beef or another, or even on fowl, sometimes adding bacon or lard or both. But the traditional *gulyás* is still prepared more or less as the wandering shepherds prepared it, though it is no longer dried in the sun; today people eat it when it is ready *(page 110)*. Its basis remains cubes of beef, preferably from the rib or shoulder, cooked with finely chopped onions and diced potatoes. Some people add fresh tomatoes or tomato purée; some use garlic; some put in sliced green peppers or hot cherry peppers; all add paprika, caraway seeds and salt. It is taboo, however, to use any flour to thicken the sauce or to add wine to lend it a French touch.

Classic *gulyás,* authorities insist, is never made of mutton or pork, and its gravy is almost never finished with sour cream. However, as with all rules, there is one exception to both these requirements: the delicious *székely gulyás (page 115)*, which may be made of a combination of meats or of pork alone, and to which sour cream is added.

Sometimes served with *gulyás* instead of the ancient *tarhonya* pellets, is a kind of noodle called *csipetke,* made from a simple egg and flour dough nipped off bit by bit between forefinger and thumb and dropped into boiling water. Some of my Hungarian friends claim they can detect from the taste of the *csipetke* whether the cook was left-handed; I am not that much of an expert.

Of the other paprika stews, two—*pörkölt* and *paprikás*—have names that mean "singed," although "braised" would be a more accurate description of their preparation. *Pörkölt* has a stronger onion flavor than *gulyás,* and uses fatter meat cut into bigger pieces. It is usually made of veal, although beef, mutton, game, goose, duck or pork are also used. The most popular *paprikás (page 117)* contains veal or chicken, although lamb, duck or even fish may be substituted. The meat, which is cut in larger pieces than for *gulyás,* is coated with a thick gravy that clings to the chunks. Sweet or sour cream is always present, sometimes mixed with a little flour, stirred in at the end just before serving. Again, there are many variations. Some people chop the onion, others slice it; some add fresh tomatoes, others add sliced green peppers or sliced potatoes.

The fourth of Hungary's notable stews, *tokány (page 111),* is certainly something you should have in your repertoire. The meat—either beef or veal—is cut lengthwise into pieces about the size of French fried potato strips. *Tokány* may contain sweet or sour cream or no cream at all, plus mushrooms, asparagus tips, peas, goose liver and parsley roots. Sometimes black pepper or marjoram is used as an enlivening agent instead of paprika; then the *tokány* is named for its spice.

In Transylvania, *tokány* contains a mixture of beef, pork, veal kidneys and mushrooms. A variety called Seven Chieftains *tokány,* after the seven chieftains who supposedly led the Magyars to Hungary in the Ninth Century, contains beef, pork and veal. *Debreceni tokány* always contains the famous sausage from Debrecen.

The cooking of any of these stews follows the same pattern. To get the onions to the subtle shade of translucent gold that marks a first-rate dish, the pot must be covered or the onions constantly stirred. Then the pot is taken away from the fire, sweet paprika is mixed with the onions, and the meat and some water are added. When the water boils away, a little more fresh water is added. The process is continued; there should be very little liquid in the kettle at any time so that the meat fries in its own fat. The liquid must not become too thin, since the idea is to obtain a strong gravy that permeates the food. For *paprikás* and some types of *tokány* you later add cream.

But try not to be confused by these Hungarian names (they seem strange because Hungarian is one of the few European tongues totally unrelated to English). Take my word for it, all the varieties of paprika dishes are superb. In the phrase of a Hungarian friend of mine, the aroma that fills your kitchen as you cook "will not make you cry for peanut butter."

Please do not entertain the thought that paprika-flavored stew is all there is to the Hungarian cuisine. There are innumerable great Hungarian dishes: notably the various cabbage dishes that have become famous throughout the rest of the world, and in some places even rival the famous *gulyás*. There is also golden-brown, roast suckling pig that should come out of the oven shining like glass; chicken fried in bread crumbs, resembling Viennese *Backhendl; fogas*, that famous fish from Lake Balaton, most distinctively Hungarian when turned in flour and paprika and fried in lard; and soups like *ujházi's*, made of tender poultry and fine noodles cooked in a thin broth with carrots, parsnips, mushrooms and celery, and delicately flavored with ginger, parsley and peppercorns.

Hungarian soups, often thickened with a *roux*, are always solid and nourishing, sometimes a main course by themselves. Take Shepherd's Wife soup, which starts with small pieces of shoulder of mutton cooked in their own fat with finely chopped onion; red paprika is added, then water, and finally, when the meat is tender, sour cream, finely chopped dill, salt and pepper and the bits of noodle called *csipetke*. The Hungarians also make a heavy, delicious soup from scraps of suckling pig and finely chopped onions fried in lard, all seasoned with red paprika, salt, ground pepper and bay leaf. When the mixture is tender, a *roux* is added, and finally the soup is finished with more seasonings and lemon juice, and sour cream is put on top. Nowadays the less traditional but very delicious fruit soup based on sour cherries, red wine and cream has become a popular way to open the meal *(page 112)*. Its subtle sweetness, faintly flavored with cinnamon, provides a cool and delicate contrast to the fiery meat dishes of the main course.

The local meat products include such specialties as *Kolozsvár* bacon, thick, spicy Debrecen sausages, smoked *Gyulai* sausage, each with a unique flavor, and of course the renowned Hungarian goose liver. It appears as a delicacy on tables all over the world, usually as an appetizer, but Hungarians use it in a variety of ways. It is fairly large—weighing between one and two pounds—and may be roasted in its own fat and

Continued on page 104

The Country Fair Flourishes in a Socialist Land

Large-scale agriculture has long been socialized in Hungary, but the country fair survives. Peasants still take their pigs to market *(above)*, offer livestock for sale *(opposite)*, trade horses *(overleaf)* and treat themselves to great outdoor meals of paprika sausage, fried pork and beer or wine, while having a fine gossip session with the neighbors. The fairs survive because even the socialized farmers on the big collective farms may own small plots on which they can raise produce or animals in their free time. The pictures on these and the following pages were taken at the fair in Dunaföldvár on the Danube south of Budapest, where farmers and their families sell the products of their plots, and also buy and sell hand-painted pictures of saints, furniture, and other household articles. The fairs are continuing centers of peasant existence, and it is at such places that some of the salient characteristics of old Hungarian country life can be seen.

98

The fairs and festivals of Hungary are a reflection of an enduring and exotic style of life and eating habits. At lunch on the grass by a food stand at the Dunaföldvár fair *(below)*, Hungarians show their delight in outdoor dining and their love of such robust food and drink as spicy paprika sausage washed down with wine. Still for sale at such fairs are hand-crafted tubs and barrels *(opposite)*, used at home for storing apples and grain and for holding the laundry. But some habits have been dying; and as a result, the government has developed a program to preserve some of the old folk customs and art. *At left:* Young girls in homemade costumes practice a traditional harvest dance.

served whole either hot or cold, often together with the heart. It may be used as a stuffing; stewed with onions, parsnips and carrots in a paprika-and-sour-cream sauce; braised with veal chops; or even cooked in a beef stew with wine (Gundel prepared it that way). Hungarian patriots and expatriates will go to any length to find goose liver, and they declaim with passion that none in the world can equal theirs.

Cabbage dishes are a staple on Hungarian dinner tables. The cabbage is often boiled with caraway seeds or pork for flavoring and may be mixed with sour cream, flour, parsley, stock and even a little vinegar before serving. But perhaps stuffed cabbage *(page 118)* is the most satisfying of all. Each leaf is wrapped around a fragrant mixture of pork, rice, eggs, spices and herbs, often covered with a light tomato sauce and served on a bed of sauerkraut. The *Kolozsvár* (Transylvanian) cabbage is layered with a thick *roux,* onion, paprika and sour cream, and often smoked sausage and bacon, with various spices. All such cabbage dishes are rich in flavor and nourishment.

Hungary has no seacoast (though it once had an admiral named Horthy who ran the country), but it has excellent fish from its rivers and lakes, and Hungarian cooks have found imaginative ways of preparing the fish. Carp is an often underrated fish, and in Hungary it can be excellent. Before World War II Gundel's would "improve on" nature by putting live carp taken from the still lakes into screened tanks that were lowered into the Danube for two weeks. The river's current would wash away the faint trace of muddiness that the still lake had left. I have eaten fine carp soup in Hungary. And then there's deviled carp *(page 120)* made with bacon, paprika, onions and tomatoes. Carp cooked *au bleu* is superb. To achieve the blue color it must be cooked immediately after being caught, in boiling water seasoned with salt, vinegar and peppercorns, then served with melted butter and parsley.

Perhaps the best fish is the perch-pike from Lake Balaton called *fogas.* It is whiter, more tender than the zander or *Schill* from the Danube (where the fish, fighting against the current, often develop muscles). Balaton *fogas* is served cold, with a salad of tomatoes and paprika, aspic and hard-cooked eggs; or it is grilled or poached in white wine and served with a crayfish *pörkölt*—the only *pörkölt* that is made *without* onions and with very little paprika, in order to preserve the full taste of the crayfish.

The season for fresh-water crayfish is any month *without* an "r," that is, from May to August. Hungarians eat a thick crayfish soup, crayfish with paprika sauce, and thin pancakes with a crayfish purée that also contains mushrooms, paprika and cream.

But when I go to Hungary I rarely order fish. I like it, but there are so many other things that I like better. High on my list of favorites is that all-purpose mixture called *lecsó (page 111).* It is simply green pepper, fresh tomatoes, fresh onions, bacon and paprika cooked together, usually in lard. It has a vivid, piquant flavor—resembling the Italian *cacciatore.* In the traditional method of preparation, the tomatoes are scalded, sometimes skinned and quartered; the peppers are cored, cut lengthwise into strips; the diced bacon is fried to a golden-brown in lard; and the finely chopped onions are stirred for just a minute. Then the paprika is added, and finally the green peppers and the tomatoes. *Lecsó* must not be made in a hurry, but stewed slowly over a low fire until the various tastes and flavors create a marvelous blend. It may be served on its own as a dip, or as an accompaniment for omelets, sausages or meats, or it may be bought as a ready-prepared cooking base.

Probably no other people on earth except the Chinese use pork in as many ways as do the Hungarians. "A chunk of pork or thin flank of pork can be added to any meat dish and undoubtedly improves the flavor of the dish," writes József Venesz, one of the great Hungarian cooks. The pork is inexpensive and of good quality. Its flavor is enhanced by the spices and herbs used in Hungarian cooking, and it tastes especially good with fried onions and peppers. Minced pork is used for stuffed green peppers and stuffed kohlrabi *(page 120),* a vegetable similar to turnip and celeriac. Pork cooked with sour cabbage makes a delicious *székely gulyás.* Pork flanks are cooked with dill cabbage; pork fillets are made in a thick paprika sauce. Other Hungarian specialties are boiled pork, served with horse-radish sauce, and jellied pork made from the head, feet and tail of the pig—cooked with mixed vegetables, onions, garlic and black pepper, sprinkled with the inevitable pinch of paprika.

For dessert Hungary offers pastries that compete with Vienna's best—and outclass them, the Hungarians say. They are adamant on the subject of *Strudel;* they maintain it really was invented in Hungary, where it is called *rétes* (although, when pressed, they concede the basic idea derives from the Turkish *baklava* pastry). The finest *Strudel* flour, with a high gluten content, originally came from Hungary (according to the Hungarian version of the story), and was imported by the Austrians. The Austrians make their *Strudel* with many different fillings, but the Hungarians fill their *rétes* with a still wider variety of things—even with cabbage that has been sautéed with ground pepper and caramelized sugar. The combination sounds strange but tastes good. Another *rétes,* one that I consider the best, is called *vargabéles* (cobbler's delight) and is made with a mixture of curd cheese, butter, sour cream, sugar, eggs, vanilla and sultana raisins.

Now that the Hungarians once more have plenty of coffee, there has been a revival of the traditional offering of a small glass of *espresso* when you go to see someone, at home or at the office, day or night. Once again coffee and coffeehouses play their important role in Budapest's social life. The city has a coffeehouse past and coffeehouse lore of its own to rival Vienna's. The Café Hungaria, once called the Café New York, is now back in business on the corner of Erzsébet and Dohány, having survived its brief postwar conversion by the Communists into a nationalized sporting-goods store.

In the early days of the century, the Café New York was a citadel of Budapest literary and amorous life. The waiter still shows you the table where Férénc Molnár, surrounded by music and the aroma of fine coffee, wrote *Liliom.* Later generations of Hungarian playwrights wrote (or at least tried to write) sophisticated comedies about adultery at Molnár's table, or other tables, but not often with his success.

Budapestians of pre-World War I days also went to the Paradise Café, on the ground floor of the Fehér Hajó Hotel, to the Café Spring and to the much older Renaissance Café. Here Sándor Petöfi, the great Hungarian

Typical of the dishes cooked outdoors at Hungary's country inns is *rabló-hus* (robbers' meat): lamb or beef on skewers, resting on trestles of fried bread, and served with potatoes and pickle slices.

poet, spoke to the representatives of the revolutionary Hungarian youth in 1848. Today young people go again to the innumerable *espresso* cafés that are always full of ideas and talk and good cheer. Hungarians are a nation of conversationalists, but they don't talk only over coffee. The wine of Hungary is a beverage of which the Hungarians are rightly proud. And the most noted wine is of course Tokay.

Tokay comes from the village of Tokaj in the Carpathian Mountains in northeastern Hungary, where the Furmint grape grows on 5,000 acres of volcanic soil. Once the best sections were owned by the Habsburgs, and "Imperial Tokay" was a royal gift. When Austrian Empress Maria Theresia sent a few casks to Pope Benedict XIV, he wrote to thank her, "Blessed is the soil which produced thee, blessed is the queen who sent thee, and blessed am I who may enjoy thee."

Tokay is still the only great wine made east of the Rhine. It is pressed from overripe grapes touched by *pourriture noble*, the "noble mold" that forms on the skins of ripening grapes in certain areas and helps to concentrate the sugar and flavor. At the most the grapes may contain 30 per cent sugar, which turns into 15 per cent alcohol. The dried grapes are collected in baskets *(puttonyos)* that hold 30 pounds each, and these baskets supply an identifying mark for the wine. The number of basket symbols printed on the label of the Tokay called Aszu indicates the number of baskets of grapes that have been used to make a certain quantity of the wine; the more *puttonyos,* the sweeter the Tokay.

The rarest Tokay of all, called *eszencia,* or essence of Tokay, is not pressed at all. The sheer weight of the ripe grapes creates just a little juice in the small barrels in which they have been placed. When the juice is exposed to the open air, it ferments. *Eszencia* often contains only 8 per cent alcohol and, despite the fact that weak wines usually spoil quickly, this one can live for many years. It is a heavy, sweet, liqueurlike wine, rath-

Also popular at inns is roast *fogas,* a pike-perch caught in Lake Balaton and the Danube. It has white flesh and is almost boneless. Tradition requires that the fish be bent into this curled shape during cooking.

er like a cordial that reminds one of honey. Even in a great year only a few bottles can be produced; understandably, it is expensive. Hungarians ascribe a miraculous rejuvenating effect to *eszencia,* which is recommended for "old men who wish to be young again."

Tokay may be Hungary's only great wine, but there are many other good ones, most bearing names that twist a tongue attuned to English. For entrées, a proper wine waiter brings a *Balatoni Rizling,* full-bodied and pleasant, or an Egri *Leánkya.* Roast veal or roast pork are accompanied by a stronger, dry wine, such as *Csopaki Rizling* or *Olaszrizling.* Strangely, many Hungarians prefer a light, dry wine such as the *Rizling* of Bácsalmás with their paprika stews; personally, I would drink a heavy red wine with such dishes, preferably an Egri *Bikavér* (bull's blood) or a *Nagyburgundi* of Villány. For poultry and feasts with suckling pig there are several fine white wines—the *Olaszrizling* of Badacsony, the *Szürkebarát* (gray friar) or the dry *Szamorodni* of Tokaj. Pastry—without which no Hungarian meal is considered complete —tastes best with a sweet wine: a *Muskotály* of Akali, a *Zöldszilváni* of Badacsony or a sweet *Szamorodni* of Tokaj.

It is their vitality and love of life that gives the Hungarians their special quality. Their peasant traditions, derived from both East and West, are in my view the richest and most vivid in Central Europe. In Hungary, life and art still are one; they are not separate and distinct as in the West. And their food and cooking are as integral to their lives as they were in olden times. In Hungary the meal of the day is a ritual, not just a matter of filling the stomach. Sometimes, Hungarians talk about the way things have changed. They are not at all sure that change means progress, but it has to be accepted. What else can you do? But however they may talk and shrug their shoulders, in their hearts the stubborn pride in an old and steadfast nation endures.

107

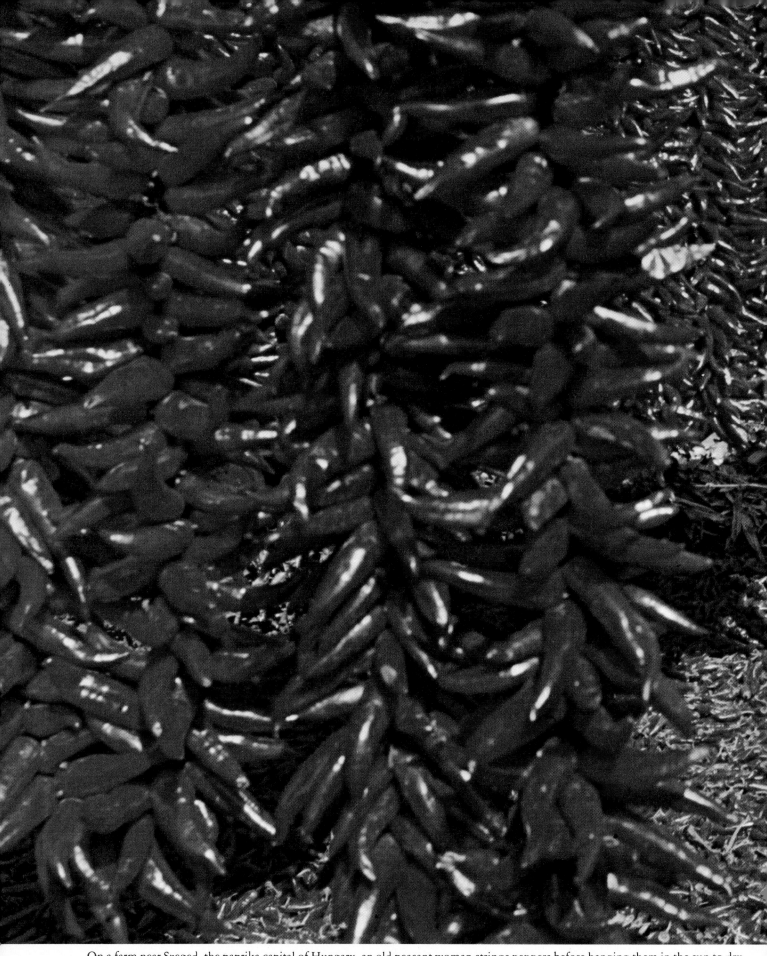

On a farm near Szeged, the paprika capital of Hungary, an old peasant woman strings peppers before hanging them in the sun to dry.

Later they will be finely ground to make the sweet, piquant condiment that is so essential to most of the country's spicy cooking.

To serve 4 to 6

2 tablespoons lard
1 cup finely chopped onions
½ teaspoon finely chopped garlic
3 tablespoons sweet Hungarian
    paprika
2 pounds shin beef, cut into 1½-
    inch cubes
½ teaspoon caraway seeds
4 cups chicken or beef stock (or
    mixed chicken and beef stock),
    fresh or canned, or 4 cups water
½ teaspoon salt
Freshly ground black pepper
2 medium-size boiling potatoes
1 pound tomatoes, peeled, seeded and
    finely chopped (about 1½ cups)
2 medium-size green peppers, with
    seeds and ribs removed, finely
    chopped
½ teaspoon marjoram

To serve 4

THE STUFFING
2 tablespoons finely chopped bacon
¼ cup finely chopped onions
½ cup chopped fresh mushrooms
    (about ⅛ pound)
¾ cup dry bread crumbs
¼ cup milk
4 anchovies, mashed
1 tablespoon finely chopped parsley

THE FISH
A 3- to 4-pound yellow pike, cleaned
    and scaled, with backbone removed
    but head and tail left on
5 tablespoons butter, melted
½ cup finely chopped onions
1 clove garlic, finely chopped
Salt

THE SAUCE
½ cup sour cream
½ teaspoon salt
Freshly ground black pepper
1 tablespoon fresh lemon juice
1 teaspoon sweet Hungarian paprika

Bogrács Gulyás
KETTLE GOULASH

Heat the lard in a 4- or 5-quart heavy saucepan until a light haze forms over it, then reduce the heat to medium and add the onions and garlic. Cook them 8 to 10 minutes, or until the onions are lightly colored. Off the heat, stir in the paprika. Stir until the onions are well coated.

Add the beef cubes, caraway seeds and stock or water to the pan and season with the salt and pepper. Bring the liquid to a boil and partially cover the pan. Simmer for 1 hour, or until the beef is almost tender.

Parboil the potatoes in boiling water for 8 to 10 minutes, or until they can be easily penetrated with the point of a sharp knife for ¼ inch or so. Peel them, cut them into 1½-inch cubes and add them, the tomatoes, the peppers and marjoram to the pan. Partially cover again and cook over medium heat for 25 to 35 minutes, or until the potatoes are done and the beef is tender. Skim off the surface fat and taste for seasoning.

Serve the goulash in deep individual plates.

Töltött Csuka
BAKED PIKE STUFFED WITH MUSHROOMS, ANCHOVIES AND BREAD CRUMBS

THE STUFFING: In a heavy 6- to 8-inch skillet, cook the bacon over moderate heat until it has rendered enough fat to coat the bottom of the skillet. Add the onions and cook for 2 or 3 minutes, then stir in the mushrooms. Cook for 3 to 4 minutes more, or until most of the mushroom liquid has evaporated. Transfer the contents of the pan to a large mixing bowl. Soak the bread crumbs in the milk until they have absorbed it, and add them and the anchovies and parsley to the bowl. Stir and mash the mixture with a wooden spoon until it is smooth and pasty.

BAKING THE FISH: Preheat the oven to 450°. Wash the fish under cold running water and dry it inside and out with paper towels. Fill the fish with the stuffing, close the opening with roasting pins, and crisscross them with kitchen string as you would lace a turkey, or sew the openings with white thread. Brush some of the melted butter on the bottom of a serving-and-baking dish large enough to hold the fish. (If you prefer to serve the fish from another dish, line the dish with a long piece of foil.) Place the fish in the dish and sprinkle the onions and garlic around it. Pour the rest of the melted butter over the fish, and bake it uncovered in the middle of the oven, basting it every 5 to 7 minutes with the pan juices.

In 40 to 45 minutes, the fish should be just firm when pressed lightly with a finger. Remove it from the oven and, if the fish is to be served from the baking dish, use a bulb baster to transfer the juices to a pan. If it is to be served from a platter, use the ends of the foil to lift it, and slide it onto the platter. Then pour the juices into a pan.

THE SAUCE: In a bowl, whisk the sour cream, salt, pepper, lemon juice and paprika together. Set the pan containing the juices on low heat and stir in the sour-cream mixture. Stir constantly while it heats. It should not boil. Taste for seasoning, then pour the sauce over the fish and serve.

Paprikás Burgonya
POTATO PAPRIKA

Cook the potatoes in boiling water for 8 to 10 minutes, then peel and cut into ¼-inch slices. In a 4-quart saucepan or casserole, heat the lard until a light haze forms over it, then add the onions and garlic. Cook for 8 to 10 minutes, or until lightly colored. Off the heat, stir in paprika. Stir until the onions are well coated. Return the pan to the heat, add stock or water, bring to a boil, and add caraway seeds, potatoes, tomato, green pepper, salt and a few grindings of pepper. Bring the liquid to a boil, stir, cover and simmer for 25 to 30 minutes until the potatoes are tender.

NOTE: The addition of Debreceni or another semisoft smoked sausage to potato paprika makes the dish a complete meal. Slice the sausage about ⅛ inch thick and add it when you add the potatoes.

Serve in a casserole as a vegetable or entrée for a luncheon dish. Top each portion with a tablespoon of sour cream.

To serve 4 to 6

2 pounds boiling potatoes
3 tablespoons lard
⅔ cup finely chopped onions
¼ teaspoon finely chopped garlic
1 tablespoon sweet Hungarian paprika
2 cups chicken or beef stock, fresh or canned, or 2 cups water
⅛ teaspoon caraway seeds
1 medium-sized tomato, peeled, seeded and chopped (about ¼ cup)
1 large green pepper with seeds and ribs removed, finely chopped
1 teaspoon salt
Freshly ground black pepper
1 pound Hungarian sausage
½ cup sour cream

Lecsó
TOMATO AND GREEN PEPPER RAGÔUT

In a 2-quart saucepan or casserole, heat the lard or bacon fat until a light haze forms over it, then add the onions and garlic and cook for 8 to 10 minutes, or until the onions are lightly colored. Off the heat stir in the paprika, continuing to stir until the onions are well coated.

Stir in the green peppers, tomatoes, salt and pepper. Cover the pan and cook for 10 minutes over medium heat. If the tomatoes have not produced enough liquid to cover the vegetables, add ¼ cup or more of purée. Cover the pan again while the purée is heating, then add the sausage, cover, and simmer for ½ hour. Lecsó should have the consistency of tomato sauce. Add the remaining purée if it needs thinning.

Traditionally, Lecsó is served in sauce dishes as an appetizer or as a luncheon dish topped with a fried egg.

To serve 4 to 6

3 tablespoons lard or bacon fat
1½ cups finely chopped onions
½ teaspoon finely chopped garlic
2 tablespoons sweet Hungarian paprika
1 pound green peppers (5 medium-sized) with seeds and ribs removed, cut into ½-inch pieces
1 pound tomatoes, peeled, seeded and coarsely chopped (1½ cups)
½ teaspoon salt
Freshly ground black pepper
½ cup tomato purée
1 pound Hungarian Debreceni sausage, cut into ⅛-inch slices

Borsos Bélszíntokány
FILLET OF BEEF STRIPS WITH ONIONS, MUSHROOMS AND PEPPERS

Heat 2 tablespoons of the lard in a heavy 10-inch skillet over high heat until a light haze forms over it. Add the meat strips and toss them about for 3 to 5 minutes, or until they are browned on all sides.

Remove the meat to a platter and add the remaining tablespoon of lard to the skillet. Turn the heat to medium and add the onions and garlic. Cook for 8 to 10 minutes, or until the onions are lightly colored. Off the heat, stir in the paprika, continuing to stir until the onions are well coated. Return the meat to the skillet and gently stir in the mushrooms and peppers. Place the pan on high heat, and when it begins to sizzle, turn the heat to its lowest point and cover the pan tightly. Simmer for 25 to 30 minutes, or until the meat shows no resistance when pierced with the point of a sharp knife. Taste for seasoning.

Tip the skillet and skim off any of the surface fat. Arrange the strips on a platter, pour the pan juices over them and serve. Borsos Bélszíntokány is usually served with rice and sour pickles.

To serve 6

3 tablespoons lard
2½ to 3 pounds fillet of beef, cut into ½-by-¼-by-3-inch strips
1 cup thinly sliced onions
¼ teaspoon finely chopped garlic
1 teaspoon sweet Hungarian paprika
½ cup chopped mushrooms (⅛ pound)
2 large green peppers with seeds and ribs removed, cut into strips ⅛ inch wide and 2½ inches long

111

To serve 6 to 8

A 3-pound frying chicken
2 medium sized whole peeled onions
  (about ½ pound)
8 cups water or chicken stock or water
  and chicken stock combined
2 cups kohlrabies diced into ½-inch
  cubes (about 4 medium-sized
  kohlrabies)
2 tablespoons butter
2 tablespoons flour
Salt
2 tablespoons finely chopped parsley

To serve 4 to 6

2 pounds of veal shoulder, cut into
  1½-inch cubes
4 tablespoons lard
2 cups finely chopped onions
½ teaspoon finely chopped garlic
1 tablespoon sweet Hungarian
  paprika
3 medium fresh ripe tomatoes, peeled,
  seeded and coarsely chopped
  (about ¾ cup), or an equivalent
  amount of canned drained
  tomatoes
1 medium green pepper, with
  seeds and ribs removed, coarsely
  chopped (about ¼ cup)
Salt

To serve 6

3 cups cold water
1 cup sugar
1 cinnamon stick
4 cups pitted sour cherries or drained
  canned sour cherries
1 tablespoon arrowroot
¼ cup heavy cream, chilled
¾ cup dry red wine, chilled

Kalarábéleves
KOHLRABI SOUP

Combine the chicken and onions in a 5-quart casserole or soup kettle and cover them, depending on the degree of richness desired, with the chicken stock, or a mixture of chicken stock and water, or water. Bring the liquid to a boil, skim off the surface scum, then reduce the heat to medium. Partially cover and cook for 40 minutes, or until tender.

Remove the chicken and strain the soup through a sieve set over a large bowl, pressing down on the onions with a wooden spoon before discarding them. Skim off the surface fat, return the stock to the pot, bring it to a boil and add the diced kohlrabies. Turn the heat to its lowest point, partially cover the pan and simmer while you prepare the chicken.

Strip the skin from the chicken and pull the meat from the bones. Cut the meat into ½-inch cubes and add them to the pot. Simmer about 20 minutes longer, or until the kohlrabies are tender.

Melt the butter in a heavy 8-inch skillet over medium heat. When the foam subsides, stir in the flour. Continue to stir until the flour is lightly browned, then add ½ cup of the stock from the pot. With a wire whisk, stir over low heat until the sauce begins to thicken, then whisk it into the pot. Simmer for 10 minutes longer. Taste for seasoning. Pour the soup into a heated tureen and sprinkle it with the chopped parsley.

Borjúpörkölt
VEAL STEW WITH TOMATOES AND GREEN PEPPERS

In a heavy 4- or 5-quart saucepan, melt the lard over medium heat, then add the onions and garlic. Cook them for 8 to 10 minutes, or until the onions are lightly colored. Off the heat, stir in the paprika, continuing to stir until the onions are well coated, then stir in the veal. Cover tightly, turn the heat to its lowest point and simmer for ½ hour.

Stir in the tomatoes and cook, covered for ½ hour longer, stirring occasionally. Then add the green peppers. Cook, covered, ½ hour more, again stirring occasionally, or until the veal is tender. The tomatoes will provide sufficient liquid. Taste for seasoning. Serve with boiled potatoes, dumplings or noodles.

NOTE: The sauce in veal *pörkölt* is like a thick gravy. Do not thin.

Hideg Meggyleves
COLD SOUR CHERRY SOUP

In a 2-quart saucepan, combine the water, sugar and cinnamon stick. Bring to a boil and add the cherries. Partially cover and simmer over low heat for 35 to 40 minutes if the cherries are fresh or 10 minutes if they are canned. Remove the cinnamon stick.

Mix the arrowroot and 2 tablespoons of cold water into a paste, then beat into the cherry soup. Stirring constantly, bring the soup almost to a boil. Reduce the heat and simmer about 2 minutes, or until clear and slightly thickened. Pour into a shallow glass or stainless-steel bowl, and refrigerate until chilled. Before serving—preferably in soup bowls that have been prechilled—stir in the cream and wine.

Served from a bowl set inside another bowl of cracked ice, cold cherry soup is made with cherries, sugar, wine and cream.

To serve 4 to 6

3 tablespoons lard
Salt
Freshly ground black pepper
8 pork chops, ¾ inch thick
    (trimmed)
Flour
1½ cups finely chopped onions
¼ teaspoon finely chopped garlic
3 tablespoons sweet Hungarian
    paprika
1 cup chicken stock, fresh or
    canned, or water
⅓ cup heavy sweet cream
⅓ cup sour cream
2 tablespoons flour
3 tablespoons finely chopped fresh
    dill

To serve 8

2 pounds sauerkraut, fresh, canned
    or packaged
A 1-pound solid piece of bacon, with
    rind
1 cup rice
2 pounds boneless pork, cut into ¾-
    inch cubes
Salt
Freshly ground black pepper
1½ cups finely chopped onions
1 teaspoon finely chopped garlic
2 tablespoons paprika
1 pound Polish, Italian or Hungarian
    sausage, cut into ⅛-inch slices
2 cups chicken stock, fresh or canned
1½ cups sour cream
¾ cup milk
½ teaspoon salt
½ teaspoon paprika

Sertésborda Kapros Paprikamártásban
BRAISED PORK CHOPS IN DILL-AND-PAPRIKA SAUCE

Sprinkle the chops generously with salt and a few grindings of pepper, then dip them in the flour and shake off the excess. In a 12-inch skillet, heat the lard over high heat until a light haze forms over it. Add the pork chops to the skillet and cook them 3 to 4 minutes on each side. Transfer the chops to a platter.

Add the onions and garlic to the fat remaining in the pan, and cook them for 8 to 10 minutes, or until the onions are lightly colored. Off the heat, stir in the paprika, continuing to stir until the onions are well coated. Return the skillet to the heat, pour in the stock or water and bring it to a boil, stirring in any brown bits that cling to the pan.

Return the chops to the skillet, reduce the heat to its lowest point, cover tightly and simmer the chops for 1 hour, or until they are tender, then arrange them on a heated platter. Combine the sweet cream and the sour cream in a mixing bowl, then with a wire whisk, beat in the flour. While still beating, pour this mixture into the skillet. Stirring constantly, simmer for 2 to 3 minutes, or until the sauce is thick and smooth. Add the chopped dill and taste for seasoning.

Pour some of the dill-and-paprika sauce over the pork chops and serve the rest in a sauceboat.

Erdélyi Rakott Káposzta
TRANSYLVANIAN LAYERED CABBAGE

Preheat the oven to 350.° Wash the sauerkraut thoroughly under cold running water, then let it stand in cold water for 10 to 20 minutes to reduce its sourness. Squeeze it dry by the handful and set it aside.

With a sharp knife, cut the bacon off the rind, leaving ¼ inch of the fat attached to the rind. Dice the bacon into ¼-inch chunks. In a heavy 10-inch skillet, cook the bacon until it is slightly crisp, then transfer it with a slotted spoon to a large mixing bowl. Pour off from the skillet all but a thin film of the fat and reserve it.

Drop the rice into 2 quarts of slightly salted boiling water. Bring the water to a boil again and cook the rice for 3 minutes. Pour it into a colander or strainer, rinse it with cold water and set it aside to drain.

Sprinkle the pork cubes with salt and a few grindings of pepper. Heat 3 tablespoons of the bacon fat in the skillet until a light haze forms over it, then add the pork cubes. Over medium heat, toss them about for 5 to 6 minutes, or until they are lightly browned on all sides. With a slotted spoon, transfer the pork to the mixing bowl with the bacon and add the onions and garlic to the fat remaining in the skillet. Stirring occasionally, cook them for about 5 minutes, or until the onions are lightly colored. Off the heat, stir in the 2 tablespoons of paprika, continuing to stir until the onions are well coated, then scrape the mixture into the mixing bowl with the bacon and pork.

Return the skillet to the heat and add the sausage and, using more of the bacon fat if necessary, cook it until it is lightly browned. Transfer the sausage to the mixing bowl and add 1 cup of the stock to the skillet. Bring it to a boil, stirring in any brown bits clinging to the bottom and sides of the pan. Then pour the stock over all the ingredients and, with a fork, toss them together gently but thoroughly.

Line a heavy 6-quart casserole with the sauerkraut, after pulling it apart with your fingers. Spread the meat-onion mixture over the sauerkraut. Spread the rice on top of that. Combine the sour cream and milk and pour the mixture evenly over the rice. Score the bacon rind and cut it into 5 or 6 equal strips. Distribute these over the top of the casserole and sprinkle with the ½ teaspoon of salt, a few grindings of pepper and paprika. Over medium heat on the top of the stove, heat the casserole until it boils or sizzles. Cook uncovered in the middle of the oven for 1¼ hours, adding the other cup of stock after 1 hour. Serve directly from the casserole.

Székely Gulyás
TRANSYLVANIAN GOULASH

To serve 4 to 6

Wash the sauerkraut thoroughly under cold running water, then soak it in cold water for 10 to 20 minutes to reduce its sourness.

Melt the lard in a 5-quart casserole and add the onions. Cook them over moderate heat, stirring occasionally, for 6 to 8 minutes, or until they are lightly colored, then add the garlic and cook a minute or 2 longer. Off the heat, stir in the paprika, continuing to stir until the onions are well coated. Pour in ½ cup of the stock or water and bring it to a boil, then add the pork cubes.

Now spread the sauerkraut over the pork and sprinkle it with the caraway seeds. In a small bowl, combine the tomato purée and the rest of the stock or water, and pour the mixture over the sauerkraut. Bring the liquid to a boil once more, then reduce the heat to its lowest point, cover the casserole tightly and simmer for 1 hour. Check every now and then to make sure the liquid has not cooked away. Add a little stock or water if it has; the sauerkraut should be moist.

When the pork is tender, combine the sour cream and heavy cream in a mixing bowl. Beat the flour into the cream with a wire whisk, then carefully stir this mixture into the casserole. Simmer for 10 minutes longer. Taste for seasoning. Serve Transylvanian goulash in deep individual plates, accompanied by a bowl of sour cream.

1 pound sauerkraut, fresh, canned or packaged
2 tablespoons lard
1 cup finely chopped onions
¼ teaspoon finely chopped garlic
2 tablespoons sweet Hungarian paprika
3 cups chicken stock or water
2 pounds boneless shoulder of pork, cut into 1-inch cubes
1½ teaspoons caraway seeds
¼ cup tomato purée
Salt
½ cup sour cream
½ cup heavy cream
2 tablespoons flour

Paprikasaláta
GREEN PEPPER SALAD

To serve 4

Preheat the oven to 450°. Arrange the green peppers on a rack and heat them in the oven for 10 to 15 minutes, or until the skin begins to discolor and blister. Remove them, wrap them in a damp kitchen towel and let them rest for 10 minutes. Strip off the skins with a small knife, then remove the stems, seeds and ribs, and cut the peppers into strips ¼ inch wide and about 3 inches long.

Combine the vinegar, sugar, salt and pepper in a mixing bowl. Add the strips of pepper, toss them with the mixture, cover and refrigerate from 2 to 12 hours. Drain them in a sieve or colander, transfer them to a mixing bowl and add the mayonnaise. Serve on lettuce as a salad or in small dishes as an accompaniment to cold meat.

3 large green peppers
2 tablespoons white vinegar
1 teaspoon sugar
1 teaspoon salt
⅛ teaspoon freshly ground black pepper
½ cup mayonnaise, freshly made or a good commercial brand

Named for a famous Hungarian family, steaks Eszterházy are braised with aromatic vegetables and colorfully garnished.

Paprikás Csirke
CHICKEN PAPRIKA

Pat the chicken pieces dry with paper towels and salt them generously.

In a 10-inch skillet, heat the lard over high heat until a light haze forms over it. Add as many chicken pieces, skin side down, as will fit in one layer. After 2 or 3 minutes, or when the pieces are a golden brown on the bottom side, turn them with tongs and brown the other side. Remove pieces as they brown and replace them with uncooked ones.

Pour off the fat, leaving only a thin film. Add the onions and garlic and cook them over medium heat 8 to 10 minutes, or until lightly colored. Off the heat, stir in the paprika; stir until the onions are well coated. Return the skillet to the heat and add the chicken stock. Bring to a boil, stirring in the brown bits from the bottom and sides of the pan.

Return the chicken to the skillet. Bring the liquid to a boil again, then turn the heat to its lowest point and cover the pan tightly. Simmer the chicken for 20 to 30 minutes, or until the juice from a thigh runs yellow when it is pierced with the point of a small sharp knife. When the chicken is tender, remove it to a platter. Skim the surface fat from the skillet. In a mixing bowl, stir the flour into the sour cream with a wire whisk, then stir the mixture into the simmering juices. Simmer 6 to 8 minutes longer, or until the sauce is thick and smooth, then return the chicken and any juices that have collected around it to the skillet. Baste with the sauce, simmer 3 or 4 minutes to heat the pieces through, and serve.

Eszterházy Rostélyos
STEAKS ESZTERHÁZY

Salt and pepper the steaks, then dip them in flour and shake them to remove the excess. Heat the lard in a 12-inch skillet until a light haze forms over it, then brown the steaks over high heat for about 3 minutes on each side. Remove them to a platter and reduce the heat to medium.

Add the onions, garlic and carrots and cook for about 8 minutes, stirring frequently, until the vegetables are lightly colored.

Off the heat, stir in the 3 tablespoons of flour, continuing to stir until all the flour is absorbed. Return the skillet to the heat, add the stock and bring it to a boil, stirring constantly with a whisk until the sauce is smooth and thick. Add the allspice, bay leaves, peppercorns, thyme, lemon peel, bacon, parsley and vinegar. Return the meat to the skillet and bring the stock to a boil again. Reduce the heat to low, partially cover the pan and simmer for 50 minutes to an hour, or until the steaks show no resistance when pierced with the tip of a small sharp knife.

Drop the parsnip and carrot strips into a saucepan of boiling, lightly salted water. Boil uncovered for 2 or 3 minutes, or until the vegetables are slightly tender, then drain in a colander or sieve. Arrange the steaks on a platter and keep them warm in a 200° oven while you prepare the sauce.

Strain the contents of the frying pan, pressing hard on the vegetables before discarding them. Skim off the surface fat from the sauce. Whisk the cream and lemon juice into the sauce and add the carrot, parsnip and gherkin strips. Simmer 2 or 3 minutes. Taste for seasoning. Pour the vegetables and the sauce over the steaks and serve at once.

To serve 4 to 5

A 3-pound frying chicken, cut up
Salt
2 tablespoons lard
1 cup finely chopped onions
½ teaspoon finely chopped garlic
1½ tablespoons sweet Hungarian paprika
1 cup chicken stock, fresh or canned
2 tablespoons flour
1½ cup sour cream

To serve 6

Salt
Freshly ground black pepper
2 pounds top round steak ½ inch thick, cut into 6 equal portions
Flour
3 tablespoons lard
1½ cups finely chopped onions
½ teaspoon finely chopped garlic
½ cup finely chopped carrots
3 tablespoons flour
3 cups beef stock, fresh or canned
3 whole allspice or ⅛ teaspoon ground allspice
3 medium-size bay leaves
4 peppercorns
⅛ teaspoon thyme
⅛-inch-wide strip lemon peel
4 slices lean bacon, coarsely chopped (⅓ cup)
2 tablespoons finely chopped parsley
¼ cup white wine vinegar
¾ cup heavy cream
1 teaspoon fresh lemon juice

THE GARNISH

2 parsnips, scraped and cut into 3-by-½-inch julienne strips
1 medium-sized carrot, cut into 3-by-½-inch julienne strips
4 sour gherkin pickles, cut into 3-by-½-inch julienne strips

To serve 4 to 6

2 pounds sauerkraut, fresh, canned
　or packaged
1 large head green cabbage (2 to 3
　pounds)
2 tablespoons lard or bacon fat
1 cup finely chopped onions
¼ teaspoon finely chopped garlic
1 pound ground lean pork
¼ cup rice, cooked in boiling salted
　water (¾ cup cooked)
2 lightly beaten eggs
2 tablespoons sweet Hungarian
　paprika
⅛ teaspoon marjoram
1 teaspoon salt
Freshly ground black pepper
1 cup water mixed with 1 cup tomato
　purée

THE SAUCE
3 tablespoons unsalted butter
2 tablespoons flour
1 cup sour cream

Töltött Káposzta
PORK-STUFFED CABBAGE ROLLS

Wash the sauerkraut in cold water, then soak in cold water 10 to 20 minutes to reduce sourness. Squeeze dry and set aside. In a large saucepan, bring to a boil enough salted water to cover the cabbage. Add the cabbage, turn the heat to low and simmer 8 minutes. Remove the cabbage and let it drain while it cools enough to handle. Pull off the large unbroken leaves and lay them on paper towels to drain and cool further.

In a 10-inch skillet, heat the lard or bacon fat on high heat until a light haze forms over it. Add the onions and garlic and cook them, stirring occasionally, until the onions are lighty colored.

In a large mixing bowl, combine the pork, rice, eggs, paprika, marjoram, the onion-garlic mixture, salt and a few grindings of black pepper. Mix well with a fork or wooden spoon.

Place 2 tablespoons of the stuffing in the center of one of the wilted cabbage leaves and, beginning with the thick end of the leaf, fold over the sides, then roll the whole leaf tightly, as you would a small bundle. Repeat with more leaves until all the stuffing has been used.

Spread the sauerkraut on the bottom of a 5-quart casserole and arrange the cabbage rolls on top of it. Add the water mixed with the tomato purée. Bring the liquid to a boil, then cover the pan tightly and cook the stuffed cabbage over low heat for 1 hour. Transfer the rolls from the casserole to a warm platter.

THE SAUCE: In a small saucepan on medium heat, melt the butter and

1　Put mixture of pork, rice, eggs and paprika on blanched cabbage leaves.

2　Fold each leaf over from the sides and start rolling from the root end.

3　Roll the leaves tightly, carefully tucking in the sides as you go.

4　The pork-stuffed cabbage roll is now shown in its completed form.

5　Place cabbage rolls on sauerkraut, add water, tomato purée and simmer.

6　Serve the stuffed cabbage rolls with their own sauce, and sauerkraut.

stir in the flour. Continue to stir until the flour browns slightly. Gradually stir in the cream, continuing to stir until the sauce is thick and smooth. Stir the sauce into the sauerkraut and simmer 5 to 10 minutes longer. With a fork or slotted spoon, lift the sauerkraut onto a serving platter. Arrange the cabbage rolls on the sauerkraut and pour some of the sauce over them. Serve the rest of the sauce in a sauceboat.

Palacsinták Barackízzel

APRICOT PANCAKES

To make about 14 pancakes

Beat the eggs lightly with the milk in a small bowl. Combine with the club soda in a large mixing bowl. With a wooden spoon stir in the flour and sugar, then add the salt and vanilla extract. Continue to stir until the batter is smooth.

Melt 1 teaspoon of butter in an 8-inch skillet, preferably a pancake skillet. When the foam subsides, ladle in enough batter to cover the bottom of the skillet thinly and tilt the skillet from side to side to spread it evenly. Cook for 2 to 3 minutes, or until lightly browned on one side, then turn and brown lightly on the other. When a pancake is done, spread 2 teaspoons of jam over it, roll it loosely into a cylinder, then put it in a baking dish in a 200° oven to keep warm until the pancakes are finished. Add butter to the skillet as needed. Serve warm as a dessert, sprinkled with nuts and confectioners' sugar.

3 eggs
1 cup milk
⅓ cup club soda, freshly opened
1 cup sifted flour
3 tablespoons granulated sugar
¼ teaspoon salt
1 teaspoon vanilla extract
4 to 6 tablespoons butter
¾ cup apricot jam
1 cup ground walnuts or filberts
Confectioners' sugar

1 Spread pancake batter thinly, tipping pan to flow batter to edges.

2 Pancakes brown in 2 or 3 minutes, then are turned to cook on other side.

Palacsinták (pancakes) are rolled up around an apricot jam filling, sprinkled with walnuts and dusted with confectioners' sugar before serving.

Töltött Kalarábé
STUFFED KOHLRABIES

To serve 4 to 6

8 to 10 medium-sized young
  kohlrabies, peeled
Leaves of 5 kohlrabies
2 tablespoons lard
½ cup finely chopped onions
½ teaspoon finely chopped garlic
½ pound ground pork
½ pound ground veal
2 tablespoons rice, cooked in boiling
  salted water (¼ cup cooked)
1 tablespoon finely chopped parsley
2 tablespoons sweet Hungarian
  paprika
⅛ teaspoon dried marjoram
2 eggs, lightly beaten
1¼ teaspoon salt
Freshly ground black pepper
⅛ teaspoon white pepper
4 cups chicken stock, fresh or canned

THE SAUCE
3 tablespoons butter
2 tablespoons flour
1 cup heavy cream
1 tablespoon finely chopped
  parsley

Slice off ¼ inch of the root end of each kohlrabi; then scoop out the pulp, creating a shell about ¼ inch thick. Chop the pulp coarsely and set it aside. Wash the leaves of 5 kohlrabies, then blanch them by dropping them into a pot of slightly salted boiling water for about 3 minutes. Drain them, chop them finely and add them to the chopped pulp.

In a heavy 8-inch skillet, heat the lard over high heat until a light haze forms over it. Add the onions and garlic and cook them for 8 to 10 minutes, or until the onions are lightly colored, then scrape them into a large mixing bowl. Add the pork, veal, rice, parsley, paprika, marjoram, eggs, a teaspoon of the salt and a few grindings of black pepper. Mix with a wooden spoon until all the ingredients are thoroughly combined.

Fill the kohlrabi shells with the meat mixture, tamping it down with a spoon and mounding it slightly. Arrange the stuffed shells in a 4-quart casserole or saucepan. Scatter the chopped pulp and leaves around them and add ¼ teaspoon of salt, the white pepper and the chicken stock. Bring to a boil, reduce the heat to its lowest point and simmer for 35 to 45 minutes, or until the stuffing is fully cooked and the sides of the kohlrabies can be pierced easily with the point of a sharp knife. Transfer the kohlrabies to a warm serving plate while you make the sauce.

THE SAUCE: In a small saucepan on medium heat, melt the butter, and with a wire whisk, stir in the flour. Continue to whisk over low heat for 3 or 4 minutes, or until the flour is lightly browned. Add the cream and whisk until the sauce is smooth and thick, then stir the sauce into the large saucepan. Simmer for 5 to 10 minutes longer, strain through a fine sieve into a large bowl, then stir in the chopped parsley. Pour the sauce over the stuffed kohlrabies and serve.

Ponty Fűszermártással
DEVILED CARP

To serve 4 to 6

3 tablespoons bacon fat or lard
1 cup finely chopped onions
2 tablespoons sweet Hungarian
  paprika
1 large green pepper, with seeds and
  ribs removed, diced into ½-inch
  pieces (about ½ cup)
1 cup chopped tomatoes, blanched,
  peeled and seeded
¼ cup dry white wine
A 5-pound carp, cleaned, scaled and
  cut into 6 or 8 steaks 1 inch thick
Salt
Freshly ground black pepper
1 tablespoon flour
½ cup sour cream

Preheat the oven to 350°. Heat the fat or lard in an 8-inch skillet over high heat until a light haze forms over it, then reduce the heat to medium and add the onions. Cook them for 8 to 10 minutes, or until lightly colored. Off the heat, stir in the paprika. Return the skillet to medium heat and add the peppers and tomatoes. Cover tightly and cook for 5 minutes, then stir in the wine.

Scrape half the vegetable mixture into a buttered 8-by-12-inch shallow baking dish, approximately 2 inches deep. Sprinkle the fish steaks generously with salt and a few grindings of pepper. Arrange them in one layer in the baking dish, and cover with the rest of the mixture. Bake in the middle of the oven for 15 to 18 minutes, or until the fish is firm to the touch and flakes easily when prodded gently with a fork.

Arrange the fish steaks on a serving platter, cover them loosely with foil and keep them warm in a 200° oven while you make the sauce.

With a wire whisk, beat the flour into the sour cream in a small mixing bowl, then stir the mixture into the pan juices. Reduce the heat and simmer on top of the stove, stirring constantly, for 4 or 5 minutes, or until the sauce is thick and creamy. Mask the carp with the sauce.

Sertésborda Hentes Módra

PORK CHOPS WITH HAM AND PICKLES

To serve 4 to 6

Pat the pork chops dry with paper towels, sprinkle them generously with salt and a few grindings of pepper, then dip them in flour and shake off the excess. Heat the lard in a heavy 10- or 12-inch skillet until a light haze forms over it, then add the chops 2 or 3 at a time. Cook them for about 4 minutes on each side, or until they are lightly browned.

Remove the chops to a platter and pour off all but a thin film of the fat. Add the onions and garlic and, stirring occasionally, cook them for 8 to 10 minutes, or until the onions are lightly colored. Off the heat, stir in the paprika, continuing to stir until the onions are well coated. Return the skillet to high heat and pour in the stock and tomato purée. Stir, bring the liquid to a boil, add the chops, and reduce the heat to its lowest point. Cover the pan tightly and simmer for about 40 minutes, or until the chops show no resistance when pierced with the tip of a small sharp knife. Turn the chops once while they are simmering.

Arrange the chops on a heated serving platter and keep them warm in a 200° oven while you make the sauce.

With a wire whisk, beat the flour into the sour cream in a mixing bowl, then whisk the mixture into the skillet. Stirring constantly, cook over low heat for 2 or 3 minutes, or until the sauce is thick and smooth. Add the ham and pickle strips and simmer 1 or 2 minutes longer, or until they are heated. Taste for seasoning.

Pour some of the sauce over the chops and serve the rest separately.

6 loin pork chops, ¾ inch thick
  (about 2½ pounds)
Salt
Freshly ground black pepper
Flour
3 tablespoons lard
1 cup finely chopped onions
1 small clove garlic, finely chopped
1 tablespoon sweet Hungarian
  paprika
1 cup chicken stock
¼ cup tomato purée
1 teaspoon flour
1 cup sour cream
6 ounces boiled ham slices, cut into 3-
  by-⅓-by-⅓-inch julienne strips
6 ounces sour gherkin pickles, cut
  into 3-by-⅓-by-⅓-inch julienne
  strips

Kohlrabi stuffed with ground pork and veal is popular in Hungary. It is served with parsley cream sauce.

V

The Influence of Czechoslovakia

Long before I knew anything about Austrian cooking I loved the *Topfenpalatschinken* (thick pancakes with curdled sweet cream) and *Streuselkuchen* (a rich crumb cake with fresh blueberries) that our cook Marie made in our home in the Moravian town of Ostrava where I was born. When I came to Vienna as a student of music in 1925, I immediately rediscovered Marie's great gastronomic creations. In Vienna, they were known as "the glories of Viennese cooking." I knew better, of course; at best, these Viennese glories were pale imitations of Marie's marvels. The "glories" had been borrowed from Moravia and neighboring Bohemia (both now part of the Czechoslovak Republic), which, of all the former provinces of the Habsburg Empire, have always had the strongest influence on Austrian, and especially Viennese, cooking. Much has been written about the famous "Bohemian cooks" in Vienna, where every "better" bourgeois house used to have an elderly woman cook who came from Bohemia. Anyhow, I feel it is about time to vindicate the art and honor of the great cooks of my native Moravia.

Marie had "belonged" to the family even before my arrival there. She had moved into my parents' home the day after they were married, as part of my mother's dowry. Grandmother, having reared 13 children, knew that an experienced cook can make or break a young household. Being a sensible woman, she had hired and trained Marie and "sent her over."

Marie had known a lot about cooking long before she met my mother's mother. She was born to cook as other people are born to write or paint. She was an instinctive cook. I never saw her read a cookbook, but her recipes had become part of her life, closely guarded from the curious and envious.

Once my mother made the mistake of bringing home a recipe for a "wonderful" cherry cake *(page 193)*. The recipe was a legacy left to my mother by an old aunt who had been very rich and lost everything, as everybody else had, in the post-World War I inflation. The only things left were a few "wonderful" recipes, and each of my aunt's nieces inherited one.

Unfortunately I cannot report how "wonderful" the recipe was. Marie never made it. For a couple of days she was so hurt that she didn't even talk to my mother. When a truce was established, she said, "*Gnädige Frau,* gracious lady, what is wrong with *my* cherry cake?" My mother remembered the lesson well, and never again gave Marie somebody else's recipe.

Frequently, guests in our home, after a particularly successful meal, would go out into the kitchen, leaving a nice tip for Marie (that was the local habit) and meekly ask her for one of her recipes. Marie turned down such demands unconditionally. She said they couldn't be written; they were only in her head. I know she spoke the truth.

Marie did many things that no highly paid housekeeper would do today. Twice a week, on Tuesdays and Fridays, she would bake bread. The evening before, she would leave the sourdough standing in the kitchen overnight; I can almost smell the sour scent of yeast as I write this. In the morning Marie would knead the dough, shape it into a round and put it into the oven. The big, white-tiled range was heated with black coal, which was mined in our town. I always tried to be in the kitchen when Marie opened the oven and took out the crusty loaf of warm, dark bread. It was baked with a mixture of wheat and rye flour and was strongly flavored with caraway seeds. It had the most marvelous smell.

Marie would smile and cut off a hard endpiece for me. She would put on a slab of sweet, golden country butter, with its slight flavor of almonds, and then she would spread a little salt on it and perhaps some pig's lard. Or if she had just prepared a fresh goose liver, she would put goose liver fat on the bread. It was wonderful.

Among my mother's friends Marie was particularly famous for her *Falsche* (false) soups and warm *Mehlspeisen* (desserts). The false soups were made with vegetable stock instead of meat stock or stock made from bones. Though false soups are not always respected by students of gastronomy, they can be very good. I happily remember Marie's potato and mushroom soups, and also her wonderful combination of the two: delicious. There were other substantial soups in Marie's repertoire—puréed with egg yolks and cream and cooked vegetables—that were almost a meal in themselves.

I especially liked it when we had a false soup at the beginning of lunch because that meant there would be something special, such as *Wiener Schnitzel* or *Lungenbraten* (a whole roast fillet of beef). Unfortunately my mother and my younger brother preferred consommé. This meant that every week we would have the boiled beef that had been cooked with the broth. Since we were a small family the piece of boiled beef would last for four or five meals—and it would not be the expensive *Tafelspitz,* a cut that is similar to our chuck or top sirloin and popular for its flavor. Let me say that Marie was very good at varying her beef broth. One day she would put in meat dumplings, then there would be tiny pancakes, noodle squares or small liver dumplings. All these I later rediscovered among the "glories" of Viennese cooking, of which that city was so proud.

Marie's loving care gave second-quality cuts and joints the taste and tenderness of the most expensive. She made a marvelous *svíčková se smetanou* (fillet of beef in a sour-cream sauce), for which she used genuine fillet when we had guests and a less expensive rump roast when we were alone; and it was hard to tell the difference between the two.

In a word, Marie could cook anything. She obviously knew the deeper meaning of the word cuisine, though she had probably never heard the word. Her pheasant, roasted in its own gravy with bacon and served with red cabbage, was superb. She prepared many varieties of stewed red and white cabbage and sauerkraut, often adding caraway seeds: there was never any taste of acidity, and elderly uncles who were on all kinds of diets and annually made their pilgrimage to the medicinal waters of Karlsbad (now called Karlovy Vary) praised Marie's kraut because it never gave them indigestion or made them feel uncomfortable.

Marie's smoked pork (called *uzené* in Czechoslovakia and *G'selchtes* in Vienna), served with potato dumplings, was mild; cured but hardly salted. Marie's pork roast, with *houskové knedlíky* (bread dumplings) and sauerkraut, was popular even with a relative of mine whose observance of Judaism was rigidly Orthodox and who otherwise never touched pork. He said it was worth a sin, and God would forgive him. The crackling on top of the pork Marie carefully scored into little squares, and then she sprinkled the whole of the roast with caraway seeds.

I can never forget Marie's sauces; they were special and in tasting them one knew instantly the sauce was Marie's and no one else's. Nowadays so many sauces lack a really distinctive character. They taste like something out of a bottle. Marie, for example, made her mushroom sauce only when fresh wood mushrooms were for sale in the market, in the late summer and autumn. These delicious mushrooms with dark-brown caps and white stems, very similar to the French *cèpes,* are hidden under and between the moss that grows near the roots of pine trees. The mushrooms were brought in to Ostrava by peasant women from the nearby Beskydy Mountains. Marie knew they must not be too big or too beautiful; the beautiful specimens (as the most beautiful apples) always attracted worms. She would never consent to the use of dried or artificially grown mushrooms. The aroma of fresh mushrooms was delicious in our house.

On Sundays Marie would cook mashed potatoes, a special treat. I always went into the kitchen to watch her. She would mash the potatoes just before they were served; she knew they must not be left standing. She would bear down on the mealy potatoes with vertical thrusts, sensing instinctively that they must never be stirred with rotary movements. (Many years later, when I knew something about gastronomy and regarded mashed potatoes, a deceivingly simple dish, as the test of a good cook, my friend Alexandre Dumaine, one of the masters of *la grande cuisine,* explained to me that potatoes must *always* be mashed with vertical thrusts.) Finally Marie added plenty of sweet butter and sweet cream. She continued mashing until potatoes, butter and cream were thoroughly blended.

Marie reached the zenith of her art when she made her *Mehlspeisen.* In my hometown the women always tried to outdo each other with their warm desserts. No one would dream of offering guests a ready-made cake that could be bought at the last minute. No, the test of a well-run household was the quality of the warm desserts, made with fresh ingredients. Marie's *Topfenknödel* (cottage-cheese dumplings) were light as a soufflé, and I would eat at least half a dozen of them. I once invited some classmates in for a dumpling-eating contest. The winner ate 34. This proved not only his astonishing physical capacity but also the airy lightness of Marie's dumplings.

The main ingredient of this marvelous specialty was a dry curd cheese (like a hard, pressed farmer's cheese) that was sold only in certain stores. Marie knew exactly the right consistency for the cheese—it must not be too creamy. Beside sieved curd cheese, the mixture contained salt, butter, eggs, and semolina or flour. Marie always said the dumplings must be simmered in water. They had to be served at once, with melted butter and sugar. In Vienna, where *Topfenknödel* are still very popular, they are often served with *Zwetschkenroester* (thickly stewed ripe plums) and toasted bread crumbs fried in butter. But it is Marie's version that I remember best.

Marie would never make apricot dumplings out of potato paste, as some other local cooks did. She said that the apricot harvest occurred just at a time when the old floury potatoes were not good for the paste. Instead she made a dough out of the inside of *Semmeln* (rolls) mixed with milk. And sometimes, she made her feathery *Brandteig* (puff paste) dumplings of flour, butter, eggs and salt. She also made marvelous *Schusterbuben* ("cobbler's boys"), pieces of yeast dough shaped like a forefinger. The dough was boiled for 10 minutes in salt water. The *Schusterbuben* were served at once, with melted butter and finely ground poppy seeds mixed with sugar. This was one of Marie's specialties that I never came across in Vienna.

On Fridays, which were meatless in our home (economy, not religion, was the reason), Marie cooked Bohemian *Dalken*, small tarts filled with marmalade, or *Kolatschen* (somewhat larger ones), or sometimes *Skubánky*, potato-paste dumplings baked in hot butter and served with cinnamon sugar. These *Mehlspeisen* were served in large heaps immediately after the false soup. Then my mother used to serve them again around 4 in the afternoon when she had invited several ladies for a *Jause*.

But all that is in the past. Today, Czechoslovak cooking is really of two kinds—one for the foreign tourists, members of foreign delegations and privileged citizens; the other for everybody else. Indeed, the Czechoslovak cuisine that one finds in foreign cities and international fairs, notably Canada's Expo '67, is without equal. But at home in Czechoslovakia the daily fare, though substantial, is quite plain and simple.

In principle every Czech who works—in a factory, in an office, in any other kind of job—eats his noon meal at a state-managed cafeteria. The catch is, of course, that he who does not work does not get this cheap meal. These government cafeterias serve very inexpensive meals since the state makes up the difference between the actual cost and the workers' contribution. A good many cafeterias offer poor food, but those that cater to the high-ranking bureaucrats are excellent. For a few crowns they serve a three-course meal that no housewife could equal at the price.

Nowadays it is not often that one gets a warm noon meal at home during the week, since almost half the country's working force consists of women. Even at night, housewives who come home after the day's work prepare a quick dinner, probably something cold or something left over from the weekend, when most of the home cooking is done.

A red-capped waiter fills mugs of beer in the garden of Prague's U Flekü brewery, which has been making beer since 1499.

Foreigners are surprised to see the crowds that throng the automat restaurants, snack bars and cafeterias in Prague at all hours. I have seen people eat warm dishes at 9 in the morning, at 4 in the afternoon, at midnight and in between. I was told that these cafeteria meals are not very nourishing—lots of carbohydrates, few proteins. A couple of hours after eating, people are hungry again. Some walk over to the Koruna restaurant in Václavské náměstí for a couple of hot sausages, or at least some slices of bread dumplings with gravy. (The dumplings are as good as they always were.) No one starves in Czechoslovakia today—but few eat excitingly.

The good small restaurants of yesterday have changed too. The food is no longer prepared by those sturdy Czech women who made the wonderful soups, roasts and desserts and who either owned the place or had worked there all their lives. You could go there every day; it was like home. Nowadays the cooks are state employees, like everybody else, and they get recipes from the authorities that must be prepared like drugstore prescriptions. They cannot create and improvise. The cooks never stay long enough at a restaurant to develop certain house specialties; they tend to move about, with the result that there is no distinction between one restaurant's food and another's—except in certain luxury restaurants. But how many Czechs can afford them? And that is why *svíčková* (fillet of beef with cream sauce) or *vépřová pečené* (pork roast) has the same taste everywhere. The good old cooking of Prague is a thing of the past.

The menus are the same in all restaurants, except in the half dozen luxury restaurants where no citizen can afford to go unless he is invited by a friend from abroad, or goes as member of a delegation. There are the same soups, the same cold appetizers, the same meat dishes, beginning with boiled beef, and other "ready dishes," all ending with the same desserts. As you might expect, it is pretty dull.

On weekends and holidays, when the families are together, some cooking is done at home. People tell me they eat too much on such occasions, "but eating is one of the few pleasures left." How well they eat depends on how much money they make. When three people in a family of four are employed, they can afford to eat well even by today's standards. It is heavy food: substantial soups, a pork roast with dumplings and sauerkraut, or *rošténky* (rump steak sautéed with onions) with potatoes, or a veal stew. The meat is drenched in gravy. On a festive occasion roast goose is served with dumplings. Green vegetables and salads are hard to get. In any case, Czechs are more interested in desserts: stewed fruit and the famous crumbly *Streusel* cake, or small cakes made from yeast dough and filled with plum jam. You would think they would be very fat people, but they are not.

This is all nourishing food, but the situation is sad when you consider that Czechoslovakia used to be one of the best-fed countries in Europe, a place where one could eat very, very well.

Since food production in Czechoslovakia is planned by the bureaucrats, as is everything else, important foodstuffs, sorely needed at home, are exported to other countries in return for industrial raw materials; or they are exported to Western countries in the interest of foreign exchange.

It is significant that the famous hams of Prague can no longer be bought there in ordinary stores. They are for sale only at the state-managed Tuzex stores—for hard-currency Tuzex bonds, or for American dollars or German marks. Lucky people who have relatives and friends abroad and get money gifts from them buy them; and, of course, foreign diplomats and tourists can also afford not only Prague ham but other things.

Compared to the Tuzex stores—which sell luxuries like Scotch whiskies, French Cognacs, South American coffee, Swiss chocolates, American canned goods, cigarettes and chewing gum, French *foie gras*, Hungarian salami and other good things—the local stores look poor, offering little beyond the bare necessities. At the Gastronom delicatessen in Prague's Příkopy, which is considered a de luxe store, I recently saw large heaps of canned Cuban lobster (which almost no one bought), third-grade Czech wines (the better varieties are all exported) and four different kinds of butter. I was told that the cheaper varieties of butter are only barely usable for cooking. Across from the Gastronom there was once—before the Second World War, an era that now seems as remote as a fairy tale to many people—the Lippert delicatessen, which offered a wonderful display of Russian caviar, truffled goose liver from Alsace, fine cheeses from Italy and Denmark, the finest Czech butter, poultry and game and fish and smoked meats and pâtés, Westphalian ham and Dutch herring and Italian *scampi* and genuine Rhine salmon and many other delicacies. Any Czech with money in his pocket could buy them. He did not have to be a diplomat or Party boss. Now Lippert's is gone, and there is a state-owned textile store in its place, selling some shoddy goods, another of the tragedies of our times.

If you walk into a butcher shop on a quiet street of a Prague suburb where foreign tourists rarely go, you will see cheap cuts of pork and beef. One is told that the better cuts are sent to the hotels and disappear in the special stores where Party bosses and other privileged people do their shopping. Once in a while word spreads in the neighborhood that there is some veal for sale, and a long queue forms within minutes—but most of the people are disappointed because the supply is soon gone. The meat is poorly displayed. No one cares. Why should they? The people working in the store are not the owner and his employees. They are state-employed and not interested at all in selling meat. If they can get a better-paid job tomorrow, perhaps working for the building trade, they will take it. As in so many places today pride in one's work is gone. It is a terrible thing to see this when one remembers how it used to be. Who knows if it will ever be different? Of course, it can be different. It can change when enough people want it.

In Paris, even though times have changed, people still talk about sauces and soufflés, in Vienna they discuss boiled beef and *Strudel*, but, alas in Prague the serious eaters seldom discuss their fabulous sausages and dumplings the way they used to before World War II. Somehow the Czechs have never promoted sausages, their most famous food product; which is surprising since they do promote their beer. The Germans, for example, have won fame for their many cold varieties of sausage, or *Wurst*, but the Czechs have failed to win comparable fame as the world champions of hot sausages. The delicious sausages known in America as frankfurters really ought to be called "Pragers," since they originated in Prague. There they are known as *párky* (pairs) because they always come in twos, like lovers. And you never can be satisfied with eating just one anyway.

Prague's *párky* look like American frankfurters but taste much better. In the old days *párky* connoisseurs ate them several times a day, having *párky*

Czechoslovakia, famous both for its glassware and the plum brandy called *slivovice*, combines the two in various ways. Both the long-stemmed glass and the outsized snifter (*above*) are appropriate for serving *slivovice*.

breaks as Americans have coffee breaks. They knew the subtle nuances in taste of *párky* made by Chmel, Zemka or other famous sausage shops. Now the names have disappeared in the anonymity of nationalized shops. And the nuances no longer exist since *párky* are manufactured by a fixed formula on assembly lines, it would seem. The recipes are worked out by civil servants instead of *párky* experts. *Párky* conformity is the rule.

The nomenclature of Prague's hot sausages was always mystifying. Besides *párky* they had *vuřty* (pronounced "vurshty," from *Wurst*), which were shorter, thicker, fatter, with a strong skin. A subspecies of *vuřty*, larded with small square pieces of fat bacon, was called *taliány* (Italians). The sturdiest variety of all, with a rather leathery skin, was called *klobásy*. When you bit into a *klobás* it fairly exploded between your teeth. The delicious juice ran down the corners of your mouth, making aristocratic fat stains on the lapels of your suit. People in Prague wore their fat stains like decorations.

All hot sausages are steamed or boiled, never grilled or broiled, in the sausage shops, which are called *uzenářství*, distinguished by their white-tiled floors and breast-high marble counters along the walls. These were and still are the cathedrals where sausage lovers worship. The sausages are steamed in big containers under the care of white-clad girls who wear thick sweaters under their nurses' coats. In winter the poor girls always have cold feet while they burn their fingers in the steam. In summer there is still the steam, but at least their feet are warm. The girls know the idiosyncrasies of their customers, who point and hold up two, three or four fingers—words are superfluous in such exalted moments—to indicate what they want and how much. The actual eating is done with a minimum of conversation.

High stacks of white plates stand next to the containers. The girls serve the desired number of sausages on a plate. Next to it they place whatever the customer likes: a roll, a piece of dark bread, raw or cooked sauerkraut, grated horse-radish or mustard, pickles or potato salad. The girls still prefer those habitués who order nothing with their *párky* but mustard and a piece of dark bread. They disapprove of people who demand Russian and other outlandish salads; and it takes nerve or ignorance to do so.

The customer pays and takes his plate to the nearest available spot alongside the wall where he places it on the marble counter. Sporty connoisseurs eat their *párky* standing up. Lazy men and fat women sit down in the back of the room. Some people order a glass of beer. The sausage shops are not permitted to sell beer, but fortunately nearly all of them are located near beerhouses, which are only too glad to have the trade.

Around midmorning the white-clad girls rushing to and from the beerhouse are a common sight in the streets of Prague. They carry a half dozen glasses in one hand without spilling a drop. The beerhouses, in turn, offer hot sausages, but no one thinks of eating them there, or at home for that matter. It is an accepted though inexplicable truth that hot sausages taste best within two yards of the container where they have been steamed. The outdoor air does not agree with them. Like many light wines, Prague's hot sausages do not travel.

I used to know people who, like myself, had *párky* for breakfast and later again in midmorning, and certainly late in the afternoon. Married men used to steel themselves for the ordeal of going home to domestic problems by having a couple of *párky*, which seemed to have the same effect on them as

Hearty stews are popular on Czech menus. The *dušené telecí na kmíně* on the opposite page, displayed with a Czech tablecloth and pottery, is composed of veal, caraway seeds and fresh mushrooms. It is served with noodles topped with toasted bread crumbs. The recipe is on page 137.

a couple of dry martinis on some family men in Manhattan. Some people hold that *párky* "taste best when it gets dark outside." This remark has a strange and Kafkaesque sound, but Prague, after all, *was* the city of Franz Kafka. And, in fact, it still is.

Although hot sausages are the great away-from-home delicacy, dumplings, that other Czech delight, are best made in one's own kitchen. Every housewife has her own recipe, and sometimes several, one for weekdays, another for Sundays and holidays.

Dumplings come in all shapes, sizes and contents, and their weight ranges from the lightness of a bubble to the heaviness of a plum pudding. In size some remind you of golf balls and others of cannon balls. Czech housewives make dumplings with bread crumbs, with potatoes, with or without flour, with semolina, with meat, with or without yeast. Nearly all dumplings are simmered in gently boiling water. Even experienced cooks are never sure how the dumplings will come out. They usually lift a sample dumpling out of the boiling water and cut it in half to see whether the dumpling is cooked right through.

I cannot remember a meal without some sort of dumplings in a Czech home. They might make their appearance in a clear consommé, as liver dumplings, or be eaten with the meat course as bread dumplings, and there are many varieties of dessert dumplings.

The most famous dumplings are *houskové knedlíky* (bread dumplings). They are still shaped in the traditional form of a longish roll. Czech housewives keep several dry, white napkins (which have been boiled to kill any germs) in their kitchens. A napkin is held under the cold faucet, squeezed out carefully, and one side is greased with soft butter. The dumpling mixture is put into the napkin and molded into the shape of a jumbo sausage. The ends of the napkin are fastened with strings. The napkin with the dumpling is suspended in a deep pot over boiling water. Many housewives let it hang from two soupspoons placed across the rim of the vessel. The salted water in the pot should be *gently* boiling. The dumpling is steamed for about 30 or 35 minutes. Then the napkin is taken out and opened, and the dumpling placed on a hot plate.

Now comes the most important part of the ritual: A Prague tradition demands that no dumpling must ever be dishonored by a steel blade, lest the appearance or taste be spoiled. You are not even supposed to touch it with a knife while eating. A taut piece of thread is used to cut off inch-thick slices. My uncle Bruno—bachelor, chamber-music player and amateur cook—used a discarded violin D string for this noble purpose.

In our home a fine variety of dessert dumplings was made with butter, egg yolks, very dry cottage cheese, a dash of salt, and just a little flour added for the sake of consistency, so they would not fall to pieces. They were as light as a soufflé, and much better than many soufflés. They were filled with sweet or sour cherries, with plums or with *povidla,* a thick plum jam, the memory of which will bring tears to the eyes of Czechs living in exile. They might also be filled with steamed apricots, or even with cabbage. Personally I preferred dumplings filled with plain air because I liked the dumpling better than its filling.

The dumplings were heaped on the largest plate available and were served with melted butter, sugar, poppy seeds, some grated cheese, ground almonds and practically anything else. I have never seen anyone spread mustard on them but I would not be very surprised if somebody did.

Beer is the national beverage of Czechoslovakia, and its excellence is attested to by Czech beer consumption, which is said to be the highest per capita in the world. The best Czech beers—the famous Pilsner, Prazdroj and Budvar—are among the best in the world. However, today they are expensive for the ordinary citizen, and so, like other first-rate products, they are exported or sold in the luxury hotels. It is easier to get a bottle of Pilsner and a slice of genuine Prague ham in Vienna than in Prague.

When I lived in Prague between the two World Wars, beer was an important topic of conversation: what kind of beer, when to drink it, how to drink it. My friends talked about beer as knowingly as the people in Burgundy talk about their wines. Everybody had his own special beer, in some favorite haunt, where the beer was drawn from the barrel. (Bottled beer was for people who did not know better.)

For a long time I went with friends to the restaurant at Prague's main railroad station, in those days called *Wilsonovo nádraží* after President Woodrow Wilson. There was a lot of coming and going, as always in railroad-station restaurants, and occasionally an employee would appear to announce the imminent departure of the express for Warsaw or for Slovakia or for Marienbad, and we were delighted because we did not have to leave. We always had the same waiter who served us something called *Mexikánský guláš* (Mexican goulash), which, if I remember correctly, was beef goulash surrounded by a rice ring and covered with minced ham and shredded red peppers: excellent. And with it came big glasses filled with beer from the Smíchov brewery. It had more body and was less bitter than Pilsner, and it was fresh, since the railroad station was practically inside the Smíchov district. Some of us wanted the beer poured slowly, into the tilted glass, so that there would be a minimum of foam. I preferred to have it poured straight in from above to get as much foam as possible. We all preferred it slightly chilled, and we all preferred to have more than one.

Most Czech beers are Pilsner-type beers, light in color and body. But there used to be two breweries in Prague that made a famous dark beer and sold it in their beer halls: U Fleků in the Kremencova district, and U Svatého Tomáše (At the Holy Thomas) in the old town. U Fleků hasn't changed; its beer hall is still a wonderful old place with dark taverns and vaulted halls where people sit in paneled rooms at long, carved tables. They started brewing their famous smoked black beer back in 1499 and have been brewing it ever since. U Fleků is one of the last authentic beer halls left in the city. U Svatého Tomáše, where the monks once made their own beer, is now a state-owned enterprise. It was always the great competitor of U Fleků. At one time the pious brethren who ran the place called proprietor Skřemenec of U Fleků a disciple of the devil. Skřemenec probably was fortunate not to have been burned at the stake.

A Prague beer hall is unique. It is impossible to compare it to a beer hall in Munich, Milwaukee or Copenhagen, or even to an English pub. The old beer halls in Prague are filled with the smell of stale beer and the musty aura of mysticism. They are dark and somber, for people who like to meditate and discuss final answers to final questions. It is no accident that Franz Kafka's K. and Jaroslav Hašek's *Good Soldier Schweik* are now Czecho-

The pause to refresh oneself with a sausage or two is an old Czech custom. Four of the country's best sausages, some fastened with little sticks, are shown above. From the left they are: *jaternice,* which can be boiled or fried; *klobásy,* eaten either cold or hot; *jelita,* also boiled or fried; and *tlačenka,* sliced and eaten cold.

slovakia's two most famous exponents of the eternal search for truth. Both searched for it, each in his own way. Except that Kafka never went to beer halls, while Hašek practically lived in U Kalicha (At the Chalice).

U Kalicha has become big business. This is a recent and regrettable development. In the old, prewar days, it was a smoke-filled beer tavern, pleasantly run down, where writers, artists, self-styled philosophers, prostitutes and men recently released from Pankrác Prison used to gather in a relaxed, cheerful atmosphere. I went there too late to meet the creator of Schweik. Hašek, today safely established as a literary genius, had died in 1923 at the age of 39. But one of his close friends and drinking companions, Michál Mareš, the writer, took me to U Kalicha, to the window table at the right side of the entrance where Hašek had spent his nights, drinking and talking and writing. We reverently drank a few liters of beer to his memory.

Today U Kalicha is for tourists. A relative of the original owner, Palivec, is working behind the beer counter, and elegant waiters in white jackets serve elegant dishes to elegant visitors. It's all very lucrative, I suppose, and very sad. I am sure Jaroslav Hašek would have hated it.

But if you want to enjoy the real magic of an old beer hall in Prague, go to U Fleků in late afternoon, when students, workers, writers, musicians and, always, girls sit at the long, carved tables, and the talk and the beer are

good. Or go to The Ostrich tavern, at the western approach to the 14th Century Charles Bridge, with its jet-black statues of the saints. The tavern has a magnificent view of Hradčany Castle, especially at sundown, when the last rays of the sun cast a golden spell over the spiky spires, and below the bridge, in Na Kampě the shadows are already dark blue.

At The Ostrich, you walk down several steps into the room, which is full of smoke and talk. The beams of the ceiling are painted with green and red vine leaves and are stained by generations of smokers. The tables are always crowded, mostly with young people. The interiors, the waiters and the atmosphere are 14th Century, though sometimes they put on the radio and play the Beatles or something similar.

In Prague no one would think of singing and shouting as in Munich's Hofbräuhaus, or of crying and dancing as in a Hungarian-gypsy wine restaurant, or swaying to the three-quarter rhythm of the music as in a Viennese *Heuriger*. A Prague beer tavern is unique. It is a place to sit quietly or to talk, a place to be alone or with others. It is a place to be as you wish. And perhaps sitting there one can feel grateful that the beer and the old beer halls of Prague, unlike the great food and cooking of the old days, are so little changed. At least some connection remains between our time and the wonderful time that used to be.

Znojemský Guláš
BEEF GOULASH WITH GHERKINS

To serve 6 to 8

3 tablespoons lard
2 cups finely chopped onions
1 tablespoon paprika
3 pounds lean boneless beef chuck,
  cut into 1½ inch cubes
1 cup dry red wine
1 cup beef stock, fresh or canned
½ teaspoon salt
Freshly ground black pepper
2 tablespoons flour
½ cup sweet gherkins cut into
  julienne strips
Salt

Preheat the oven to 350°. Heat the lard in a 5-quart flameproof casserole until a light haze forms over it, then add the onions. Cook them over medium heat for 8 to 10 minutes, or until they are lightly colored. Off the heat, stir in the paprika, continuing to stir until the onions are well coated. Add the beef and pour the wine and beef stock over it. Stir in the salt and a few grindings of pepper. Bring to a boil, then cover tightly and bake in the middle of the oven for 1 hour.

Remove the casserole from the oven and with a spoon skim off about 2 tablespoons of the surface fat. Combine this with the 2 tablespoons of flour, then stir the mixture into the casserole. Return the casserole to the oven and cook for 30 to 40 minutes longer, or until the beef shows no resistance when pierced with the tip of a small sharp knife. Arrange the beef on a platter. Skim the surface fat from the casserole, add the gherkins and heat for 2 or 3 minutes longer. Taste for seasoning. Pour the sauce over the beef and serve.

Dušené Zelí
BRAISED CABBAGE WITH BACON

To serve 6

1 tablespoon lard
1 cup finely chopped onions
½ cup diced bacon (¼-inch dice)
A 3-pound head green cabbage, cored
  and shredded
1 teaspoon caraway seeds
¼ cup white vinegar
1 cup water
1 teaspoon salt
1 teaspoon sugar
Freshly ground black pepper

Heat the lard in a 3-quart saucepan over high heat until a light haze forms over it, then add the onions. Cook them 8 to 10 minutes, or until lightly colored. Stir in the bacon and cook about 5 minutes, or until lightly browned, then add the cabbage, mixing it thoroughly with the bacon and onions, and stir in the caraway seeds. Cover and cook for about 5 minutes over medium heat. Pour in the vinegar and water and season with the salt, sugar and a few grindings of pepper. Bring the liquid to a boil, cover tightly and cook for about 30 minutes over very low heat, stirring occasionally. The cabbage should be moist (but not soupy) when done. If it seems dry during the cooking, add a tablespoon or so of water.

Bramborová Polévka
POTATO SOUP

To serve 4 to 6

2 pounds (about 4 medium-sized)
  boiling potatoes
6 tablespoons butter
1 cup chopped celery
¼ cup diced parsnips (½-inch dice)
1 cup finely chopped onions
1 cup diced carrots (½-inch dice)
2 tablespoons flour
1 quart chicken stock, fresh or canned
¼ teaspoon marjoram
½ teaspoon salt
Freshly ground black pepper
½ cup chopped mushrooms, fresh
  or dried (dried mushrooms should
  be soaked and drained)

Cook the unpeeled potatoes for 6 to 8 minutes in boiling water to cover, then peel and dice them into ½-inch chunks. Melt the butter in a heavy 4-quart saucepan or a soup kettle over medium heat. Add the potatoes, celery, parsnips, onions and carrots. Let the vegetables cook, uncovered, in the butter, stirring them occasionally, for about 10 minutes, or until they are lightly browned. Sprinkle the flour evenly over the vegetables, then stir them until they are all well coated with flour.

Add the stock, marjoram, salt, a few grindings of pepper and mushrooms. Bring the soup to a boil on high heat, stirring almost constantly. Reduce the heat to very low and partially cover the pot. Simmer for 25 to 30 minutes until the potatoes are tender. Taste for seasoning.

Serve in individual soup bowls or in a heated soup tureen.

Dušené Telecí na Kmíně
VEAL RAGÔUT WITH CARAWAY SEEDS

Sprinkle the veal cubes with salt and a few grindings of pepper. Over medium heat in a 10- or 12-inch skillet, melt the butter. When the foam subsides, add the onions and cook them 6 to 8 minutes, or until translucent. Stir in the veal cubes and sprinkle the flour and caraway seeds over them. Stir again to coat the veal evenly with the mixture. Cover tightly and cook over very low heat for 10 minutes, shaking the pan every now and then to keep the veal from sticking. Stir in the stock, bring to a boil and reduce the heat to low. Add the mushrooms, cover and simmer for 1 hour, or until the veal is tender. Add more stock by the tablespoon if the veal seems too dry or the stock too thick. Taste for seasoning and serve. Veal ragôut is traditionally served with buttered noodles.

2 pounds boneless shoulder of veal cut into 1-inch cubes
Salt
Freshly ground black pepper
3 tablespoons butter
½ cup finely chopped onions
2 tablespoons flour
1½ tablespoons caraway seeds
1½ cups chicken stock
1 cup thinly sliced fresh mushrooms

Bramborové Knedlíky
POTATO DUMPLINGS

In a large saucepan, bring 5 quarts of water to a boil. In a mixing bowl, combine the riced potatoes, flour, salt, farina or semolina, egg and milk. Mix them together with a wooden spoon until they form a smooth paste. Dust your hands with flour and form the mixture into balls about 1 inch in diameter.

Drop the dumplings into the boiling water and bring to a gentle boil again. Simmer the dumplings for about 10 minutes, or until they rise to the top.

To make 12 to 14 dumplings

5 medium-sized potatoes, boiled in their jackets, cooled, peeled and riced (about 2¾ cups riced)
⅓ cup flour
1 teaspoon salt
¼ cup farina or semolina
1 egg, lightly beaten
2 teaspoons milk

Kapr na Černo
CARP IN BLACK SAUCE

Preheat the oven to 350°. In a heavy 1-quart saucepan, melt the butter. When the foam subsides, add the celery, carrots, parsnips and onions. Cover, reduce the heat to low and simmer for about 10 minutes.

In a heavy 2-quart saucepan, mix the granulated sugar with the water. Without stirring, cook over medium heat for about 3 minutes, or until the sugar caramelizes into a thick dark syrup. Pour in the vinegar, bring it to a boil, and stir until the caramel has dissolved and the vinegar is reduced to about ⅓ cup. Add 2½ cups of water and bay leaves, thyme, peppercorns, allspice, lemon peel, currant jelly and the steamed celery, carrots, parsnips and onions. Partially cover the pan and simmer over low heat for about ½ hour, then add the beer, grated gingersnaps and brown sugar. Cook over medium heat for about 5 minutes, or until the sauce thickens slightly. Strain through a sieve, pressing down hard with a wooden spoon on the vegetables and condiments before discarding.

With a pastry brush or paper towel, lightly butter a 3- or 4-quart casserole suitable for use as a serving dish. Arrange the carp steaks on the bottom, pour the sauce over them, then sprinkle with chopped prunes, raisins and slivered almonds. Bake the steaks uncovered in the middle of the oven 10 to 15 minutes, or until they are just firm to the touch. Baste the fish once or twice as they bake.

Serve the fish, garnished with lemon wedges, from the baking dish.

To serve 4 to 6

2 tablespoons unsalted butter
⅓ cup diced celery
½ cup diced carrots
½ cup diced parsnips
½ cup finely chopped onions
2 tablespoons granulated sugar
1 tablespoon water
1 cup red wine vinegar
2½ cups water
2 bay leaves
⅛ teaspoon thyme
5 peppercorns
5 whole allspice
2 slices lemon peel, ½ inch wide
2 tablespoons red currant jelly
½ cup light beer
⅓ cup grated gingersnaps
A 4-pound carp cut into 6 eight-ounce steaks about 1 inch thick
1 tablespoon light brown sugar
⅓ cup pitted and chopped prunes
¼ cup chopped seedless raisins
1 tablespoon slivered almonds

Roast goose, stuffed with sauerkraut and surrounded by bread dumplings, is a festive special-occasion bird in Czechoslovakia.

Houskové Knedlíky

BREAD DUMPLINGS

To make about 12 dumplings

4 tablespoons butter
3 cups bread cubes, cut in ½-
    inch chunks
3 tablespoons finely chopped onions
10 tablespoons flour
2 tablespoons finely chopped parsley
½ teaspoon salt
⅛ teaspoon nutmeg
¼ cup milk

Melt 3 tablespoons of the butter in a heavy skillet. When the foam subsides, add the bread cubes. Toss them about in the butter until they are brown on all sides, then set them aside.

Add the rest of the butter to the skillet and when it has melted, stir in the onions. Cook them 3 or 4 minutes, until they are lightly colored, then scrape them into a large mixing bowl. Stir in the flour, parsley, salt and nutmeg, and moisten with the milk. Knead lightly to form a dough. Gently fold in the bread cubes and let the mixture stand for about 30 minutes.

Divide the dough in half and, with your hands, knead and form it into 2 long, sausagelike rolls about 2 inches in diameter. (They will each be 5 to 7 inches long.)

Carefully place the rolls in an 8-inch saucepan half full of boiling salted water. Cook them gently over medium heat for 20 to 25 minutes, turning them once with a large spoon or 2 slotted spoons. Remove them to paper towels to drain. Cut them into ½-inch slices while they are still hot. Serve them immediately with roast goose *(page 139)* or any meat dish that has a gravy or sauce.

138

Pečená Husa se Zelim

ROAST GOOSE WITH SAUERKRAUT

Preheat the oven to 325°. Pull out all the loose fat from inside the goose and dice it into ½-inch chunks. In a small saucepan simmer the fat with a cup of water, covered, for about 20 minutes. Uncover the pan and boil the liquid completely away. The fat will then begin to sputter. Continue to cook until the sputtering stops. Strain the fat into a bowl and reserve. Discard the browned fat particles.

Drain the sauerkraut, wash it well under cold running water, then, to reduce its sourness, soak it in cold water for 10 to 20 minutes. Squeeze it dry by the handful. Heat 6 tablespoons of the goose fat in a heavy 10- or 12-inch skillet and add the onions and sauerkraut. Stirring occasionally, cook uncovered for about 10 minutes. Transfer the sauerkraut mixture to a large mixing bowl. Add the apples, potato, ½ teaspoon salt, caraway seeds and a few grindings of pepper.

Wash the goose inside and out with cold running water, pat it dry with paper towels and sprinkle the cavity generously with salt and a few grindings of pepper. Fill the goose with the sauerkraut stuffing, sew up the openings with needle and thread, and truss the legs with cord. Set the goose, breast up, on a rack in a large roasting pan. Cook it in the middle of the oven for 2 to 2½ hours, or 20 to 25 minutes a pound. With a bulb baster, occasionally remove the grease that drips into the pan. The goose is done when the juice from a punctured thigh runs pale yellow.

When the goose is done, remove it to a serving platter and cut away the thread and cords. Transfer the stuffing to a serving dish. Let the goose rest on the platter for at least 15 minutes before carving it.

To serve 6

An 8- to 10-pound goose
1 cup water
4 pounds fresh, canned or packaged
   sauerkraut
2 cups finely chopped onions
2 cups finely chopped apples
1 cup grated raw potato
½ teaspoon salt
1 tablespoon caraway seeds
Freshly ground black pepper
Salt

Svíčková na Smetaně

FILLET OF BEEF WITH SOUR-CREAM SAUCE

Place the beef in a 4- or 5-quart casserole or saucepan and add the onions, celery, carrots, parsnips, bacon, peppercorns, allspice, bay leaves, salt, a few grindings of pepper and the thyme. Dribble the melted butter evenly over the meat and vegetables. It is customary to marinate the meat in this mixture for at least 24 hours. However, this step may be omitted.

Preheat the oven to 450°. Bake the fillet, uncovered, in the middle of the oven for 25 to 30 minutes, or until the vegetables and meat are lightly browned, turning the meat once during this time. Lower the temperature to 350°. Pour 2 cups of stock, first brought to a boil in a saucepan, into the casserole and bake for 1 hour longer, turning the meat occasionally. Add more stock only if the liquid seems to be cooking away too rapidly. Arrange the finished beef on a platter and keep it warm in a 200° oven while you make the sauce.

THE SAUCE: Pour the contents of the casserole through a sieve, pressing hard on the vegetables with a wooden spoon before discarding them, then return the stock to the casserole. Bring the sauce to a simmer over medium heat. In a mixing bowl, add 2 tablespoons of the sauce to the sour cream, then beat in the flour with a wire whisk. Stir the mixture into the casserole. Cook for 3 or 4 minutes without boiling. Add the lemon juice. Taste for seasoning. Serve the beef sliced and the sauce separately.

To serve 6

3 pounds fillet of beef or eye round,
   rolled and tied securely at 1-inch
   intervals
½ pound onions, sliced
1 cup diced celery
⅔ cup diced carrots
1 cup diced parsnips
¼ cup diced bacon
8 peppercorns
4 whole allspice
2 bay leaves
1 teaspoon salt
Freshly ground black pepper
¼ teaspoon thyme
1 tablespoon melted butter
2 cups beef or chicken stock, fresh
   or canned (plus ½ cup if needed)

THE SAUCE
1 tablespoon lemon juice
2 cups sour cream
2 tablespoons flour

1 Start a fruit dumpling by placing a plum or apricot on a dough square. Fold edges over the fruit.

2 Gently roll the dough into a smooth ball, being careful that the fruit does not pop out of the dough.

3 After the dough has risen, boil the dumplings in water and serve with melted butter, sugar and cinnamon.

To make 12 dumplings

THE DOUGH
2 packages active dry yeast
Pinch of sugar
¼ cup lukewarm water
¼ cup milk (room temperature)
½ teaspoon vanilla extract
¼ teaspoon grated lemon peel
¼ cup sugar
½ teaspoon salt
3 egg yolks
2 cups all-purpose flour

THE FILLING
12 damson or Italian plums or 12 apricots, pitted
Granulated sugar

THE TOPPING
½ cup butter (1 quarter-pound stick), melted
Granulated sugar
Cinnamon

Kynuté Ovocné Knedlíky
YEAST FRUIT DUMPLINGS

Sprinkle the yeast and the pinch of sugar over the lukewarm water. Be absolutely sure the water is lukewarm (110° to 115°)—neither too hot nor too cool to the touch. Let the mixture stand for 2 or 3 minutes, then stir it to dissolve the yeast. Set the container in a warm, draft-free place—such as a turned-off oven—for 2 or 3 minutes, or until the solution has begun to bubble and has almost doubled in volume.

In a mixing bowl, combine the milk, vanilla extract, lemon peel, sugar, salt and the yeast solution, then stir in the egg yolks, one at a time. Stir in 2 cups of the flour, ½ cup at a time, to make a medium-firm dough.

Remove the dough to a floured board or table and knead it by pulling the dough into an oblong shape, folding it end to end, then pressing it down and pushing it forward several times with the heels of the hands. Turn the mass of dough slightly toward you and repeat the process—pulling, folding, pressing and pushing. Continue, sprinkling more flour on the dough and the working surface if either becomes sticky, until the dough is smooth and elastic. This will take at least 10 minutes.

Put the dough into a large lightly buttered bowl, dust the top of it lightly with flour and cover it with a kitchen towel. Let it stand in a warm, draft-free area for 35 to 45 minutes, or until the dough has doubled in size and no longer springs back when it is poked with a finger.

Put the fruit in a glass bowl and add sugar to sweeten to taste.

Punch the dough down, then roll it out on a floured board and knead it again for 1 minute. With a floured rolling pin, roll it into a 12-by-16-inch rectangle ¼ inch thick. With a pastry cutter or sharp knife, cut the dough into 12 four-inch squares.

Lay one plum or apricot in the center of each square. Dust your hands with flour, fold the dough over the fruit, then roll it into a ball. The dough wrapping must be secure enough not to come apart while the dumplings boil. Set the dumplings on a platter or baking sheet, cover with a cloth and let them rise in the unlighted oven for 10 minutes.

Bring 3 quarts of salted water to a bubbling boil in a 4-quart saucepan. With a large spoon, carefully place 4 of the dumplings in the water. Cover the pan, leave the heat high, and let the dumplings boil for 6 minutes. Turn them with the spoon and let them boil for 6 minutes longer, then remove them with a slotted spoon to paper towels to drain. Repeat the process with the rest of the dumplings, 4 at a time.

Dribble the melted butter over the dumplings and sprinkle them with sugar, then with cinnamon. Serve fruit dumplings while they are warm.

Fazolové Lusky na Paprice
GREEN BEANS PAPRIKA

To serve 4

2 quarts water
1 teaspoon salt
1 pound green beans, cut into 1-inch pieces (about 3 cups)
4 tablespoons butter
3/4 cup finely chopped onions
1 tablespoon sweet Hungarian paprika
2 tablespoons flour
1 cup sour cream
1/2 teaspoon salt

In a 3-quart saucepan or soup kettle, bring 2 quarts of water and a teaspoon of salt to a bubbling boil over high heat. Drop the beans in by the handful. Bring the water to a boil again, reduce the heat to medium and cook the beans, uncovered, for 10 to 15 minutes, or until they are just tender. Drain them immediately in a sieve or colander.

Melt the butter in a heavy 10-inch skillet, and when the foam subsides, add the onions. Cook for 4 or 5 minutes, or until they are translucent. Off the heat, stir in the paprika, stirring until the onions are well coated.

With a wire whisk, beat the flour into the sour cream, then stir the mixture into the skillet with the onions and add the salt. Simmer on low heat for 4 or 5 minutes, or until the sauce is smooth and creamy. Gently stir in the beans; simmer about 5 minutes longer, or until heated through.

Dušené Houby
SAUTÉED MUSHROOMS

To serve 4

6 tablespoons butter
1/2 cup finely chopped onions
1 pound fresh mushrooms, thinly sliced
1/2 teaspoon caraway seeds
Salt

Melt the butter in a heavy 10-inch enameled or stainless-steel skillet over medium heat. When the foam subsides, add the onions. Stirring occasionally, cook them for 4 to 6 minutes, or until they are translucent, then add the mushrooms and caraway seeds. Toss the mushrooms about in the butter until they begin to give off their juice. Bring the juice to a boil and, stirring constantly, cook briskly, uncovered, 4 or 5 minutes longer, or until all the juice has evaporated. Taste for seasoning. Serve sautéed mushrooms hot as an accompaniment for meat or egg dishes.

Liptavský Sýr
LIPTAUER CHEESE

To make approximately 2 cups

8 ounces cottage cheese
8 tablespoons (1 quarter-pound stick) unsalted butter, softened
1 tablespoon sweet Hungarian paprika
Freshly ground black pepper
1/4 teaspoon salt
2 teaspoons caraway seeds
1 teaspoon dry mustard
1 teaspoon chopped capers
1 tablespoon finely chopped onions
1/2 cup sour cream (plus 1/4 cup if a dip is desired)
3 tablespoons finely chopped chives

With a wooden spoon rub the cottage cheese through a sieve into a mixing bowl. Cream the butter by beating it against the side of a mixing bowl with a wooden spoon. Beat in the cheese, the paprika, a generous grinding of black pepper, the salt, caraway seeds, mustard, capers, onions and sour cream.

Continue beating vigorously with a wooden spoon or by using an electric mixer at medium speed until the mixture forms a smooth paste.

If the Liptauer cheese is to be used as a spread, shape it into a mound and decorate it with the chives, or shape it into a ball that may be rolled in the chives. Refrigerate it for 2 hours, or until it is firm.

To make a Liptauer dip, stir the extra sour cream into the paste with a wooden spoon or beat it in with an electric mixer. Sprinkle the chives over the dip after it has been poured into a serving bowl.

VI

The Cooking
of Yugoslavia

With the old walled city of Dubrovnik as a colorful background, Yugoslavian seafood and wine are displayed on the terrace of the Hotel Argentina. The large fish in the foreground are dentex. On the plate are Adriatic lobsters and a bass, with two fish bearing the interesting name John Dory.

The Yugoslavs are marvelous. I love them—they are full of energy and the movement of life. I have always seen them as people of violent extremes, but fortunately all the Yugoslavs I know are my friends. Everything they do is done with fervor and gusto; however you want to characterize it, it is life. And to be sure, their cooking reflects all of this.

One of the difficulties in trying to understand Yugoslav cooking or Yugoslav anything springs from the complexity of the country. Geographically, it ranges from the rugged, beautiful southern seacoast with a soft, Mediterranean climate to the eastern mountains with their severe winters. To the north, the fertile grain-producing Vojvodina plain below the Hungarian border is Yugoslavia's breadbasket. In the south there are olive trees, figs, orchards, vineyards and tobacco fields.

It must be remembered that until 1918 there was no Yugoslavia as we know it now. The new country was put together from a hodgepodge of nations and provinces. Some of these had been under the influence of the Habsburgs, some under the Turks, and some had experienced both forms of domination. It can be said quite fairly that Yugoslavia as we know it today is a composite of Central European and Middle Eastern tradition and culture—and, certainly food and cooking.

The people of Yugoslavia belong to five principal nationalities—Serb, Slovene, Croatian, Montenegrin and Macedonian—and speak three main languages—Slovene, Serbo-Croatian and Macedonian. And they include Muslims, Jews, and Christians of the Serbian Orthodox and Roman Catholic Churches. This heterogeneous population is combined in the Socialist

Federal Republic of Yugoslavia as six republics—Croatia (which includes most of the Dalmatian Coast), Slovenia, Bosnia and Herzegovina, Montenegro, Macedonia, and Serbia (which includes Vojvodina)—plus the autonomous region of Kosovo—Metohija. Understandably, the Yugoslavians are regional in spirit. A man is proud not of the fact that he is a Yugoslav, but that he is a Serb, Macedonian or Dalmatian. And he is right, for this is his real heritage.

The various ethnic groups not only speak their own dialects, they have their own newspapers and radio stations; their own customs, traditions, crafts and arts, folklore, dances, melodies—and, of course, their own cooking. *Borba*, the biggest Yugoslav newspaper, has two editions; one is printed in the capital city of Belgrade, in the Cyrillic letters of the ancient Slav alphabet (used in Serbia, Bulgaria and Russia), the other in Roman letters in Zagreb, the country's second-largest city.

The menu at the Metropol Hotel in Belgrade is printed in English, Serbo-Croatian, French and German. The orchestra that plays at dinner offers Viennese waltzes, a selection from *My Fair Lady*, Hungarian gypsy melodies and—best of all—Bosnian folk songs. The fish section of the menu includes boneless sterlet from the Danube, trout "as you like it" from fast-flowing mountain streams, and lobster from the Adriatic. The Dalmatian ham tastes slightly like Italian *prosciutto*, only more piquant. There is a cosmopolitan selection of specialties from Italy, France and the United States. There are also Greek meat dumplings, and poached eggs Portuguese style. The Austrian influence is unmistakable in the clear soup with semolina dumplings, breaded breast of veal, *Sachertorte*, *Doboschtorte*, and *Rehrücken*, the long chocolate cake decorated with blanched almonds to look like saddle of venison. Just in case you want something local, you can order a Serbian chicken soup, suckling pig, grilled saddle of lamb, Serbian chicken pilaf, grilled paprika in oil, *kajmak* (strong salted cheese), *kačkavalj* (a hard white curd cheese), and a genuine *nutpita* (a *baklava*-like pastry, whose *Strudel* dough is usually filled with walnuts). You can also get excellent fresh Danube sturgeon, from which the famous black caviar comes. It is a seemingly endless variety of influences. But it is also those influences that make the food, and the city of Belgrade, so completely fascinating.

Until 1876, when the Serbs won their freedom after 500 years of Turkish rule, the Sava River close to Belgrade was the border between Turkey and Austria-Hungary. Belgrade somehow has never lost the charged atmosphere that it knew as a center of strife in those brisk times.

A short walk along Belgrade's principal avenue, called Terazije, is a wonderful experience. *Terazije* means "scale," and refers to the time when the Turks ruled Belgrade and customs officers were posted at one end of the thoroughfare with scales to weigh the belongings of incoming travelers. Terazije is crowded with all sorts of people. There are young students in fashionably slim trousers, elderly gentlemen who look like Austrian bureaucrats or Parisian *boulevardiers*, wild-eyed Macedonians in colorful native costumes, peasant women carrying geese for sale, children, pretty girls of course; in short, a sort of synthesis of bustling life in a city that is part European, part Middle Eastern, part old and part new. It is so exciting to me that I never tire of strolling there.

On Terazije stands the Moskva Hotel, of which I am very fond, though for reasons that will become evident, I no longer go there. In the early postwar years it was the place to stay; practically anything might, and almost everything did, happen there. American correspondents living at the Moskva were amused or shocked (depending on their moods) by the unpredictable behavior of the hotel's heat, water and electricity. The waiters were proud, defiant individuals who accepted large tips with indifference bordering upon impertinence. They never deigned to say "thanks." On one sweltering summer day the radiators in my room suddenly became hot—adding the Moskva's insult to the local climate's injury. The following winter the radiators stopped heating during a terrible cold wave. The water supply was just as whimsical. When a guest on the third floor took a bath, second-floor guests had no water. A patron who took a room with bath discovered too late that the tub was not connected and therefore useless. But a room with bath was a status symbol in Belgrade in those days, and favored guests were glad to have one, water or no, whether the tub was connected or not.

The power supply was uncertain. Some guests disliked the hotel's Turkish-style breakfast coffee and preferred to make their own on electric plates graciously installed by the management. Unfortunately the electrical system did not permit more than two people to make coffee at the same time. If a third turned on his electric plate, the fuse in the corridor would blow. The guests had to telephone to each other in order to coordinate their coffee-making operations.

I remember the time when the third-floor corridor got a new concrete floor. All outer doors on the corridors were removed until the concrete hardened under the doorsteps. Meanwhile the rooms were closed by their inner doors—all except one, which lacked an inner door. That room's occupant, a melancholy junior statesman on the staff of the United States Embassy, had to live and sleep in full view of all passersby. But that didn't bother anyone—not at the Moskva.

Once when I ordered breakfast for 8 o'clock and somebody pounded my door at 5:15 a.m., I really was not surprised. A laconic waiter entered, placed the breakfast tray on the table and departed, ignoring my verbal protest. I had my breakfast, and later listened to a noisy argument down the corridor where another guest had ordered breakfast for 5:15 because he had to make a plane. I went back to bed. I could not sleep any more but I felt better when I heard, later on, that the other guest had missed his plane and had to stay over.

We stayed at the Moskva because of its manager, Vladimir Tomasic, a dignified, white-haired man with the elegant bearing of a captain of the old Austrian cavalry (which he had been). He spoke about a dozen languages and had the gift of saying a lot in any of them without ever making a commitment. He had convinced himself and his guests that the Moskva was one of world's great hotels. After all, the American bar downstairs featured something called Scotch Wiski (it was distilled in Dalmatia and by some remarkable coincidence bore an unmistakable resemblance to *šljivovica*, the famous Yugoslav plum brandy). It was a drink that I have found no difficulty living without.

But Tomasic was able to get excellent *scampi* from the Adriatic coast.

Continued on page 148

Dinner in Dubrovnik

Standing in the garden of her home in Dubrovnik, Mrs. Jozip Radojevic, wearing a traditional Dalmatian costume of the area, holds a trayful of freshly picked plums, apricots and cherries that will be served at the end of an elaborate dinner she is preparing for her family and guests. A resourceful hostess, she is known as one of the best cooks in Yugoslavia's "tourist belt." Sometimes these local fruits appear at her table in cakes or *Strudel*. The garden is not only a favorite dining area but Mrs. Radojevic also uses it as an outdoor kitchen.

Meat grilled on skewers is popular all over the Balkans as well as the Middle East. But different regions do it differently. Mrs. Radojevic is preparing Serbian *ražnjići (recipe and picture, pages 162-163)*, a veal and pork dish, on decorative skewers. Her nephew later cooked the meal over an open fire in the garden.

Mrs. Radojevic puts ground coffee and sugar in her coffee pot. She will add hot water to make a strong, thick, sweet brew, like Turkish coffee.

These large prawns, with their delicate flavor, were better than the best shrimp and we would have them grilled, with a little melted butter on top. Tomasic also arranged for fresh goose liver, broiled in butter, with boiled rice. A bottle of *dingač*, a full, red wine from Dalmatia, went with this dish. After such a meal you could not complain simply because the elevator had broken down or water had to be carried up in buckets. You could almost believe Tomasic's defence of the Moskva.

Tomasic had an elegant way of dealing with complaints. "Other hotels in Europe were terrible at the end of the war and have deteriorated since," he would say. "Remember, gentlemen, that to stay at the Moskva is a spectacular honor which carries certain obligations."

Dear Tomasic has since departed for the beyond where he probably runs a hotel for whimsical angels, and now when I am in Belgrade I stay at the Metropol, one of the most luxurious hotels in the Communist world. It is a spectacular, gleaming-white structure whose profusion of marble and mirrors would make it right at home in Cannes or Miami Beach. The building was designed to be the headquarters of the People's Youth of Yugoslavia. Later, the government wisely decided that it was much too fancy for the People's Youth. I, along with many others, am most grateful for this intelligent decision.

Certainly things have changed in the years since the Communists first took over. Efforts to create a homogeneous, monolithic state have eased somewhat. Although collective farms in the low-lying arable land have altered the nature and scope of agriculture, peasants in the barren hilly areas still work small holdings as they have for centuries. At the same time, the government animosity toward creature comfort, so marked just a few years ago, has begun to relax. There is even a rising interest in the pleasures of the cuisine. The atmosphere has become free enough to accommodate occasional lively discussions in Yugoslavia as to whether there really *is* such a thing as Yugoslavian cooking; that is to say, an authentic, indigenous cuisine. These debates, frequently conducted with the assistance of strong beverages, are as a rule gingery and one does well to remain impartial, or out of them entirely.

There is indeed a Yugoslav cuisine, although it naturally (and in my opinion, fortunately) reflects the past—the history, folklore and tradition of these colorful individualists. Yugoslav cooks, while suffering the humiliations imposed by erstwhile enemies and occupiers, have learned a good many things from them, as well as from neighbors and friends. In Bosnia and Herzegovina and in Macedonia, the Turkish influence remains strong. On the Dalmatian coast and in Montenegro there is a marked Italian flavor to the food. In northern Croatia and parts of Serbia the cooking is more Hungarian, whereas in Slovenia, which belonged to Austria until 1918, the influence of Vienna prevails and one finds many Austrian specialties. Of all the provinces, Serbia is easily the richest in distinctive regional dishes, with its fish stews, grilled meats, hearty meat and vegetable casseroles, cheeses, the delicious farmer's bread, *pogaca*, pumpkin pie and mouth-watering *Strudel*.

All Yugoslav cooking is sturdy and direct; basically it is peasant cooking, heavy, spicy, full of strong flavors. Almost everybody has a farm

Besides beauty, the Dalmatian coast offers many delicious food specialties: ham that has been rubbed with salt, pepper and garlic and smoked for up to two months; cheese cured in olive oil; country bread baked under a bed of live coals; and wine from the nearby vineyards.

background; a great many people in the cities still have relatives back on the family farm. The popular dishes are the ones their grandmothers and mothers cooked at home, often for many people. Yugoslav recipes for many dishes harken back to farm meals in their use of the country's wonderful fresh produce—tomatoes, peppers and eggplant. Meat specialties, too, are often glorified farm dishes—ragôuts of small pieces of meat (pork, beef or mutton are best-liked), with vegetables, prepared in oil and baked in the oven. *Djuveč,* the savory Serbian meat and vegetable casserole *(page 161)* is delectable; so is *podvarku,* roasted turkey hen; and *sarma,* which means stuffed sauerkraut leaves (it is different from shredded sauerkraut); this dish can also be made with fresh cabbage. These are good, solid dishes that have the unmistakable exotic flavor of the region; they have not yet been "modernized" to the point where they taste like just about anything else.

In Bosnia the great specialty is *lonac,* which means "pot" in Serbo-Croatian because it is made in a special deep earthenware pot. It is a rich, succulent stew of beef, pork, lamb, calf's feet, bacon, parsnips, carrots, cel-

ery, onions, potatoes, white wine, vinegar, garlic and parsley. After initial preparation taking at least three hours, it is baked for four hours. But Bosnia's housewives never seemed to resent the time it takes to make *lonac;* their hospitality is evident from the fact that a proper *lonac* is always made for at least 10 people. Another Bosnian specialty is *šiš-ćévap* (as they call their shish kabob): *šiš* is a Turkish word that means "spit."

Perhaps the most famous Bosnian delight is *musaka,* minced meat and vegetables roasted in the oven, covered with a thick sauce made of milk and beaten eggs. Although this may be found in homes and restaurants all around the Mediterranean, the Yugoslavs still think of it as one of their great dishes. And they are right.

Grilled meats have always been a popular part of the diet, and they are so good that they are often found in neighboring countries where restaurants present "Yugoslav specialties." Among the grilled dishes are *ćevapčići* (grilled meatballs made of beef that is ground several times until it can be kneaded like a dough), *ražnjići* (veal and pork kabobs), and *pljeskavica* (grilled meat patties of pork and veal). The meat (either pork, beef, lamb or veal) is roasted on a square grill over branches of grape vine, or more prosaically, charcoal. Fancy modern restaurants have an electric grill, which is a pity since much of the flavor is lost. All grilled meats are strongly spiced and served with chopped onion and often with pieces of small green peppers. Grilling is not reserved solely for meat; in areas near the Albanian border, where Oriental customs are still strong, they put small pieces of *Planinski sir,* a hard mountain cheese, on small spits, grill them, and eat them with bread and warm milk.

There is fine fish in the rivers of Yugoslavia and along the seacoast. Sardines, mackerel, bonito, tunny and the so-called bluefish are the most common, but the Adriatic Sea is said to contain 365 different varieties of fish. As a result, Yugoslavs have always been enthusiastic fishermen. Mihailo Petrović is a colorful case in point. Famous as a mathematician and amateur musician in Belgrade in the 1930s, Petrović was much prouder of his master fisherman's diploma (awarded to him by the fishermen's guild for his skill with the rod) than of his university diplomas. When Petrović wasn't writing a book on higher mathematics or playing the fiddle, he was to be found fishing near his house at the confluence of the Sava and the Danube. He would cook the fish he caught right away, *bouillabaisse* style, in a large copper container. His fish soup, or *alaska čorba,* was famous partly because no one else knew the exact ingredients. When he was about to add spices and other little things, Petrović would quickly distract his guests' attention—by having a string quartet play or some such diversion—and add his "secret" ingredients. He probably added olive oil, onions, garlic, tomatoes, bay leaf, thyme, parsley, peppercorns and white wine, among other things.

In common with the Viennese, the Yugoslavs love sweets. In fact, their *Strudel,* or as they call it *pita,* appears to have reached them from three sides—from Austria to the west, Hungary to the north, and Turkey to the east. *Pita* can be made with a variety of fillings, savory and sweet, varying slightly according to the region. The Turkish varieties are made with honey. *Baklava,* a Turkish-style *Strudel* made with walnuts or al-

The produce market at Dubrovnik (*opposite*) is almost opulent in its fine display of cherries, apricots, cucumbers, string beans and lettuce, as well as milk and eggs. Women from all parts of town gather here each day to shop and keep up with the gossip. Such places have not changed over the centuries. The market—no matter the time or place—remains a vibrant center of life.

Seen through an ancient wall is one of Dubrovnik's bastions, which now houses several museums and an aquarium. Dubrovnik has within it a walled city, where almost 6,000 people live. No motor vehicles are permitted there. Here one strolls to a favorite restaurant or café or stands watching the fishermen bring in some of the 365 different kinds of Adriatic fish that go into the soups and stews the people of Dubrovnik eat.

monds and covered with sugar syrup, is frequently encountered in Yugoslavia. Another Yugoslavian delicacy influenced by the Middle East is *kadaif;* long, thin noodles with nuts and almonds, heavily soaked in syrup like *baklava.* And there is the delicious *dul-pita* (rose *Strudel*), which is not made with roses, but nuts. It does look like a rose in full bloom when it is baked, and it takes the typically Oriental poetry of its name from this. It is superb.

In certain places, notably Bosnia and Macedonia, many housewives still practice the art of making their own paper-thin crisp pastry for *pitas.* But nowadays the sweet dessert *pitas* and the *kadaifs* are often bought ready-made at the local bakery—or at least the prepared pastry is used to simplify the long, complicated process.

All Yugoslavs seem to love *ratluk.* And who can blame them? The name is a corrupted form of the Arabic *rahat-lokoum,* which means "a little sweet that causes pleasure." And that is just what it is. This delicious hard *gelée* is made of sugar, starch, water, almonds and rose oil. The dried, sliced almonds are put into a mixture of syrup and starch; lemon juice and a few drops of rose oil are added, and the mixture is left to cool in an enameled dish. Later it is cut into small squares, and dusted with sugar and rice. But go easy on the *ratluk* that you will be offered in a Yugoslav home. It is too rich to be eaten in quantity, and if you over eat you will regret it. An appropriate Yugoslav proverb says, "The honey is sweet but don't bite yourself in the finger."

I have already said that hospitality is sacred in Yugoslavia. One notes this especially in those households that keep the old religious custom of *slava*—the annual celebration of the day commemorating a family's patron saint. For such a family, *slava* is the greatest holiday of the year. In the pre-World War II days, wealthy families would place small newspaper ads inviting all their friends and throw lavish open-house parties that sometimes lasted two or three days. But in postwar times, during what is now known as the "Russian" era—the period until 1948, when Marshal Tito broke with the Soviet Union—no Yugoslav dared observe the "bourgeois" *slava*. Nowadays one reads in the papers that Mr. and Mrs. Dusic will be "at home tomorrow"—the code for inviting friends to their *slava*. When a fellow tells his associates at the office that he expects to be sick for a couple of days, they smile and promise to drop in and help him get well again. Even good Communists now celebrate the *slava*. After all, why shouldn't they? It's a lovely custom whatever your politics.

There are various interesting rituals in Yugoslav homes for greeting a guest. In Slovenia he is offered applesauce and stewed fruit, in Bosnia and Herzegovina he gets black coffee and *ratluk*, in Serbia and Macedonia he gets a *sljivovica* (plum brandy) and black coffee, and also *slatko* (the thick, sweet preserve usually made from plums) and the traditional glass of water. (In the Hofmannsthal-Strauss opera *Arabella* the heroine brings her fiancé, who hails from this part of the world, a glass of fresh water as a hospitable token of her love.)

Slatko is extremely popular. It is a Serbian specialty and it is always made at home; it is neither jam, marmalade nor stewed fruit, but fruit slowly cooked in thick syrup. The fruit must remain whole and retain its natural color. While it is being cooked, the container may be slightly jogged to prevent the mixture from sticking and burning, but the fruit must never be touched with a spoon or it might come apart. The syrup must be thick; two pounds of sugar are used for two pounds of fruit. When the syrup no longer flows down from a spoon, but drops off in thick pearls, the mixture is ready. The foam is taken off the top, the container is closed with a wet napkin and left for 12 hours until the syrup is hard. (It can also be left for two years.) Although plums are the usual base for *slatko* it is made of all kinds of fruit and even of some flowers—white violets, May roses and acacia blossoms. Many people use watermelons, unripe figs and green unskinned walnuts. The container of *slatko* is always served with ceremony; it is placed on a large tray, together with a glass of water for each guest, and each glass has a silver spoon lying across its rim.

All Yugoslavs are great coffee drinkers. Black coffee, made either in Serbian or Turkish style, is served all day. Both methods produce coffee with a similar taste, but their preparation differs. Both are cooked in a *dshesva*, a long-handled copper vessel with a lip and no cover. To make one cup of Serbian coffee you need one and a half cups of water, a lump of sugar and one and a half teaspoons of finely ground coffee (the best is from beans roasted at home). The cold water and the sugar go into the *dshesva*. When the water starts to boil, a little is poured away into another vessel. Then the coffee is thrown into the boiling water. It must boil up just once, whereupon the hostess removes the *dshesva* and adds the rest of the water that was kept in the other container. Then she covers the *dshesva* with its copper lid, waits 30 seconds, and pours the coffee into small cups in front of the guests.

In Bosnia, where memories of the Turkish rule are still strong, people prefer Turkish coffee. The finely ground coffee is put into the dry, heated *dshesva*. The water is boiled in a second *dshesva* and poured over the coffee, and the copper vessel is held over the flame just until the coffee boils. It is removed at once and served in the *dshesva*. Sugar is served separately. The guests either put the sugar into their cups and pour the coffee on top, or they nibble the sugar with their coffee. All this is helpful to know because wherever you go, you will be offered coffee, and your host or hostess will be pleased when you do the right thing.

Everybody likes cheese in Yugoslavia. In the formerly Austrian regions of Slovenia and Croatia they eat cheese at the end of the meal. In Serbia they often start out with some cheese, and sometimes they have a piece of smoked beef or smoked pork with cheese. Soft cheeses are made mostly of sheep's milk. Depending on where they are made, these cheeses are called *Zlatiborski sir* or *Javorski sir*. In deference to a presumed Western taste for milder cheeses, visitors are often offered either a Gervais-type cream cheese or Imperial, cream cheese mixed with butter.

The most popular cheese in Serbia is *kăckavalj,* a pungent hard cheese, without holes, but with many layers that are slightly crumbly in texture. It is made of sheep's milk, or sometimes of a mixture of sheep's and cow's milk. *Kăckavlj* was contributed by the nomadic tribesmen who brought it with them from the East, where so many good things come from. There are many varieties, the best-known of which is *Pirotski kăckavalj* from Pirot in eastern Serbia. Top quality *kăckavalj* is served as *meze* —a Turkish word that means "nibbles"—with a drink. The harder varieties are grated like Italian *Parmigiano* and used for cooking. Thin slices are sometimes breaded and served as an appetizer.

Another popular milk product from Serbia is *kajmak*. Many housewives make their own; it's simple. Boiled milk (cow's milk or sheep's milk) is left to cook in a *karlice,* a flat, large vessel. After it cools, the cream is taken from the top. Every day the milk is cooked again and the layer of cream is taken off and placed into a wooden container called a *čabrica*. Fresh *kajmak* is white and mild. Later it ferments, salt is added, and it takes on a yellow color. The great Serbian specialty, *gibanica,* the delicious cheese pie made with crisp *Strudel* pastry, is filled with ripe *kajmak*. It is a delightful dish, but made best with the local products.

Bread, the inevitable accompaniment to cheese, reaches a superb form in Serbian *pogaca,* or farmer's bread. Yugoslav housewives say cryptically that "the dough must be neither too hard nor too soft." They flatten it to the size of a well-dusted,round baking plate, cover the dough and leave it for 15 minutes. Some brush the dough with egg yolk before baking. It is first cooked in a hot oven for half the cooking time, and then the heat is reduced. *Pogaca* is served instead of conventional bread in long, narrow strips—warm, often with *kajmak*.

No report on Yugoslavia would be complete without mention of *šljivovi-ca*, the country's national drink and its contribution to the international family of famous beverages. *Šlijivovica* is made from plums. Yugoslavia has more plum trees than any other country on earth—over 75 million. Most of them grow in the plum belt that stretches through the middle of the country, from eastern Bosnia to western Serbia. The most famous plum variety is called *požegača*—a large oval blue fruit, sweet and juicy, with a delicate bloom. The plums are not picked for *šljivovica* making until the trees are at least 20 years old.

Serbian poets talk ecstatically about the Bosnian *požegača* plums, which are covered with an ashlike powder when they are ripe. It is not always easy to get the smooth, mellow *šljivovica* made from the *požegača* variety, but if you are lucky and find a peasant who produces it in small quantities in his village home, it can be very good. There are two types of *šljivovica*, the so-called "soft" plum brandy containing only 25 per cent alcohol and the better-known strong *šljivovica*, which is distilled twice until it becomes a spirit of at least 40 per cent alcohol; the very best is sold at 50 per cent alcohol, which means 100 proof. Small producers use wooden fermentation vats and pot stills, and they age the spirit in oaken casks for at least three years until it takes on a velvety, mellow quality. It is a marvelous libation, and one that you might expect in such a lively country.

I remember a story about two Yugoslav friends who wanted a little snack. One did the shopping and came back with 9.50 dinar (about 75 cents) worth of *šljivovica* and 0.50 dinar worth of bread, and the other said, "You shouldn't have bought so much bread!" Actually, the Yugoslavs are disciplined drinkers, except when they sit around in groups and get excited, or when they are celebrating; but then, there is always a reason for celebrating something. And even if there were not some*thing* to celebrate, one can always celebrate life, the wonderful fact of being alive and here. What could possibly be better than that?

In exuberant moments, a Yugoslav likes to smash his glass against the wall, a tradition that several years ago began to annoy penurious officials. Signs went up in the coffeehouses announcing that henceforth anybody smashing his glass would be fined. Since the fine was equivalent to only 66 cents the signs were taken as invitations instead of warnings. The waiter would sweep up the pieces, and the exuberant customer would pay up and order more *šljivovica*. Things got so bad that one coffeehouse manager called the police, and the glass smasher was taken to court, where he informed the judge that he'd already paid his fine and couldn't be punished twice for the same misdeed. The judge agreed. Now new signs inform customers that "willful, intentional smashing of glasses is contrary to good public behavior." My friends sadly conclude that the country is getting soft.

And if you are offered "tea from Šumadija" on a cold winter night, be careful. It contains no tea. You burn half a pound of sugar in a container, and heat a pint of *šljivovica* in another container until it simmers. You pour the *šljivovica* over the burned sugar, which caramelizes. Dust with sugar and add two teaspoonfuls of honey. A Yugoslav friend tells me you should use soft *šljivovica*. But he uses the strong one.

A Countryside Feast

In Pobreze, a five-family village in the Dinaric Alps near Dubrovnik, the family of wine grower Nino Uskokovic prepares to entertain friends. *At left:* Luce Uskokovic bakes bread in one of the oldest forms of indoor baking. The dough loaf is placed under the dome-shaped lid and hot coals are piled on top. The little black cans on the wall will be used to roast coffee beans. Meanwhile in the garden *(above)* Luce's husband, Vlaho, barbecues a lamb over an open fire.

Watched by a family pet, Luce makes final preparations
(*opposite*) for the meal. The lamb, crisp and brown, has
been cut into manageable pieces with a hatchet and
knife and piled on a board. Behind the lamb is the
homemade bread, and at the left are plates of green
salad. At the wooden trestle table (*above*) Papa Nino
Uskokovic pours a glass of *Dalmatinsko crno vino*, or
Dalmatian red wine, for Luce, his daughter-in-law.
Also at the table are Luce's husband Vlaho and a
neighbor. The wine is cut heavily with water. In the
oval dish (*center*) are potatoes, which along with
quartered raw onions are important to the meal.

To serve 4 to 6

1 pound small white beans (Great
    Northern, navy or pea beans)
2 tablespoons lard
1 cup finely chopped onions
½ teaspoon chopped garlic
2 teaspoons sweet Hungarian paprika
1 teaspoon hot paprika
2 cups chicken stock, fresh or canned
1 teaspoon finely chopped hot red
    peppers
2 pounds boneless smoked pork butt,
    cut into ½-inch cubes

Pasulj
PORK AND BEAN CASSEROLE

An hour before you plan to cook the beans, cover them with cold water in a 2-quart saucepan or soup kettle and bring the water to a boil. After 1 or 2 minutes, turn off the heat and let the beans soak, uncovered, in the hot water for about an hour.

In a 4- or 5-quart casserole or soup kettle, heat the lard over medium heat until a light haze forms over it. Add the onions and garlic and cook them, stirring occasionally, until the onions are lightly colored. Remove the casserole from the heat and stir in the sweet and hot paprika, continuing to stir until the onions are well coated. Drain the beans and add them, the chicken stock, the red peppers and pork cubes to the casserole.

Return the casserole to medium heat and bring it to a boil, stirring gently once or twice. Cover tightly and reduce the heat to its lowest point. Simmer for about 1 hour and 15 minutes, then remove the cover and simmer for 15 minutes longer. The sauce should be thick and should coat the beans and pork lightly. If the sauce seems thin, boil vigorously, uncovered, until it thickens to the desired consistency.

Serve *pasulj* directly from the casserole.

NOTE: Since the pork may be salty, no salt should be added to the *pasulj* until it is done and can be tasted for seasoning.

To serve 6 to 8

A 7-pound leg of lamb, boned and
    tied
1 teaspoon salt
1 cup vinegar
2 cups water
3 bay leaves
2 cups sliced onions
6 peppercorns
2 sprigs parsley
½ teaspoon thyme
2 tablespoons lard
4 large fresh tomatoes, coarsely
    chopped, or 1 large can tomatoes,
    drained
3 slices bacon
Salt

Jagnjeći But
MARINATED LEG OF LAMB

Rub the leg of lamb with the salt and put it in an earthenware or enameled casserole. In a saucepan, combine the vinegar, water, bay leaves, onions, peppercorns, parsley and thyme. Over high heat, bring to a boil, cool to lukewarm, then pour over the lamb. Marinate the lamb, uncovered, in the refrigerator for 6 to 24 hours, turning it every couple of hours.

Preheat the oven to 350°. Remove the lamb from the marinade and pat it dry with paper towels. Heat the lard in a heavy 12-inch skillet until a light haze forms over it, then add the lamb. Cook it for 15 to 20 minutes, or until it is brown, turning it every 5 minutes with two wooden spoons. Place it in a casserole or roasting pan just large enough to hold it. Strain the marinade into a bowl and add the contents of the strainer, 1½ cups of the marinade and the tomatoes to the casserole. Lay the bacon slices over the lamb. Bring the liquid to a boil on top of the stove, then cook, covered, in the middle of the oven for about 2 hours, checking occasionally to see that the liquid is barely bubbling. (Reduce the heat if necessary.) When the meat shows no resistance when pierced with the point of a small sharp knife, remove it to a platter. Strain the cooking juices through a sieve into a saucepan, pressing down hard on the vegetables before discarding them. Skim the surface fat and bring the juices to a boil on top of the stove. Taste for seasoning. To serve, slice the lamb, and arrange it on a serving platter. Mask the slices with some of the sauce and serve the rest in a sauceboat.

Djuveč

LAMB CHOP AND VEGETABLE CASSEROLE

Preheat the oven to 350°. Pat the lamb chops dry with paper towels, sprinkle them with ½ teaspoon of the salt, a few grindings of pepper and a little thyme. In a heavy 12-inch skillet over high heat, melt the lard until a light haze forms over it, then add the chops. Cook them about 2 minutes on each side, or until they are lightly browned. Remove them to a warm platter.

Add the onions and garlic to the hot fat in the skillet and, stirring occasionally, cook them over medium heat for 8 to 10 minutes, or until the onions are lightly colored. Remove them from the skillet with a slotted spoon and set them aside. Pour the chicken stock into the skillet. Bring to a boil, scraping in any brown bits that cling to the bottom and sides of the skillet. Then remove the skillet from the heat.

Spread half of the onion-garlic mixture over the bottom of a 6-quart casserole attractive enough to be used as a serving dish. Cover the mixture with the potatoes, the green peppers and half the tomatoes. Season with ½ teaspoon of salt, a few grindings of black pepper, thyme and the crumbled bay leaf. Add the other layer of onion-garlic mixture and the rest of the tomatoes.

Pour the stock from the skillet into the casserole and arrange the lamb chops over the vegetables. Bring the casserole to a boil on top of the stove, cover it tightly, bake in the middle of the oven for 25 minutes, then remove the cover and continue to cook in the oven for 15 minutes longer.

Djuveč, which is a favorite Yugoslavian dish, is served directly from the casserole in which it is baked.

To serve 4

4 lamb loin chops, 1 inch thick (about 6 ounces each)
1 teaspoon salt
Freshly ground black pepper
Thyme
3 tablespoons lard
3 cups onions, sliced about ⅛ inch thick
¼ teaspoon finely chopped garlic
¼ cup chicken stock, fresh or canned
1½ pounds (about 4 large) potatoes, peeled and sliced ¼ inch thick
3 large green peppers, with seeds and ribs removed, and sliced into rings (about 1½ pounds)
2 pounds tomatoes, peeled and sliced about ¼ inch thick (about 8 medium tomatoes)
½ bay leaf, crumbled

Lovački Djuveč

HUNTER'S STEW

In a 10- or 12-inch skillet, cook the bacon over medium heat for 6 to 8 minutes, or until it has rendered most of its fat and is slightly crisp. Remove the bacon with a slotted spoon, reserve it and pour off all but a thin film of the fat from the skillet.

Add the onions and, stirring occasionally, cook them for 3 or 4 minutes, or until they are slightly translucent, then add the garlic and carrots and cook for 5 or 6 minutes longer.

Return the reserved bacon to the skillet, stir in the water and vinegar, and add the beef cubes, the salt, and a few grindings of black pepper. Reduce the heat to its lowest point and simmer, covered, for about 1 hour, or until the beef shows only a slight resistance when it is pierced with the tip of a small sharp knife.

Gradually stir in the rice and add the sliced peppers and 1 cup of the beef stock. Bring the liquid to a boil, then reduce the heat to low, cover and simmer for 20 minutes, or until the rice is tender but not mushy. Taste for seasoning. If at any point the rice becomes too dry or shows signs of sticking to the bottom of the pan, add the remaining beef stock.

Lovački Djuveč is usually served as a main dish, accompanied by a mixed green salad.

To serve 4 to 6

8 slices bacon, chopped
1½ cups finely chopped onions
1 teaspoon finely chopped garlic
1 cup scraped and sliced carrots
2 cups water
¼ cup red wine vinegar
3 pounds boneless beef chuck, cut into 2-inch cubes
½ teaspoon salt
Freshly ground black pepper
1 cup converted rice
2 medium-sized green peppers, with seeds and ribs removed and cut into slices ¼ inch wide and 2 inches long (about 1½ cups)
1¼ cups beef stock
Salt

Ražnjiči, at the top in the picture above, are cubes of veal and pork interspersed with bay leaves. *Ćevapčići (bottom)* are sausagelike patties made of ground beef and ground lamb. Both are cooked on skewers. In Serbia, where they originated, they are grilled over smoldering branches of grapevine.

Ražnjiči
VEAL AND PORK BARBECUE

Pat the veal and pork cubes dry with paper towels, sprinkle them with salt and a few grindings of pepper and mix them well with the oil and onions in a large bowl. Cover and refrigerate for at least 3 hours, stirring them every now and then. Remove the cubes to a plate and reserve the marinade for later use.

To prepare *ražnjiči* for cooking, arrange the veal and pork cubes alternately on skewers—either small bamboo skewers or 6- to 8-inch trussing skewers—with half a bay leaf separating each pair of cubes. Broil *ražnjiči* in a preheated oven broiler, 4 to 6 inches from the flame, or on an outdoor grill, for 10 minutes on each side, or until the cubes show no pink in the center when one is cut into. The pork should not be undercooked. With either method, baste the *ražnjiči* with the marinade while they are broiling.

Ražnjiči may be removed from the skewers before they are served, or served on the skewers. Sprinkle the chopped onions over them just before serving.

To serve 4 to 6

1 pound boneless veal, cut into
  1½-inch cubes
1 pound lean boneless pork, cut into
  1½-inch cubes
Salt
Freshly ground black pepper
2 tablespoons vegetable oil
1 cup thinly sliced onions
15 small bay leaves, broken in half
2 tablespoons finely chopped onions

Ćevapčiči
SKEWERED LAMB-AND-BEEF SAUSAGE ROLLS

Heat the lard in an 8-inch skillet over high heat until a light haze forms over it. Reduce the heat to medium, add the onions and garlic and, stirring occasionally, cook them for 6 to 8 minutes, or until the onions are lightly colored. Scrape them into a large mixing bowl.

Add the lamb, beef, egg white, salt and paprika. Mix well with your hands or a wooden spoon.

Shape the mixture into small cylinders approximately 1 inch in diameter and 2 inches long and arrange them on a plate. Cover the plate with wax paper or plastic wrap and then refrigerate it for at least an hour before cooking, or until the meat mixture has become firm.

Arrange the cylinders on 6- to 10-inch metal skewers, 4 or 5 to a skewer, leaving at least ¼ inch space between them and running the skewers through the sides, not the ends, of the cylinders.

Like most other meats cooked on skewers (kabobs) this Yugoslav favorite can be cooked in one of three ways.

Broil the *ćevapčiči* on a charcoal grill or in a preheated oven broiler that is 4 to 6 inches from the flame. Another method is to fry them over high heat in a heavy 12-inch skillet in which 2 tablespoons of lard have been heated to the smoking point. If the *ćevapčiči* are broiled on a grill or in an oven broiler, cook them about 8 minutes on each side, or until they are dark brown on the outside and well done on the inside. If *ćevapčiči* are cooked in a skillet, they should be turned every so often, a skewerful at a time, with a wide metal spatula.

Ćevapčiči may be served on the skewers so that the diners may remove them or they may be removed from the skewers before serving. Sprinkle the meat sausage rolls with the finely chopped onion just before serving. *Ćevapčiči* may also be served as a cocktail hors d'oeuvre. A spicy accompaniment to *ćevapčiči* are tiny hot peppers.

To serve 6

1 tablespoon lard
½ cup finely chopped onions
½ teaspoon finely chopped garlic
1 pound ground lamb
1 pound ground beef chuck
1 egg white, lightly beaten
1 teaspoon salt
1 tablespoon sweet Hungarian
  paprika
2 tablespoons lard (optional)
2 tablespoons very finely chopped
  onions

To serve 4 to 5

1½ pounds sauerkraut
A 3-pound frying chicken, cut up
Salt
7 tablespoons bacon fat or lard
½ cup finely chopped onions
¼ teaspoon finely chopped garlic
1 tablespoon finely chopped hot chili
  peppers
Freshly ground black pepper
½ cup chicken stock

To serve 4

Salt
A 3-pound carp or scrod, cut into 8
  six-ounce steaks about 1 inch thick
Flour
4 tablespoons butter
2 tablespoons vegetable oil
1 pound onions, peeled and thinly
  sliced
1 pound tomatoes, peeled, seeded and
  chopped (about 1½ cups)
½ cup dry white wine
1 tablespoon vinegar
1 teaspoon chopped small bottled
  tabasco peppers
¼ teaspoon white pepper

To serve 2 to 4

1 large eggplant (about 1½ pounds)
3 large green peppers (about 1 pound)
1 teaspoon salt
Freshly ground black pepper
½ teaspoon finely chopped garlic
2 tablespoons lemon juice
6 tablespoons vegetable oil
2 tablespoons finely chopped parsley

Podvarak
CHICKEN AND SAUERKRAUT

Wash the sauerkraut under cold running water, then soak it in cold water 10 to 20 minutes to reduce its sourness. Squeeze it dry by the handful.

Wash the chicken pieces quickly under cold running water, pat them dry with paper towels and salt generously. Over high heat, in a heavy 10-inch skillet, heat 4 tablespoons of the fat until a light haze forms over it. Brown the chicken pieces a few at a time, starting with the skin sides down and turning them with tongs. As each browns, remove to a platter and add a fresh piece to the pan until all the chicken is done. Set aside.

Heat the rest of the fat in the skillet until a light haze forms over it and add the onions and garlic. Cook them for 2 or 3 minutes, or until the onions are slightly translucent. Add the sauerkraut, chili peppers and a few grindings of black pepper. Cook uncovered for 10 minutes over medium heat. Using the tongs, lay the chicken pieces on top of the sauerkraut and pour the stock over the chicken. Bring the liquid to a boil, then reduce the heat to low and cook, covered, for 30 minutes, or until the chicken is tender. Serve the sauerkraut on a platter with the chicken, either surrounding it or as a bed for it.

Brodet na Dalmatinski Način
FISH DALMATIAN STYLE

Salt the fish steaks on both sides; dip in flour and shake off the excess.

In a heavy 12-inch skillet, melt 2 tablespoons of the butter and 1 tablespoon of the oil. When the foam subsides, add the fish and cook for 2½ minutes on each side, or until lightly browned. Remove to a platter.

Heat the rest of the oil and butter in the skillet, and when the foam subsides, add the onions. Cook them for 3 to 4 minutes, or until they are translucent. Add the tomatoes, wine, vinegar, tabasco peppers and white pepper. Bring to a boil and stir. Return the fish to the skillet and simmer, tightly covered, for 10 to 15 minutes. Arrange the fish steaks on a platter and pour the sauce over them and serve.

Srpski Ajvar
SERBIAN VEGETABLE CAVIAR

Preheat the oven to 500°. Place the eggplant and green peppers on a rack set in a baking pan. Bake the green peppers for 25 minutes, then remove them. Bake the eggplant 15 to 20 minutes longer, or until it is tender. Wrap the eggplant in a damp towel and let it stand for about 10 minutes to loosen its skin. Peel the green peppers, remove and discard the seeds and ribs, then chop the peppers very finely and transfer them to a glass mixing bowl. Peel the eggplant, chop it very finely and squeeze it dry in a kitchen towel.

Add the eggplant, the salt and a few grindings of black pepper to the chopped green peppers in the mixing bowl. Then, with a wooden spoon, stir in the garlic, lemon juice and vegetable oil, mixing all the ingredients together thoroughly. Taste for seasoning.

Chill and garnish with the parsley. *Srpski ajvar* is served as a relish.

Šljiva Slatko
PLUM PRESERVES

To make 4 cups

4 cups sugar
2 pounds damson plums, sliced in
  half and pitted
3 tablespoons lemon juice

Slatko is a Serbian specialty consisting of pieces of large fruit or whole small fruits, such as cherries or berries, that hold their shape during cooking. To avoid breaking up the fruit, do not stir it but shake the pan often to prevent sticking or burning. The most popular *slatko* is made from plums. To prepare it, combine the sugar and plums in a 2- to 3-quart saucepan, with the plums on the bottom. Cover tightly and cook on medium heat for 10 minutes, then shake the pan gently to distribute the sugar evenly. Replace the cover and cook over medium heat for 15 to 20 minutes longer, or until all the sugar is dissolved.

Add the lemon juice and boil for 8 to 10 minutes, or until the liquid thickens to a thin syrup that, if tested, registers 234° on a candy thermometer or forms a soft ball when a little is dipped into cold water.

Off the heat, skim off any foam on top of the fruit with a wooden spoon, then cover the pan and let the plums stand for 12 hours at room temperature before serving. If the *slatko* has become watery during this time, boil it again for a short time, and cool it again.

Because of the syrup in which it is cooked and kept, *slatko*, refrigerated in a covered glass container, will keep for as long as two years. It may be served as a simple dessert or with fruit dumplings *(page 140)*, or it may be served like preserves, with rolls or bread.

Using a pound of sugar for each pound of fruit, you can make *slatko* from various kinds of fruits, such as cherries, strawberries and blackberries.

NOTE: The plums are usually juicy enough so that it is not necessary to add liquid, but if the liquid seems scanty after 20 minutes of cooking, add 1 tablespoon of water.

Lubenica Slatko
WATERMELON PRESERVES

To make 10 cups

4 pounds watermelon rind
4 pounds granulated sugar
1½ cups water
2 whole lemons, thinly sliced and
  seeded
3 four-inch pieces vanilla bean

Remove the rind's outer green skin and the inner pink flesh until only the lightest part remains. Cut it into ½-inch cubes. (It should make about 10 cups.)

Cover the watermelon rind with cold water in a 4- or 5-quart saucepan. Bring the water to a boil, then pour it off and repeat the boiling, beginning with more cold water. Repeat once again, the third time simmering for 20 minutes before draining the rind in a sieve.

Return the rind to the pan and cover it with the granulated sugar and 1½ cups of water. Add the lemon slices and the vanilla bean. Shaking the pan frequently, cook over medium heat until the sugar has melted. Then simmer uncovered for about 2 hours, or until the syrup registers 234° on a candy thermometer or forms a soft ball when a little of it is dropped into cold water.

Watermelon *slatko* will keep for as long as a year when it is refrigerated in a glass container. Serve it either in a small dish as a dessert or as you would serve preserves.

In Yugoslavia, *slatko* is served very ceremoniously. The bowl containing it is placed on a tray, along with a glass of water and a silver spoon for each guest.

VII

The Pastry Paradise

A plate of Rigó Jancsi squares is surrounded by romantic symbols of gypsy life—cards, a violin and a rose. The deliciously rich chunks of chocolate cake are named for a 19th Century gypsy violinist who, legend says, broke the hearts of princesses with ease and equanimity. But the confection is much more tangible than legends are, and equally enjoyable.

T he world's finest *pâtisserie* comes from Vienne," France's greatest chef, the late Fernand Point, once told me. The genius of the Restaurant de la Pyramide in Vienne, a city south of Lyon, did not mean his own Vienne but the Austrian Vienne—the city of Vienna.

Vienna has been endowed with its love of bread and pastries for over 500 years. Five years before Columbus discovered America, an anonymous Viennese baker invented the *Kaisersemmel* (the Emperor's roll), known in less civilized places as the "Vienna roll." Emperor Frederick V had ordered a batch of rolls to be distributed among the children, with the Emperor's likeness stamped on each roll, and the famous *Kaisersemmel* was the result. Handmade rolls that are round with the top crust divided into four sections are still called *Kaisersemmel* in Vienna, though they no longer bear the Emperor's picture, since Austria is now a republic.

Given this glorious and persistent tradition, it is no small thing to be a baker in Vienna. Vienna's *Lebzelter* (gingerbread makers), for instance, had their own guild in 1661. There were also sugar bakers, restricted by law to the use of "burnt sugar, burnt almonds, biscuits and zwieback"; and chocolate makers, marzipan makers, cake bakers and candymakers. As for producers of bread, they were divided into ordinary breadmakers, *Semmel* roll bakers and "luxury bakers." Today it is different. Bakers call themselves makers of *Weiss und Schwarzgebäck*, meaning that they bake both white rolls and dark breads.

Vienna's pastry lore is as rich as the city's musical tradition, for local pastry lovers have perpetuated all kinds of legends. No one can be sure

whether Vienna's addiction to sweets stems from the marriage of some Byzantine princess into the Babenberg family or dates from the time of the
Archduke Ferdinand of Habsburg, grandson of King Ferdinand of Aragon,
who came to Vienna in 1526 from Spain. His cortège consisted of Spanish and Burgundian noblemen who had in their entourage some Burgundian pastry makers. Actually, the first sugar bakers had previously appeared
in 1514 at the court of Emperor Maximilian I. In any case, Vienna's pastries are a synthesis of these foreign influences, as is almost everything
else in this city where so many nationalities have passed through or settled. In 1762, Mozart's father, a skeptical man, wrote, "Are all people
who come to Vienna bewitched so they have to stay here? It rather looks
like it." To me, his question is still apt.

Three hundred years ago, an anonymous Viennese cook scooped the
cream off the milk and carefully whipped it into *Schlagobers*—whipped
cream. In Vienna, whipped cream is not only used in countless pastries
and on top of many *Torten* (flat-topped, round cakes), but sugared whipped
cream is served as a dish by itself. Hopeless *Schlagobers* addicts pile more
whipped cream even on top of their whipped cream. There are few Viennese
who pass a day without a little *Schlagobers;* they seem to need it as a French-
man needs wine. They have it with morning coffee, or with their dessert, or
in some pastry, or "in between"; there is always an excuse for it. You can't
blame them: it's marvelous.

Another delight of Viennese pastry lovers is *Faschingskrapfen (page 32)*.
Faschingskrapfen have been a Viennese marvel since 1615, the year that
they were first available, under the name *Cillikugeln*, after a Frau Cäcilie,
who made them. They are light, round fried yeast cakes, and they have
been inadequately described in English as carnival doughnuts.

Of course, this is all wrong. There is no carnival in Vienna but there is
Fasching, a very different kind of affair. Fasching begins the day after
Epiphany (early in January) and lasts until Shrove Tuesday (the last day before Lent). Vienna's Fasching is more civilized, intimate and *gemütlich*
than the boisterous Karneval times in Cologne, Mainz and Munich, or
the Fasnacht in Basel, with their street parades, wild speeches, commercial-
ized fun, heavy drinking, and almost-anything-goes spirit. Vienna's Fasching is frankly devoted to the pleasures of wine, women and song, and,
naturally, waltzing. There are hundreds of balls during the Fasching
weeks, and many Viennese socialites go to two or three every week. The
best-known is the Opernball, when the stage and auditorium of the Vienna State Opera become a giant ballroom.

No ball is possible without a buffet and on each buffet there are *Faschingskrapfen*. No one knows how many *Krapfen* are consumed during
the merry-go-round of Fasching. But Fasching wouldn't be what it is without the feathery fried cakes that look like doughnuts and taste so much
better. During 1815, the year of the Congress of Vienna, over 10 million
Faschingskrapfen were said to have been eaten. Some were broken in half
by young girls and given to their young men. The young men were
trapped since a broken *Krapfen* was considered a token of engagement.

The making of *Krapfen* is a most important event in Viennese households. A *Faschingskrapfen* expert recently explained to me that the most
important thing to remember before you start is to have your kitchen

warm. There must be no cool draft. If you go out for a minute, be sure not to leave the door ajar. *Everything* should be warm—the ingredients, the mixing bowl, the pastry dough, even your hands. Apart from the basic yeast dough, you need apricot jam, good and firm, and the very best fat you can get for frying. In Vienna they used to use any combination of fats from beef, pork or goose for the frying of *Faschingskrapfen*. Today many people buy pure lard though it browns the *Krapfen* rather fast. And so, one has to be quite careful.

The *Krapfen* are turned as they fry in a half inch of sizzling fat until they are a golden color on both sides, with a white band around the middle where the fat has not reached. After being well drained, the *Krapfen* are served, still warm, with some vanilla-flavored confectioners' sugar sprinkled over them. And they are absolutely delicious.

There is one place in Vienna where they fry the *Krapfen* in butter. Everybody will tell you that it can't be done, that the butter will burn. But nothing is impossible at Demel's—though I've never been able to figure out how they manage to do it.

There are over 1,500 pastry shops in Vienna making and serving pastries and sweets. The 800-odd coffeehouses and 1,100 restaurants also serve pastries and sweets. But the fine art of pastry making has generally fallen on bad times in Vienna and elsewhere. In the Iron Curtain countries sweetmeats are sometimes condemned by misanthropic commissars (though not by their wives) as "food for the idle Capitalists." Restrictions,

The fanciest cake in Vienna, the *Spanische Windtorte (below and on the cover)*, is made simply of egg whites beaten with sugar into a meringue. Meringue rings form the cake proper and meringue piping swirls around its sides and top in rosettes and curlicues. The cakes and buns at the right are also delicious, but no match for the *Windtorte's* elaborateness.

rationing and other limitations have ruined such once-great confectioners as Rumpelmayer in Dresden and Felsche in Leipzig. Berger in Prague (once famous for its chocolate parfaits and light creams) has been nationalized, and so have Budapest's most famous confectioner, Gerbeaud (now called Vörösmarty), and Kapsa in Bucharest.

Even where the ingredients are plentiful in the Western world, people have become calorie conscious. A generation told to watch the bathroom scales and to stick to fruit juice and steak feels guilty at the mere sight of a *Schaumrolle* (a puff-paste roll filled with whipped cream) or a layered *Doboschtorte* (a rich, chocolate-filled cake with a caramel topping, *page 195*). Some three-star *Konditoreien* (confectioners) nonetheless carry on: Hanselmann in St. Moritz, Sprüngli in Zurich, Florian in Venice, Zauner in Ischl. But the greatest of all is still Demel's in Vienna.

Demel's, being the ranking pastry shop in Vienna and Austria, is naturally the world's champion. A great many good things have come to an end in Vienna, but not Demel's. It is not simply a pastry shop but the greatest temple of *la grande pâtisserie* this side of paradise. It represents the Viennese *Lebensart*, its manner of living, its sweet way of life. Even Viennese who never go to Demel's (it is pretty expensive) feel reassured by its still being there. They often stop in front of the shop windows and with a warm glow in their hearts wistfully gaze at those sweet masterpieces. The feeling is that, as long as Demel's and the Opera and St. Stephan's Cathedral stand, everything will be all right.

Around Christmas Demel's shows beautiful fairy-tale landscapes such as Tyrolean chocolate chalets surrounded by creamy meadows and marzipan glaciers. At Easter time there are lovely bunnies and chocolate eggs. For years the place won every culinary honor with its delicious assortments of *Torten*, made from centuries-old recipes.

In 1786 one Ludwig Dehne, a sugar baker's apprentice from Württemberg, who had come to the Mecca of pastry making for a postgraduate course, opened his shop across from the stage door of the old Burg Theater. The present owner of Demel's, Baron Federico Berzeviczy-Pallavicini, keeps several metal containers in which coffee and ice cream were carried to the box holders of the Burg Theater. Admirers took their leading ladies to Dehne's Burg Theater Sugar Bakery for beautifully shaped ice-cream creations, *Hobelspäne* (shavings), as the rich but fragile "carpenter's curl cookies" are aptly described, and various kinds of small *Krapfen* (cookies or cupcakes), some sweetened with honey and spices.

After Dehne's death his widow was named court caterer and the shop became the official sugar baker of the imperial household. But Dehne's grandson, Anton August, deserted the honest craft of pastry baking for a career in politics. In 1857 he sold his shop to his first assistant, Christoph Demel. When the old Burg Theater was torn down 30 years later, Demel moved his pastry shop to its present location in the Kohlmarkt.

Demel's is not only a national monument but also Austria's culinary conscience. Supreme quality has always been their creed. To get the finest ingredients, Demel's will go to great lengths, sending all over the world for what they need. Of course, everything is made in the house. They even make their own chocolate, mixing selected cocoa beans and sugar for 72 hours. They produce something so delicious that it might be called "the beginning and the end of chocolate"—genuine cocoa beans dipped in chocolate. At Demel's each of the pastry cooks is a specialist. Some of them make puff pastry and others make cake mixtures. No electric beaters are used; at Demel's they are convinced that only a cake mixture artfully beaten by hand can have the needed consistency and "warmth." They use 80 pounds of the finest butter daily.

There are always problems to be solved—such as how best to make dough patties filled with wild strawberries, a summertime creation. Originally Demel's put the fruit on the dough and the patties got wet and sticky. In Germany, some pastry shops "isolate" the dough with a thin chocolate coating, but at Demel's they know better than to blend chocolate and strawberries. After many months of experimenting they found out that only a very thin coat of hot apricot marmalade would separate fruit and dough.

At Demel's the former Habsburg Empire has its sweet resurrection. They have borrowed and perfected the best pastry recipes from all corners of the old Austro-Hungarian realm. Other fine things have also been appropriated from abroad: *brioches, soufflés, madeleines* and *croissants* from France; *kulic* (a large *brioche*) from Russia; *Baumkuchen* (tree cake) from Germany, a delicate creation of many layers of the thinnest dough showing concentric rings like a real tree trunk.

At Demel's they make dozens of different *Torten* every day. In Vienna they say, "A *Torte* is a round cake, but not every round cake is a *Torte*." On an average day you may find the rum punch *Torte, Indianer Torte, Josephinen Torte, Pralinen Torte, Giselatorte,* chocolate cream *Torte,* the various *Linzertorten,* the *Nusswaffeltorte* (the exception because it is square), the macaroon *Torte* (either soft or hard), the bread *Torte,* the *Neapolitaner Torte,* the *Breslauer Torte* (almonds and sour cherries). There are especially light specimens, such as the *Sandtorte* and the *Konserventorte* (made of a fluffy biscuit dough), and heavier *Torten* such as the *Annatorte* and the *Dory Torte* (extra thin, filled with chocolate cream, and extra good). History is reflected in the *Nelsontorte* and the *Austerlitztorte.* There is also a *Demeltorte*—a rich, crisp pastry filled with glazed fruit.

Among the best-known specialties of the house are the various *Strudel* and the *Indianer,* which is made everywhere in Vienna—though nowhere as well as at Demel's. Another baker's wife is credited with the *Indianer;* in fact, the baker's wife plays a big role in Viennese pastry history, as in French love lore. In 1850 a Hindu tightrope walker, called an *Indianer* by the Viennese, was the great sensation locally. He performed on a tightrope suspended from two towers, balancing with the help of a long stick that had a black ball at each end. Not far from where he performed there lived a baker named Krapf and his wife, Frau Cilli. The story goes that the baker told his wife to stop staring like crazy at that *Indianer* up there. Thereupon Frau Cilli got mad, and threw a lump of dough at her husband. It missed Herr Krapf but mercifully landed in a pan of hot fat and puffed up. Frau Cilli, no fool, filled it with cream, dumped it in hot chocolate and called it *Indianer.* Another authentic Viennese delight was born. The only trouble with the story is that, like so many cooking tales, it is misleading. The *Indianer* is baked, not fried. But the story persists and at least illustrates the legendary aspect behind so much of Viennese cooking.

On a large table in the front room of Demel's there are innumerable des-

Continued on page 176

The Best in Sugar Bakeries

The famous sugar bakery, Ch. Demel's Söhne in Vienna's Kohlmarkt, is out of
the Baroque world of the Old Empire, a place resplendent with mirrors and
silver, black marble tables and chandeliers in swirling white wrought iron. But
Austrians judge it not by the décor but by its unrivaled pastries—a good
example of which is the *Gugelhupf,* a fluted coffee cake *(opposite)* that goes so
well with whipped-cream rolls and coffee topped with more whipped cream
(Schlagobers)—or by luscious candies *(above)* wrapped in fanciful paper designed
by Demel's owner, the Baron Federico Berzeviczy-Pallavicini.

As this fantastic display demonstrates, the temptations in Demel's baroque rooms are too delightful to be resisted. On stands above the silver tray *(from left): Punschkrapferln, Butterteigtascherl;* a *Gugelhupf* and some *Butterteigkipferln;* on the silver tray, *Burgtheater Linzer* and *Erdbeertörtchen;* on stands at rear of the counter, a *Topfentorte,* a *Kaffeecremetorte,* a *Kaffeebuttercremetorte,* a plate of *Schaumrollen, Stachelbeertörtchen* and a *Kirschtorte;* on stands in foreground: *Nusschnitten, Indianerkrapfen,* an *Annatorte* and a *Punschtorte;* and on the counter, *petits fours, Jubiläumskrapfen* and *Erdbeerkrapfen.*

serts: notably the *Gugelhupf*, a tall, sugar-dusted cake with fluted walls and a hole in the middle, made in various sizes, and the *Rahmkuchen*, a light spongecake covered with whipped cream. On the shelves are many other marvels including the *Indianer*, the *Hahnenkamm* (puff-paste *brioches* with marmalade) and the *Rehrücken* (mock saddle of venison). This chocolate cake is baked in a special tin *(illustration, page 194)*, covered with chocolate icing and decorated with spiky strips of blanched almonds to look like the larding on a saddle of venison.

The most famous of Vienna's pastries—at any rate, outside Vienna—is the *Apfelstrudel (page 187)*. Yet the *Apfelstrudel* is not of Viennese origin. It was the Hungarians who took their incredibly thin *Strudel* dough from the great Turkish delicacy *baklava* and then filled it with apples. For centuries, *Apfelstrudel* has been the pride of Hungarian housewives and the test of

Honey-cake valentines, shaped as hearts and inscribed "To heart from heart with heart," are on sale at a fair at Kalocsa in Hungary. The cakes, fashioned by itinerant bakers who follow the fairs, are glazed and decorated with sugar piping and souvenir pictures and mirrors.

great pastry chefs. But it is in private homes that the superb quality of Hungarian *Strudel* is best seen.

Károly Gundel, the restaurateur, attributed the success of *Strudel* in his country to the excellent quality of Hungary's wheat flour: "The flour should be neither wet nor freshly ground," he wrote. "It is recommended to use *glattes Nullerweizenmehl*" (smooth wheat flour).

The Viennese, using their own flour, make an *Apfelstrudel* that at its best is the equal of the finest Hungarian product. Several years ago, I was privileged to watch the making of a *Strudel* dough in Demel's kitchen. I now understand why Demel's *Ausgezogener,* or pulled-out *Apfelstrudel,* became so famous in Vienna. I had been asked to be there at 6 o'clock in the morning. By then people already had been working for two hours. As I parked my car (in those days you could still park in the Kohlmarkt, which is *verboten* today) I was immediately struck by the fine fragrance of chocolate and *Butterteig* (puff paste) emanating from within. Following the sweet scent, I arrived in the kitchens. The equipment, the interiors and the people were old and cheerful. I was shown a sink made of dark stone, vintage 1888. Modern refrigerators had been installed—reluctantly —years ago. A new gas-and-electric baking oven was still viewed with distrust by older members of the staff, who knew the wisdom of baking with a wood fire but nevertheless had adapted to modern times.

At Demel's the making of the *Strudel* dough is a sacred ritual. (In Vienna it is said that you should be able to read your newspaper through a *Strudel* dough, which must be as thin as onionskin.) The ritual is performed every morning by two white-coated "professors" of *pâtisserie.* They have the steady hand and cool concentration of brain surgeons (or, at any rate, of actors performing the roles of brain surgeons in a film). The dough had been made and kneaded and finished an hour before my arrival and was "resting." It looked smooth and silky. Such dough, one of the *Strudel* makers said, will acquire some elasticity and then can be handled more easily. Of course, one has to know how.

A brief lecture on flour followed. The *Strudel* maker talked scientifically about the two distinctive types of flour used in Vienna: *glatt* and *griffig* flour. The first kind is slippery and smooth; the second is rougher and grainier, like a fine semolina. There are two schools of thought among Vienna's *Strudel* makers: some prefer the one flour and some the other, and some, I regret to say, mix both kinds. It is such minutiae that make it difficult to translate the inner meaning of a recipe, because elsewhere flour may be just flour. In any case, *Strudel* flour should have a high gluten content. As we see, *Strudel* making requires knowledge and finesse.

In the Demel kitchen there was a large table covered with a floured white tablecloth. The *Strudel* makers put the pastry in the middle of the cloth and slowly rolled it out in all directions with a floured rolling pin. Then they began to work the dough with their hands. Slowly, gently and steadily they pulled out the dough with their floured hands until it became thin, thinner and, finally, thinnest. It covered the tablecloth completely until the edges of the dough were hanging over the edges of the table. In most private homes this is the moment of tension: one wrong move and the dough will tear.

I quickly realized that this could not happen at Demel's. The *Strudel* makers were not tense; they were indeed rather businesslike and sure of themselves. (Later I was told that they had made the *Strudel* every morning for almost 30 years. They were like tightrope artists who know exactly what they are doing.)

When the dough was nothing but a thin film, the surface was brushed with melted butter, and the *Strudel* makers spread fried bread crumbs over approximately two thirds of it. Then they covered it with apple slices, a mixture of sugar and raisins, and a little powdered cinnamon. The uneven edges were trimmed with kitchen scissors.

There were quite a few other *Strudel* makers working in the kitchen, but it was very quiet. Standing at one side of the table where they had spread the apples, the *Strudel* makers took two corners of the tablecloth in their hands, lifting it gradually to coax the *Strudel* into a roll. They rolled it up tightly and steadily, and they closed the ends of the dough so the filling wouldn't fall out during the baking.

When the long *Strudel* was rolled and gently placed on a baking sheet, the men twisted it into a horseshoe shape and "painted" it, dipping their brushes into strained melted butter and carefully covering every part of the dough. Then they put it into the oven. While it was baking they brushed it lightly a few more times with butter. About half an hour later they took it out of the oven, ready for serving. *Strudel* should always be served freshly made. Once it gets cold and the butter has congealed, the poetry is gone, as in a collapsed soufflé. It has a stale taste.

Although apple is the traditional filling, Viennese bakers sometimes fill the *Strudel* with some seasonal fruit: stoned sweet cherries, damsons or sour cherries instead of apples. And, of course, all year round they make the rich *Rahmstrudel*, which is prepared with sweet or sour cream and milk, the *Topfenstrudel* with soft-curd cheese, the poppy-seed *Strudel* (the poppy seeds are cooked with sugar and milk) and the *Nuss-Strudel* (one uses ground walnuts instead of poppy seeds). From Hungary comes the cabbage *Strudel* filled with finely chopped cabbage that has been roasted in fat with sugar. An 1849 Viennese cookbook even gives the recipe for a *Schwammstrudel*, with stewed mushrooms. Most of the varieties are made with traditional thin *Strudel* pastry, but a few are made with yeast.

As popular as the different *Strudel* among those who worship at the shrine of Viennese pastry are all the various *Torten*. Perhaps nowhere else in the world are these marvels of the baker's art so numerous and so delicious.

The most famous of all *Torten* in Vienna (though, in my opinion, not the best) is the *Sachertorte*. This tasty delight has created more myths, and still creates more arguments, than any other Viennese pastry. Many people all over the world associate it with Vienna, though few have seen it, and even fewer have tried a "genuine" *Sachertorte*.

It is not true, as one legend has it, that the *Sachertorte* was invented by the notorious Frau Anna Sacher. This formidable, cigar-smoking owner of the Hotel Sacher irritated His Majesty, the ascetic Emperor Franz Josef I, by encouraging the frivolous goings-on between the youthful archdukes and the lithe, lissom members of the Vienna Opera ballet. In fact, the *Sachertorte* had been invented in 1832 by the founder of the Sacher line, Franz, while he was serving as Prince Metternich's chef.

"He bothered me all the time to invent something new, as though my pastries were not good enough," Franz Sacher said. "So I just threw some ingredients together and that's it." "He" was Prince Metternich, and "it" became the *Sachertorte*. Fortunately the Prince didn't demand that it be called *Metternichtorte*. He might have, if he had foreseen its worldwide success, but even a Metternich cannot foresee the future.

Since then there have been countless recipes for the "Original" *Sachertorte*. It is the only *Torte* on earth that became the issue of a celebrated court case, which created more excitement in Vienna and consumed more newspaper space than a minor war. The issue was: who had the right to call his product the "genuine" *Sachertorte*—the Hotel Sacher, which traded on the family connection with the *Sachertorte*'s creator, or Demel's, which had bought the right to fix the "Genuine *Sachertorte*" seal (in finest bittersweet chocolate, of course) on its *Torten?* Demel's had acquired the right from Edouard Sacher, the grandson of creator Franz Sacher and the last scion of the dynasty. The recipe was published, with Edouard Sacher's permission, in *Die Wiener Konditorei,* by Hans Skrach. It starts out with 14 egg yolks, just to give you an idea of its scope.

Basically the *Sachertorte (page 186)* is a chocolate sponge mixture, baked in a buttered, flour-dusted, round cake tin. Demel's version is covered first with hot apricot marmalade and then with bittersweet chocolate icing. The Sacher's version is sliced in half and filled with apricot jam.

The question kept the public and the courts of Vienna busy for seven long years. It is known in Vienna as the "Sweet Seven Years' War." Eventually, Austria's highest court decided that the Hotel Sacher had the right to make and sell the "Genuine *Sachertorte*." That was the end of the lawsuit, but not of the popular argument. Demel's promptly announced they were going to sell the *Ur-Sachertorte,* the very first version. Since then a great many people, including some prominent members of the Sugar Bakers' Guild, have spoken out in favor of Demel's. Both Demel's and the Hotel Sacher send their *Sachertorten* in wooden boxes all over the world, and one can only say that both versions are light, delicate and distinctive.

Vienna's leading chefs are no help when it comes to defining the proper recipe for the *Sachertorte*. A former Demel's man puts the apricot jam inside, a method frowned upon by other experts. Another famous chef diplomatically avoids the issue and comes up with an Austrian compromise: you may or may not fill the *Torte* with marmalade or whipped cream! No *Sachertorte* purist would ever touch such a thing.

Note: at Demel's you are always asked whether you want whipped cream with your *Sachertorte*. Informed scientific opinion in Viennese *Sachertorte* circles says that a fine *Sachertorte* becomes even finer with a little whipped cream served on the side.

There are several variations of the sculptured *Gugelhupf* beloved by Viennese pastry eaters. It can be made from yeast dough or a spongecake mixture; some are marbled variations of plain and chocolate sponge.

Emperor Franz Josef I preferred the small, intimate *Gugelhupf* made by Katharina Schratt, the famous Burg Theater actress with whom he fell in love when she was 33 and he was in his early fifties. The Schratt story is one of the great legends of Vienna, the favorite topic of Vienna's Sunday supplement readers and an important contribution to the city's gastronomic lore. Frau Schratt made her *Gugelhupf* all by herself, and it was always fresh-

Continued on page 182

Molds for Edible Art

In most parts of Central Europe the honey-cake baker has been done in by the more sophisticated pastries provided by the sugar baker. But small numbers of stubbornly traditional honey-cake bakers survive in Hungary, still kneading honey into their flour and still forcing the dough into hand-carved antique wooden molds such as those seen here. The thick, malleable dough retains the imprint of the design through the baking process. The cakes were the original predecessors of today's picture magazines and art reproduction books; in times past they were the only graphic art circulating among the common people. They were decorative, long lasting, and whenever one finally got tired of the picture, one had the pleasure of eating it.

18TH CENTURY PAIR OF ARISTOCRATS

17TH CENTURY MOUNTED TRUMPETER

16TH CENTURY ORPHEUS WITH LYRE

17TH CENTURY KING LEOPOLD I

18TH CENTURY ADORATION OF THE MAGI

17TH CENTURY SAMSON AND THE LION

19TH CENTURY HUSSAR ON HORSEBACK

ly baked at 4:30 in the afternoon when the Emperor came to her for their *Jause*. Unfortunately, history tells us nothing of the quality of Frau Schratt's *Gugelhupf*.

Perhaps one of the most notable examples of the wild extravagance and decorative skill of the Viennese bakers is the *Spanische Windtorte*, as it is called for some quaint and mysterious reason that has never been adequately explained, at least to this writer. This fantastic creation of nothing but sugar, egg whites and whipped cream *(cover photograph)* is built up in layers of piped rosettes and shells into a veritable extravaganza of meringue. Although the *Windtorte* is something usually attempted only by the professional baker, it can be made in the home *(page 196)* provided one has the skill and patience.

Some of the best pastry is still made by Hungarians. And although Hungarian *pâtisserie*, like that of Vienna, is not what it used to be, the tradition still remains strong in spite of the limitations imposed by the government. There is, after all, no reason why one cannot bake the delicacies of a former era at home; and it is here, in the home, that Hungarian baking is truly unique. Included in many ancient chronicles are descriptions of the shops of the confectioners and pretzel bakers of old Budapest. One pastry baker named János Kertsok had his shop in the present Kristóf tér. This was the famous Neugebohren, which also had a coffeehouse, on Sebestyén utca. On Budapest's Castle Hill, Russwurm was a well-known pastry shop. And on the square called Szinház tér (now Vörösmarty tér) there was the king of Budapest's confectioners, Kugler. He later sold his popular shop to Gerbeaud, a Swiss confectioner who made Gerbeaud's a world-famous institution, the only such enterprise that was said to have been a serious competitor of Demel's.

Gerbeaud's now belongs to the state, as does everything else, and was renamed Vörösmarty, after the famous 19th Century Hungarian poet. Between the two landmarks of Gerbeaud's in the middle of the city and Gundel's restaurant in Varosliget, the city park, scene of Molnár's *Liliom*, there runs a wonderful subway, the oldest and smallest in Central Europe. It was built by a Swiss firm in 1896 to celebrate 1,000 years of Hungary's existence. It is a lovely little subway, consisting of pleasant two-car trains.

Old habitués of Gerbeaud's claim that it is as good as ever; some go so far as to call it "the world's greatest pastry shop." An American guidebook published by a former citizen of Budapest says of it, "As good as Demel's in Vienna—the once distinguished still meet there." The second part of the statement is right—Gerbeaud's is still the meeting place of elderly ladies who once were very elegant and distinguished cavaliers whose noble bearing contrasts with their shiny elbows. It is still a lovely place and was recently redecorated in its old familiar style with chandeliers, dark oil paintings, intimate salons and lace curtains. Most habitués order just a cup of coffee and linger over it for a long time, rather anachronistic figures who talk more about the past than the present. They have a proprietary attitude; they know they once belonged there and still do, and they ignore the *nouveau riche* customers who can afford to order three pieces of *dobos torta*, the layered cake that is a Hungarian specialty.

I visited both Gerbeaud's (Vörösmarty) and Gundel's on my latest trip to Budapest. While both institutions try their very best, any comparison with the past would be folly. True, at Gerbeaud's they still make good *rétes* (as they call their *Strudel*), chocolate and *dobos torta,* but *torta* for *Torte* Gerbeaud's is no match for Demel's. And at Gundel's the only truly excellent thing I had was a *palacsinta,* Gundel's famous crêpe, filled with a delicate stuffing of walnuts, raisins and sweet cream.

I must say that for me nothing was ever more delicious than the pastries we used to have at Christmas in my hometown in Moravia. I remember how for weeks before the holidays our house used to be filled with the most wonderful scents—butter? chocolate? vanilla? almonds?—emanating from the oven. Housewives in Ostrava would compete with each other in making cookies—*Vanillekipfel* (small vanilla crescents)—biscuits, *Kokosbusserln* (coconut kisses) and *Bischofsbrot* (bishop's bread, a shallow cake made of eggs, flour, sugar, butter, with lots of raisins and almonds). And there were ambitious *Torten* such as *Malakov Torte* (a *Torte* made of fluffy, light ladyfingers and a fruit cream) and, above all, the traditional braided Christmas *Striezl* loaf. It was richer than the usual plain Sunday *Striezl* and was deliciously covered with almonds, hazelnuts and raisins. People would send *Striezl* to each other as gifts, a pleasant memory of a time when one didn't go into a store to buy Christmas presents and cross a name off a check list, but gave something that one had done with one's own hands, and created out of one's own self.

As the holidays approached, the delicious aroma from the kitchen became more intense, and the pace of baking increased. All large plates, tureens, silver boxes and glass bowls were filled with pastries. It seemed inconceivable that all these sweet things would ever be eaten. But Christmas was the time of hospitality, people visiting and being served some pastry —even before lunch—and any home that couldn't offer these small, delicious mountains of crescents, biscuits, chocolate-covered things and *petits fours* would feel disgraced. The competition was terrific, and it was never settled. No husband in his right mind would dare tell his wife that somebody else's *Torte* was better.

The great aim was to create a recipe that no one else could duplicate. The recipes were handed down as oral tradition from grandmother to mother to daughter. I learned that subtle and unfathomable differences were made in the exchange value of different cakes and *Torten.* When my mother sent a dear friend her *Doboschtorte (Dobos torta* in Hungary) and in turn received "only" a *Linzertorte* (the single-layered cake filled with raspberry jam and covered with latticed strips of dough), she was not pleased. The reasons were never explained to me; it might be the expense involved or the amount of work. As a boy I attributed the intrinsic value of the *Doboschtorte* to its many layers. Today I know that my mother was right. It is, of course, less work to make a *Linzertorte.*

It is a lovely thing, to give a present that one has made with some effort; something less easy than to go into a store and buy what a machine has thrown together. We children were told to draw, or paint, or sew, or make something for our parents. And our mothers baked nice things and sent them to their friends. It was a delightful custom. I hope it will come again. I hope very much that people will again make things, cook and bake for themselves, and for one another. Life is, after all, more real that way, more nourishing to body and to spirit as well.

To make 35 cream slices

THE CAKE

2 tablespoons butter

2 tablespoons flour

3 ounces unsweetened chocolate

¾ cup (1½ quarter-pound sticks) unsalted butter, softened

½ cup sugar

4 eggs, separated

Pinch of salt

½ cup sifted all-purpose flour

THE FILLING

1½ cups heavy cream

10 ounces semisweet chocolate, broken or chopped into small chunks

4 tablespoons dark rum

1 teaspoon vanilla extract

THE GLAZE

1 cup fine granulated sugar

⅓ cup water

7 ounces semisweet chocolate, broken or chopped into small chunks

Rigó Jancsi
CHOCOLATE CREAM SLICES

Preheat the oven to 350°. With a pastry brush or paper towel, butter an 11-by-17-inch jelly-roll pan and sprinkle the flour over the butter. Tap the edge of the pan on a table to knock out the excess flour.

Melt the chocolate over low heat in a heavy 1-quart saucepan or in the top of a double boiler placed over simmering water. Set the chocolate aside to cool to lukewarm. Cream the butter and ¼ cup of the sugar by beating them against the side of a mixing bowl with a wooden spoon, continuing to beat until the mixture is light and fluffy. Add the melted chocolate and beat in the egg yolks, one at a time.

In another mixing bowl, preferably of unlined copper, beat the egg whites and a pinch of salt with a wire whisk or rotary beater until the whites cling to the beater; add the remaining ¼ cup of sugar and beat until the whites form stiff, unwavering peaks. With a rubber spatula, stir about ⅓ of the whites into the chocolate base, then pour the chocolate mixture over the rest of the whites. Sprinkle the flour lightly on top. Gently fold the flour into the mixture until no white streaks are visible.

Pour the batter into the prepared jelly-roll pan, spreading it evenly with a rubber spatula. Bake in the middle of the oven for 15 to 18 minutes, or until the cake shrinks slightly away from the sides of the pan and a knife inserted in the middle comes out clean. Remove the cake from the oven, loosen it from the pan by running a sharp knife around the sides, and turn it out on a rack to cool.

THE FILLING: In a heavy 1-quart saucepan, combine the cream and chocolate, and stir over medium heat until the chocolate dissolves. Then reduce the heat to very low and simmer, stirring almost constantly, until the mixture thickens into a heavy cream. Pour it into a bowl and refrigerate for at least 1 hour. When the mixture is very cold, pour in the rum and vanilla and beat with a wire whisk or a rotary or electric beater until the filling is smooth and creamy and forms soft peaks when the beater is lifted from the bowl. Do not overbeat or the cream will turn to butter.

Cut the cake in half to make two layers, each 8½ inches wide. Over one layer spread the filling, which will be about 2 inches thick. Set the other layer on top. Refrigerate on a rack for about 1 hour.

THE GLAZE: Meanwhile, make the glaze. In a heavy 1-quart saucepan, heat the sugar, water and chocolate over medium heat, stirring constantly, until the sugar and chocolate are dissolved. Remove the pan from the heat, cover and let the glaze cool for about 20 minutes.

Set the rack holding the cake on a jelly-roll pan and, holding the saucepan with the glaze in it about 2 inches above the cake, pour the glaze over it. Refrigerate the cake on the rack for 10 to 20 minutes longer, or until the glaze is firm.

Serve *Rigó Jancsi* by cutting it into 35 small equal pieces, 5 in each row across and 7 in each row down. For cutting, use a sharp knife that has been dipped in warm water. Rinse the knife and dip it again in warm water before each cutting.

Indianerkrapfen
PUFFS WITH WHIPPED CREAM

Preheat the oven to 400°. Sift the flour and cornstarch into a bowl.

Beat the egg yolks lightly with a fork and add the vanilla extract. With a wire whisk or a rotary or electric beater, beat the egg whites until they begin to foam, then, 1 tablespoon at a time, beat in the sugar. Continue beating until the whites form stiff, unwavering peaks.

Mix about ¼ of the egg whites into the yolks with a rubber spatula, then reverse the process and pour the yolk mixture over the rest of the whites. Sprinkle the flour and cornstarch on top of the yolks, then fold gently until no trace of flour remains.

Lightly butter and flour a 12-cup muffin tin. Turn the tin over and strike it on the table to remove any excess flour.

Pour the batter into the cups, filling each cup ⅔ full. Bake in the middle of the oven for 12 minutes, or until the cakes are lightly browned. Remove from the oven and run a knife around each cake to loosen it, then lift them from the tin and cool on a cake rack.

THE FILLING: Whip the cream until it begins to thicken, add sugar and vanilla and whip until cream holds its shape firmly. Refrigerate.

With a sharp knife, slice around each cake almost to the bottom, leaving a ¼-inch rim around the circumference. Pull out the insides of the cakes, leaving thin shells. Fill each cake shell with the whipped cream, then refrigerate for 1 hour.

Another method: cut off a ¼-inch slice from the top and remove the insides. Replace top after filling.

THE GLAZE: Combine the chocolate, cream, sugar, water and corn syrup in a heavy saucepan. Stir them together over low heat until the chocolate melts and the sugar dissolves. Raise the heat to medium and cook without stirring for about 5 minutes longer.

Remove the pan from the heat and stir 3 tablespoons of the hot mixture into the lightly beaten egg. Then beat the egg mixture briskly into the chocolate mixture and add the vanilla.

Transfer the cakes upside down to a cake rack set on a jelly-roll pan (or right side up if using alternate method) and pour over them the warm glaze from the saucepan. Refrigerate to chill the glaze, and serve.

To make 12 puffs

THE BATTER
¼ cup all-purpose flour
¼ cup cornstarch
4 eggs, separated
½ teaspoon vanilla extract
¼ cup sugar

THE FILLING
1½ cups heavy cream, chilled
1 tablespoon sugar
1 teaspoon vanilla extract

THE GLAZE
4 ounces unsweetened chocolate
⅔ cup chilled heavy cream
1 cup sugar
4 tablespoons water
2 tablespoons white corn syrup
1 egg, lightly beaten
1 tablespoon vanilla extract

1 To make *Indianer* you first bake cupcakes (made with eggs, cornstarch and flour) and then hollow them out with a sharp knife.

2 Next, fill the cupcakes to the edge with whipped cream, refrigerate them for at least an hour, then place them upside down on a cake rack.

3 Pour the chocolate glaze over the cupcakes and refrigerate again. When the glaze has cooled, remove them from the rack and serve from a platter.

To make 1 nine-inch round cake

6½ ounces semisweet chocolate,
    broken or chopped in small chunks
8 egg yolks
8 tablespoons (¼-pound stick)
    unsalted butter, melted
1 teaspoon vanilla extract
10 egg whites
Pinch of salt
¾ cup sugar
1 cup sifted all-purpose flour
½ cup apricot jam, rubbed through
    a sieve

THE GLAZE
3 ounces unsweetened chocolate,
    broken or chopped into small
    chunks
1 cup heavy cream
1 cup sugar
1 teaspoon corn syrup
1 egg
1 teaspoon vanilla extract

To make filling for 1 six-foot *Strudel*

1 pound creamed cottage cheese,
    sieved
5 egg yolks, lightly beaten
¼ teaspoon salt
1 lemon peel, grated
¼ cup Cream-of-Wheat
½ cup seedless white raisins
1 cup sugar
5 egg whites

Sachertorte
SACHER CAKE

Preheat the oven to 350°. Butter two 9-by-1½-inch round cake pans and then line them with circles of wax paper. Butter the paper circles, sprinkle them with flour and shake off the excess.

In the top of a double boiler, melt the chocolate, stirring occasionally with a wooden spoon. In a small mixing bowl, break up the egg yolks with a fork, then beat in the chocolate, melted butter and vanilla extract.

With a wire whisk or a rotary or electric beater, beat the egg whites and pinch of salt until they foam, then add the sugar, 1 tablespoon at a time, continuing to beat until the whites form stiff, unwavering peaks on the beater when it is lifted from the bowl.

Mix about ⅓ of the egg whites into the yolk-chocolate mixture, then reverse the process and pour the chocolate over the remaining egg whites. Sprinkle the flour over the top. With a rubber spatula, using an over-and-under cutting motion instead of a mixing motion, fold the whites and the chocolate mixture together until no trace of the whites remains. Do not overfold.

Pour the batter into the 2 lined pans, dividing it evenly between them. Bake for 25 to 30 minutes, or until the layers are puffed and dry and a toothpick stuck in the center of a layer comes out clean.

Remove the pans from the oven and loosen the sides of the layers by running a sharp knife around them. Turn them out on a cake rack and remove the wax paper. Let the layers cool while you prepare the glaze.

THE GLAZE: In a small heavy saucepan, combine the chocolate, cream, sugar and corn syrup. Stirring constantly with a wooden spoon, cook on low heat until the chocolate and sugar are melted, then raise the heat to medium and cook without stirring for about 5 minutes, or until a little of the mixture dropped into a glass of cold water forms a soft ball. In a small mixing bowl beat the egg lightly, then stir 3 tablespoons of the chocolate mixture into it. Pour this into the remaining chocolate in the saucepan and stir it briskly. Cook over low heat, stirring constantly, for 3 or 4 minutes, or until the glaze coats the spoon heavily. Remove the pan from the heat and add the vanilla. Cool the glaze to room temperature.

When the cake layers have completely cooled, spread one of them with apricot jam and put the other layer on top. Set the rack in a jelly-roll pan and, holding the saucepan about 2 inches away from the cake, pour the glaze over it evenly. Smooth the glaze with a metal spatula. Let the cake stand until the glaze stops dripping, then, using two metal spatulas, transfer it to a plate and refrigerate it for 3 hours to harden the glaze. Remove it from the refrigerator ½ hour before serving.

Topfen Strudelfülle
COTTAGE CHEESE FILLING FOR STRUDEL

In a mixing bowl, stir together the cottage cheese, egg yolks, salt, lemon peel, Cream-of-Wheat, raisins and sugar. In another bowl, beat the egg whites with a wire whisk or a rotary or electric beater until they form soft peaks. Stir about ¼ of the whites into the cheese mixture, then fold in the rest with a rubber spatula. Proceed as with other *Strudel* fillings.

186

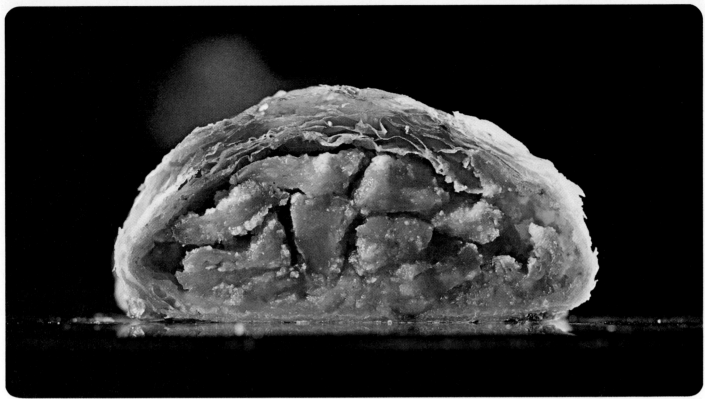

Strudel crust is light and flaky. The filling here is apple slices, but other sweets, meats and even vegetables and cereals are often used.

Apfel Strudelfülle
APPLE STRUDEL FILLING

To make filling for 1 six-foot *Strudel*

8 large green cooking apples (about
  5 pounds) peeled, cored and cut
  into ½-inch slices
¾ cup sugar
2 teaspoons cinnamon
¾ cup seedless white raisins
1 tablespoon grated lemon peel
¾ cup ground almonds

In a large mixing bowl, combine the apples, sugar, cinnamon, raisins and lemon peel. Sprinkle the 3-inch strip of *Strudel (page 188)* nearest you with the ground almonds, then distribute the apple mixture evenly along the strip to within 2 inches of the ends, then lift the tablecloth on that side and use it to roll the dough around the filling, jelly-roll fashion. Brush the top of the roll with melted butter and sprinkle it with bread crumbs, then cut into sections that will fit comfortably on your baking sheets. Bake in the middle of a preheated 450° oven for 10 minutes, then reduce the heat to 400°. Bake for 20 minutes, or until the *Strudel* is crisp and brown.

    NOTE: Cut the quantities in half to make one phyllo *Strudel* roll.

Kirschen Strudelfülle
CHERRY STRUDEL FILLING

To make filling for 1 six-foot *Strudel*

8 cups sour pitted cherries, fresh or
  canned (drained)
2 cups sugar
2 teaspoons grated lemon peel
¾ cup ground almonds

Combine the cherries, sugar and lemon peel in a bowl. Sprinkle the almonds onto the 3-inch strip of *Strudel (page 188)* nearest you.

    Spread the cherries evenly along the strip to within 2 inches of the ends, then lift the tablecloth on that side and use it to roll the dough around the filling, jelly-roll fashion. Brush the top of the roll with melted butter and sprinkle it with bread crumbs, then cut into sections that will fit comfortably on your baking sheets. Bake in the middle of a preheated 450° oven for 10 minutes, then reduce the heat to 400°. Bake for 20 minutes or until the *Strudel* is crisp and brown.

Strudel

To make 1 six-foot *Strudel* (cut into sections)

¾ cup lukewarm water
1 large egg, lightly beaten
¼ teaspoon white vinegar
2 tablespoons butter, melted
2½ cups bread flour (all-purpose flour will not do)
¾ teaspoon salt
Melted butter
Bread crumbs

Preheat the oven to 450°. In a small mixing bowl, combine the water, egg, vinegar and butter, all of which should be at room temperature, then add the mixture to the flour and salt in a large mixing bowl. Stir by hand for about 5 minutes or by using an electric mixer with a pastry arm for about 3 minutes, or until the mixture becomes a firm dough.

Form the dough into a ball and transfer it to a floured surface to knead it. Traditionally, *Strudel* dough is kneaded by repeatedly lifting it up about 2 feet and throwing it against the table, continuing for about 10 minutes, or until the dough becomes smooth and elastic. However, the dough can be kneaded like other doughs—by pulling it into an oblong shape, pressing it down and pushing it forward several times with the heels of the hands, then turning it slightly and repeating the process until it is smooth and elastic. This usually takes about 10 minutes.

Form the dough into a ball again, place it on a floured surface, cover it with a warm (but not hot) inverted metal or earthenware bowl and let it rest for 30 minutes.

Meanwhile, cover a large table (about 6 by 4 feet) with a tablecloth, and sprinkle the cloth generously with flour. With a pastry brush, coat the top of the dough with melted butter. Roll it out to a thickness of about ⅛ inch, then begin stretching it over the backs of your hands. Working quickly, continue lifting the dough and stretching it by pulling your hands apart until it is almost paper-thin and drapes over all 4 sides of the

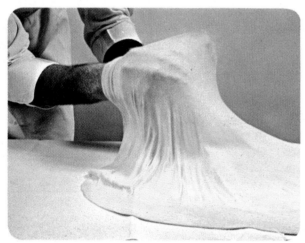

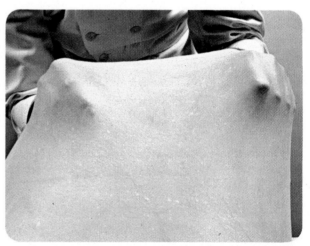

1 On a floured cloth roll out the *Strudel* dough, pull it with backs of your hands until it stretches into a sheet over the table and is as thin as can be without tearing.

2 When dough is ready *(above)* oil or butter it and then *(below)* cover it with bread crumbs. The thicker edges beyond the table top must be neatly and evenly trimmed.

table. With scissors, trim off the thick outer edges of the *Strudel* dough.

Brush the stretched dough generously with melted butter and then sprinkle it with bread crumbs. Place whatever filling you plan to use *(pages 59, 186 and 187)* along the edge nearest you, in a 3-inch strip, to within 2 inches of the ends, then lift the tablecloth on that side and use it to roll the dough around the filling, jelly-roll fashion. Brush the top of the roll with melted butter and sprinkle it with bread crumbs. With a sharp knife, cut it into sections that will fit comfortably on your baking sheets.

Lightly butter 1 or 2 large baking sheets, place the sections on it, seam sides down with the aid of a metal spatula. Bake in the middle of the oven for 10 minutes, then reduce the heat to 400°. Bake for 20 minutes longer, or until the *Strudel* is crisp and brown.

NOTE: Prepared *Strudel* dough (phyllo) is available in many areas. The usual package of prepared dough contains 4 sheets, designed to be made into 2 *Strudel* rolls, both of them together holding about as much filling as the one long roll made from the recipe above.

To prepare packaged *Strudel* dough, preheat the oven to 400°, then unroll one sheet on a large damp kitchen towel and, using a pastry brush, coat it with butter, then sprinkle it with bread crumbs. Unroll a second sheet over the first and similarly coat it with butter and sprinkle it with bread crumbs. Spread the filling along a 3-inch strip of the dough nearest you and use the towel to roll it up, jelly-roll fashion. Bake in the middle of the oven for 25 to 30 minutes, or until golden brown.

3 Now place the filling, prepared before you started working the dough, along the whole length of the dough *(above)* to within 2 inches of the ends. The floured cloth *(below)* is lifted to make the dough roll over and over on itself until it is all rolled up. The ends are then sealed and the *Strudel* is cut in even sections to fit comfortably in the oven.

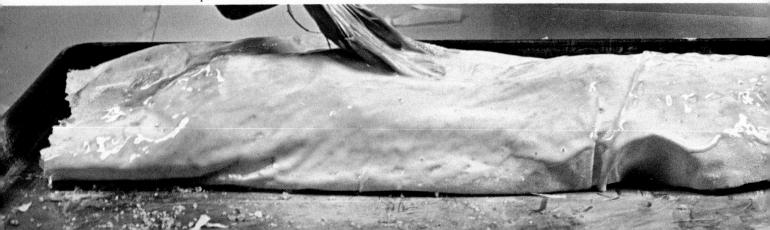

Four Fabulous Cakes

In Vienna a cake is more than just a cake. It is a creation that allows free rein to the cook's creativity. Four of the more famous ones are: *Haselnusstorte (left)*, made with beaten eggs and ground hazelnuts; *Doboschtorte (center bottom)*, a many-layered spongecake filled with chocolate cream and glazed with caramel sugar; *Rehrücken (center top)*, a mock saddle of venison with almonds and unsweetened chocolate; and *Linzertorte (far right)*, which is shown in more detail on page 192.

To make 1 nine-inch cake

1½ cups all-purpose flour
⅛ teaspoon ground cloves
¼ teaspoon cinnamon
1 cup finely ground unblanched
    almonds
½ cup sugar
1 teaspoon grated lemon peel
2 hard-cooked egg yolks, mashed
1 cup unsalted butter (2 quarter-
    pound sticks), softened
2 raw egg yolks, lightly beaten
1 teaspoon vanilla extract
1½ cups thick raspberry jam
1 egg, lightly beaten
2 tablespoons light cream
Confectioners' sugar

Linzertorte

LINZER CAKE

Sift the flour, cloves and cinnamon together into a deep mixing bowl, then add the almonds, sugar, lemon peel and mashed egg yolks. With a wooden spoon, beat in the butter, raw egg yolks and vanilla extract. Continue to beat until the mixture is smooth and doughy. Form the dough into a ball, wrap it in wax paper or plastic wrap, and refrigerate it for at least 1 hour, or until it is firm.

Remove about ¾ of the dough from the wrapping and return the rest to the refrigerator.

With a paper towel or pastry brush, lightly butter a round 9-by-1- or 1½-inch false-bottomed cake pan. Add the dough (if it is too firm, let it soften a bit) and, with your fingers, press and push it out so that it covers the bottom and sides of the pan, making a shell about ¼ inch thick. Spoon in the raspberry jam and spread it evenly over the bottom of the shell with a spatula. On a floured surface with a floured rolling pin, roll out the rest of the dough into a 6-by-9-inch rectangle ¼ inch thick.

With a pastry cutter or sharp knife, cut the dough into strips ½ inch wide, 2 of them 9 inches long and the rest 8 inches long. Lay one of the 9-inch strips across the center of the jam and flank that strip on each side with one of the 8-inch strips placed halfway between the center and sides of the pan. Rotate the pan about ¼ of the way to your left and repeat the pattern with the other 3 strips, so that they create Xs with the first 3 in a latticelike effect.

Run a sharp knife around the top of the pan to loosen the part of the bottom dough that extends above the strips. Press this down with your fingers into a border about ¼ inch thick. Lightly beat the whole egg with the cream and, with a pastry brush, coat all the exposed pastry. Refrigerate for ½ hour.

Meanwhile preheat the oven to 350°.

Bake the *Torte* in the middle of the oven for 45 to 50 minutes, or until it is lightly browned. Set the pan on a large jar or coffee can and slip down the outside rim. Let the *Torte* cool for 5 minutes on the bottom of the pan, then sprinkle it with confectioners' sugar. *Linzertorte* should cool to room temperature before being served.

1 *Linzertorte* starts with a dough of flour, ground nuts, butter, sugar, spices and lemon peel pressed into a round cake pan as if for a pie.

2 Fill the crust with jam, top it with crisscrossed dough strips, and run a knife around the edge.

3 Now fold in the edge over the cross strips to make a border around the *Torte* about the same width as the strips. Then bake until light brown.

Bublanina
SPONGECAKE WITH CHERRIES

Preheat the oven to 350°. With a pastry brush or paper towel, butter the bottom of a 9-inch layer-cake pan. Pour the cherries into a sieve or colander and let them drain while you prepare the batter.

In a mixing bowl, with a wire whisk or a rotary or electric beater, beat the egg whites with the salt until they foam, then beat in the sugar, a tablespoon at a time. Continue to beat until the whites form stiff, unwavering peaks when the beater is lifted from the bowl.

Beat the egg yolks lightly with a fork, then add the lemon peel, lemon juice and vanilla extract. Mix about ¼ of the beaten egg whites into the egg yolks, then reverse the process and pour the yolk mixture over the remaining whites and sprinkle the flour on top. With a rubber spatula, fold until no traces of the whites remains. Do not overfold.

Pour the batter into the pan and spread the cherries evenly over it. Bake in the middle of the oven 35 to 40 minutes, or until the cake is golden brown and springy to the touch. Cool in the pan before serving.

To make 1 nine-inch cake

1 cup canned pitted sweet black cherries
3 eggs, separated
Pinch of salt
½ cup sugar
½ teaspoon grated lemon peel
2 teaspoons lemon juice
½ teaspoon vanilla extract
½ cup sifted all-purpose flour

Haselnusstorte
HAZELNUT CAKE

Preheat the oven to 275°. In a large bowl, beat the egg yolks and the whole egg together with a wire whisk, or rotary or electric beater, continuing to beat until the mixture is thick and light yellow in color. Gradually beat in ½ cup of the sugar, then the nuts and the bread crumbs. Continue to beat until the mixture forms a dense, moist mass.

In another bowl, beat the egg whites with the wire whisk or rotary or electric beater until they begin to foam, then add ¼ cup of the sugar, 1 tablespoon at a time. Continue to beat until the whites form stiff, unwavering peaks when the beater is lifted from the bowl. With a rubber spatula, mix about ¼ of the whites into the hazelnut mixture, then sprinkle the flour over it and gently fold in the rest of the whites. Continue to fold until no trace of the whites remains. Be careful not to overfold.

Butter and flour a 10-inch springform pan. Turn the pan over and strike it on the table to remove excess flour. Pour the batter into the pan, smooth the top with a spatula and bake in the middle of the oven for 45 to 50 minutes, or until it shrinks away slightly from the sides of the pan. Remove the upper part of the pan as soon as you take it from the oven. Let the cake cool, then slice it into two equal layers, using a long, sharp, serrated knife. (The cake will fall somewhat after it is removed from the oven.)

THE FILLING: Whip the chilled cream with a wire whisk or rotary or electric beater until it begins to thicken. Add the sugar and vanilla and continue to whip until the cream holds its shape firmly.

Reconstruct the cake by first placing the bottom layer on a sheet of wax paper at least 18 inches square. Spread whipped cream on top to a thickness of ½ inch and place the other layer over it. With a spatula, completely mask the cake with the rest of the whipped cream.

THE DECORATION: Scatter the ⅓ cup of hazelnuts on the wax paper around the cake. Then lift a small portion of the paper and toss the nuts on to the cake. Repeat until all the nuts are used. Serve at once.

To make 1 ten-inch cake

6 eggs, separated
1 whole egg
1 cup ground hazelnuts
¾ cup sugar
⅓ cup bread crumbs
1 teaspoon flour

THE FILLING
1½ cups heavy cream
1 tablespoon sugar
1 teaspoon vanilla extract

THE DECORATION
⅓ cup ground hazelnuts

To serve 10

¼ cup bread crumbs
5 egg whites
½ cup sugar
5 egg yolks
2 whole eggs
½ teaspoon cinnamon
2½ tablespoons finely chopped
   citron
¼ pound grated almonds (about ¾
   cup)
⅓ cup grated unsweetened chocolate
   (about 2¼ ounces)

THE CHOCOLATE GLAZE
⅔ cup heavy cream
5 tablespoons unsalted butter
Pinch of salt
1 cup sifted dark, unsweetened cocoa
1⅓ cups sugar
1 teaspoon vanilla extract
1 cup blanched almonds

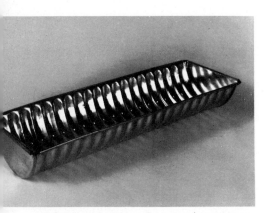

Rehrücken (saddle of venison) molds are available in sizes from 10 to 14 inches.

Rehrücken
MOCK SADDLE OF VENISON CAKE

Rehrücken, a word that in German means "saddle of venison," is also used to designate an Austrian cake with a long tradition behind it. The cake is like a saddle of venison only in its shape, and for many generations, molds made in the shape of a stylized saddle of venison have been manufactured especially for making this fanciful cake. These special molds are fluted and have deep indentations down the middle. Many Austrian traditionalists still use the special mold for making Rehrücken, *but the cake can be made in a deep loaf pan. The almonds that are used to decorate the icing of the cake are meant to suggest the strips of bacon or salt pork inserted into genuine saddles of venison to lard them.*

To make the cake, preheat the oven to 350°, then with a paper towel or pastry brush, lightly butter a 4-by-12-inch loaf pan or a *Rehrücken* mold and dust it heavily with bread crumbs. Invert the pan and shake it to remove the bread crumbs that do not adhere to the butter.

With a wire whisk or rotary or electric beater, beat the egg whites until they foam, then beat in ¼ cup of the sugar, 1 tablespoon at a time. Continue beating until the whites form stiff, unwavering peaks when the beater is lifted from the bowl.

Combine the yolks, the whole eggs and the rest of the sugar in a large mixing bowl. With the same beater you used before, beat until the mixture is pale yellow and quite thick. Then beat in the cinnamon, citron, almonds and chocolate. Continue beating until all the ingredients are thoroughly blended.

With a rubber spatula, mix about ¼ of the egg whites into the batter, then reverse the process and pour the batter over the rest of the whites. Using an over-and-under cutting motion instead of a mixing motion, fold them together until no trace of the whites remains.

Pour the batter into the prepared loaf pan or *Rehrücken* mold and bake it in the middle of the oven for 25 to 30 minutes, or until the cake shrinks slightly away from the sides of the pan, is golden brown and is springy to the touch.

Remove the cake from the oven and let it cool for 2 or 3 minutes. (In cooling, this very delicate cake may shrink slightly or fall a bit in the center, but in neither event will its final shape be affected.) Turn the cake out on a rack, set the rack on a jelly-roll pan and let the cake cool further while you make the chocolate icing.

THE CHOCOLATE GLAZE: In a small heavy saucepan, combine the cream, butter, salt, cocoa and sugar. Cook the mixture over very low heat, stirring constantly, for about 5 minutes, or until the icing is smooth and thick. Remove it from the heat and stir in the vanilla extract. Let the icing cool for about 5 minutes, then holding the saucepan about 2 inches above the cake, pour the icing over it evenly.

Press the almonds upright into the icing about an inch apart, in a regular pattern. (Try rows of 5 or 6 almond halves across and 10 lengthwise.) Let the cake cool completely (for about 45 minutes) before serving. Slice *Rehrücken* so that one of the shorter rows of almond halves decorates each serving.

194

Doboschtorte

DOBOS CAKE

To make 16 slices

THE CAKE: Preheat the oven to 350°. Cream the butter and sugar by beating them together against the side of a mixing bowl with a wooden spoon. Beat in the eggs, then stir in the flour and the vanilla extract. Continue to stir until the mixture becomes a smooth, firm batter.

With a pastry brush or paper towel, butter the underside of a 9-inch layer-cake pan, then dust it with flour. Strike the pan against the edge of a table to knock off the excess flour. With a metal spatula spread the batter as evenly as possible over the underside of the pan to a thickness of ⅛ inch. Bake in the middle of the oven 7 to 9 minutes, or until the layer is lightly browned around the edges.

Remove from the oven and scrape off any batter that has dribbled down the sides of the pan. Loosen the layer from the pan with a spatula, put a cake rack over it and invert. Wipe the pan with a paper towel, butter and flour it again and repeat the baking process with more batter. (You may, of course, bake as many layers at a time as you have 9-inch cake pans.) Continue until all the batter is used. You should have 7 exactly matching layers.

THE FILLING: In a small saucepan, combine the sugar, cream of tartar and water. Stir over low heat until the sugar is completely dissolved, then turn the heat to moderately high and boil the syrup without stirring until, if tested, it registers 238° on a candy thermometer, or until a drop of the syrup in cold water forms a soft ball.

Meanwhile, in a mixer, or by hand with a rotary or electric beater, beat the 8 egg yolks for 3 or 4 minutes, or long enough to thicken them and lighten them somewhat in color.

Pour the hot syrup into the eggs, continuing to beat as you pour in the syrup in a slow, steady stream. If you are using a mixer, beat at medium speed until the mixture cools to room temperature and changes to a thick, smooth cream. This usually takes from 10 to 15 minutes.

If you are beating by hand, set the mixing bowl in a pan of cold water to hasten the cooling and add the syrup a little at a time. Continue to beat until the cream is cool, thick and smooth, then beat in the cocoa and vanilla extract. Last, beat in the butter, adding it in small pieces until it is all absorbed. Refrigerate while you make the glaze.

THE GLAZE: First, place the most attractive of the cake layers on a cake rack set on a jelly-roll pan, then mix the sugar and water together in a small heavy saucepan. Without stirring, cook until the sugar dissolves, boils and begins to darken in color. Swirling the pan, continue to boil until the caramel becomes a golden brown, then pour it over the layer. With a buttered knife, quickly mark the glaze into 16 equal wedges, cutting nearly, but not quite, through to the bottom of the glaze. This mirrorlike layer will be the top of the *Torte*.

ASSEMBLING THE TORTE: Place a cake layer on a serving plate and, with a metal spatula, spread chocolate filling over it to a thickness of ⅛ inch, then top with another cake layer. Continue with the other layers, finishing with a layer of filling and the glazed top. Use the rest of the chocolate filling to cover the sides of the cake, smoothing it on with a spatula and refrigerate. To serve, slice along the lines marked in the glaze.

THE CAKE

½ pound unsalted butter, softened
1 cup granulated sugar
4 eggs, lightly beaten
1½ cups all-purpose flour
1 teaspoon vanilla extract

THE FILLING

1⅓ cups sugar
¼ teaspoon cream of tartar
⅔ cup water
8 egg yolks
½ cup dark unsweetened cocoa
2 teaspoons vanilla extract
2 cups (1 pound) unsalted butter, softened

THE GLAZE

⅔ cup sugar
⅓ cup water

THE SHELL
8 egg whites
½ teaspoon cream of tartar
2½ cups superfine sugar

THE DECORATION (optional)
4 egg whites
¼ teaspoon cream of tartar
1¼ cups superfine sugar
6 candied violets

THE FILLING
1½ pints heavy cream
2 tablespoons sugar
¼ cup Cognac
3 cups strawberries, raspberries or
   blueberries, washed and hulled

Spanische Windtorte
SPANISH WIND CAKE

THE SHELL: Preheat the oven to 200°. With a pastry brush or paper towel, lightly butter two 11-by-17-inch baking sheets, sprinkle them with flour, tip them from side to side to spread the flour evenly, then invert them and strike them on the edge of a table to knock out the excess. Invert an 8-inch plate or layer-cake pan on the floured surface of one baking sheet and tap it with your hand, making a ring to serve as a guide in making the layers of the shell. Repeat the process on the first sheet and outline 2 similar rings on the other sheet, making 4 guide rings in all, none of them touching one another.

With a wire whisk, or rotary or electric beater, beat the 8 egg whites with the cream of tartar until they begin to foam, then gradually beat in 2¼ cups of the sugar, continuing to beat for at least 5 minutes, or until the whites form stiff, unwavering peaks when the beater is lifted from the bowl. With a rubber spatula, gently fold in the remaining ¼ cup of sugar. Fit a No. 8 plain-tipped pastry tube onto a large pastry bag and fill the bag with the meringue. Pipe a ½- to ¾-inch-thick circle of the meringue just inside one of the marks on the baking sheets and continue it in a closed spiral that ends in the center of the ring (this will be the bottom of the *Torte*). Carefully smooth the top of the spiral with a spatula. Then make plain rings of meringue about ¾ inch thick just inside the 3 other circles on the baking sheets. Bake them in the middle of the oven for 45 minutes, then gently slide them off on racks to cool.

To make a top (optional) for the *Torte*, make another spiral layer like the first one and bake for 45 minutes. (The top is used to make a more spectacular Spanish Wind cake like the one on the cover of this book.)

Construct the shell by piping about a teaspoon of the meringue onto each of 5 or 6 equidistant spots around the edge of the bottom circle to serve as a cement, then fit one of the rings over this. Continue the process with the 2 other rings, one on the other. When the shell is completed, set it on a baking sheet and let it dry out in the 200° oven for about 20 minutes or longer if necessary. Let the shell cool.

THE DECORATION (OPTIONAL): Use a flat spatula to apply the rest of the meringue in the pastry bag to the outside of the shell to make it smooth, then return it to the oven to dry for another 20 minutes. Meanwhile prepare more meringue, if you plan to use it, following the directions for the first batch. Fit a No. 6 star tube onto the pastry bag, put the meringue into the bag and make swirls and rosettes on the outside of the shell and on the circle to be used as a top (optional). Return both circles to the oven again to dry for about 20 minutes. If you wish to decorate the shell with candied violets, pipe small dabs of meringue around the center of the shell, and one dab in the center of the top spiral circle, and secure the violets on them.

THE FILLING: Whip the chilled cream until it begins to thicken, then gradually beat in the sugar. Continue to beat until the cream is firm enough to hold its shape softly, then beat in the Cognac, and last, fold in the berries with a rubber spatula.

Gently spoon the filling into the shell. If you have prepared the top spiral, lay it gently on top.

Mastering Vienna's Pastry Magic

Most beautiful of Vienna's round cakes, a baroque triumph in conception, design and execution, besides tasting of heaven, is the *Spanische Windtorte* (see the front cover and page 169). Austrians call many super-elegant things Spanish, and so the mixture of egg whites beaten with sugar, known as meringue in most places, is "Spanish wind" in Austria and is the basis of this fantastic cake. Folded into its sweetened whipped cream may go many luscious things—strawberries, crushed macaroons, toasted hazelnuts, candies and shaved bitter chocolate. The sides are *geschnörkelt* (curlicued) in rosebuds and seashells, decorated with crystallized violets, and the cake is topped by a curvy cornice.

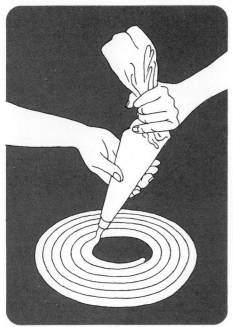

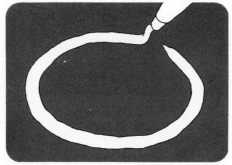

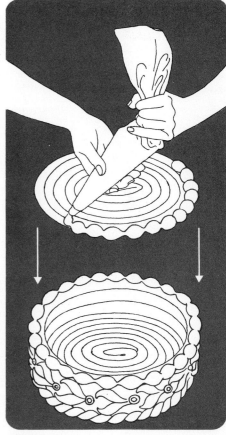

1 On 2 greased and floured 11-by-17-inch cookie sheets mark 4 guide rings by inverting an 8-inch cake pan. Inside 1 ring, using a No. 8 plain-tip pastry tube, spiral meringue into center to form cake's bottom.

2 Now make 3 once-around circles of meringue close inside the 3 remaining guide rings on the sheets, making sure they do not touch. Bake all for 45 minutes at 200° and then remove to racks and allow to cool.

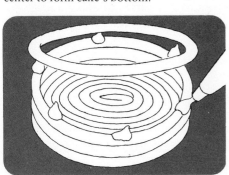

3 Make a second spiraled disk to form the top. While it is baking, construct the shell by using 6 teaspoon-sized dabs of uncooked meringue to join the rings to each other and to the bottom. Bake for 20 minutes.

4 The cake also may be prepared without decoration. But to decorate it, spread the remaining meringue around the sides to create a smooth wall. When ready the shell must go into the oven to dry for 20 minutes.

5 Now using a No. 6 star-tipped pastry tube and a fresh batch of meringue, decorate the sides and create a border for the top. Bake 20 minutes, cool, fill with whipped cream and fruit and add the top.

Glossary

Austria

AM ROST (ahm rohst): grilled

ANNATORTE (ah-na-TOR-teh): a chocolate cake topped with the thinnest chocolate curls

APFEL (ahp-fel): apple

AUFLAUF (AWF-lowf): soufflé: not quite as light as the French equivalent

BACHFORELLE (bakh-for-rel-leh): brook trout or *forelle blau* (fohrel-leh bl'ow): blue trout; the traditional method of preparation which requires freshly caught fish of certain varieties only—those with small scales like salmon or trout. The natural film which covers the scales turns blue when boiled in vinegar and stock

BACKHENDL (BAHK-hen-del): traditional Viennese delicacy made from young spring chicken cut into four and dipped in flour, egg and bread crumbs before frying

BAUERNSCHMAUS (B'OW-ernsh'mouse): Peasant's feast: sauerkraut garnished with smoked and boiled pork and pork sausages

BAUERNSPECK (B'OW-ernshpek): home-cured bacon

BEIN (bine): leg. **BEINFLEISCH** (bineflysh): a favorite cut of boiled beef

BRANDTEIG (BRAHNT-tyge): puff paste; French *pâte à choux*

BRATEN (BRAH-ten): roast; to roast

BUCHTELN (BOOKH-teln): jelly buns

DOBOSCHTORTE (DOH-bosh-torteh): see under Hungary, **DOBOS TORTA**

EI (eye): egg

EINBRENN (INE-brenn): a *roux* made with flour and butter or beef suet

EINGEMACHTES (INE-geh-MAHK-tes): served in a white sauce or fricassée

EINGETROPFTES (INE-geh-TROPF-tes): a popular garnish for the beef broth made by pouring a light pancake batter into hot soup

EIERSCHWAMMERLN (eye-er-SHWAHM-merln): wood mushrooms like the French chanterelles

ERDBEEREN (EHRD-beh-ren): strawberries

FALSCHE (FAHL-SHEH): used to describe soups which are made from vegetables without meat stock as a base; also for any dish which makes use of an inferior cut of meat as a substitute for a better one

FLECKERLN (FLEK-erln): small squares of noodle dough used as a garnish for the beef broth

FLEISCH (flysh): meat

FRÜHSTÜCK (frew-stewk): breakfast

GEBACKEN (geh-BAHK-en): fried

GEFÜLLTE (geh-fewl-teh): stuffed

GEKOCHT (geh-KOKHT): boiled; cooked

GESOTTEN (geh-ZOHT-ten): simmered

GRIESS (grees): farina

G'SELCHTES (geh-zelch-tess): smoked pork

GURKEN (GOOR-ken): cucumbers

HASELNUSS (HAH-zell-noos): hazelnut, filbert

HEURIGER (HOY-rig-er): this year's pressing of wine; also used for the inns around Vienna where the wine is drunk

HUHN (hoon): chicken

INDIANERKRAPFEN (in-dee-AHN-er-KRAP-fen): puffs with whipped cream

JAUSE (YOW-zeh): afternoon gathering for coffee and cakes

JUNGFERNBRATEN (YOONG-fern-BRAH-ten): pork roast from a young pig

KAFFEE (kah-FAY): coffee

KALBSHAXE (KAHLBS-hahkseh): veal shank

KALBSHIRN (KAHLBS-hearn): calf's brains

KIPFEL (KIP-fel): crescent-shaped roll

KIRSCH (keersch): cherry brandy

KIRSCHEN (KEER-shan): cherries

KNÖDEL (K'NUH-del): dumpling
KÖCHIN (KUHK-heen): cook

KONDITOREI (kohn-dee-toh-RYE): pastry shop

KRAPFEN (KRAHP-fen): doughnuts

KREBSE (KREB-seh): river crayfish

KREN (kren): horseradish

KROKETTEN (kroh-KET-ten): croquettes made of chopped meat or vegetables and coated with bread crumbs

KUCHEN (KOO-khen): cake

LEBER (LEHB-er): liver

LEBKUCHEN (LEHB-koo-khen): gingerbread

LINZERTORTE (LIN-t'ser-TOHRteh): a cake made from a short dough usually with ground al-monds or hazel nuts and chocolate, filled with jam and covered with latticed strips of pastry

LUNGENBRATEN (LOONG-en-BRAH-ten): fillet of beef

MAJORAN (mah-YOR-an): marjoram

MAKRONEN (mah-KRO-nen): macaroons

MARILLEN (mah-RIL-len): apricots

MEHLSPEISEN (MEHL-shpy-sen): desserts

MELONEN (meh-loh-nen): melons

MILCH (milsh): milk

NOCKERLN (NOK-erln): a cross between noodles and dumplings; Italian *gnocchi*

NUDELN (NOOD-eln): noodles

PALATSCHINKEN (PA-laht-SHINken): thin pancakes made from an egg batter like the French *crêpes* which may be filled with a variety of fillings; the most popular are cottage cheese and apricot jam

PILZE (PILL-tse): mushrooms

PUNSCH (poonsh): punch
PUNSCHTORTE (poonsh-TOHRteh) is so-called because part of it is soaked in a punch mixture often made with rum

REHRÜCKEN (REH-rew-ken): venison, or the long chocolate cake known as the mock saddle of venison and made in a special tin. It is decorated with rows of blanched almonds which are stuck along the top to look like the fat with which the real roast of venison would be larded

REIS (RICE): rice

RESTEKÜCHE (RESS-teh-KEWkeh): leftover cookery

RINDFLEISCH (RINT-flysh): beef

RINDSUPPE (RINT-zoop-peh): beef broth

RIESLING (REES-ling): dry white wine like the German Riesling

ROLLEN (ROL-len): rolls that are filled

SACHERTORTE (ZAHK-er-TOHRteh): the rich chocolate cake with chocolate icing first made by Franz Sacher, Prince Metternich's chef. It has become one of Vienna's most celebrated delicacies and was responsible for the controversy between Demel's and the Hotel Sacher about who had the right to sell the "genuine" Sachertorte. It is traditionally eaten with whipped cream (*Schlagobers*)

SALAT (sah-laht): salad

SARDELLE (zar-DEL-leh): anchovy

SAUERKRAUT (ZOW-er-kraut): fermented shredded cabbage

SCHAUM (sh'owm): whipped froth or mousse; the head on a glass of beer

SELCHFLEISCH (ZELSH-flysh) smoked pork

SCHINKEN (SHIN-ken): ham

SCHNEE (shnay): beaten white of egg

SCHNITZEL (SHNIT-zel): a very thin cut of meat prepared in various ways. It is traditionally veal but may be pork or even beef

SCHLAGOBERS (SHLAH-go-bers): whipped cream traditionally served with pastry

SCHMARRN (shmarn): nonsense. It is used to describe a thin egg pancake often torn into pieces, like *Kaiserschmarrn*

SCHWEIN (shvine): pork

SEMMEL (ZEM-el): roll

SOSSE (ZOHS-seh): sauce

SPECK (shpek): bacon, boiled and smoked

STRUDEL (SHTROO-del): paper thin layers of pastry dough filled with a variety of things from meat, cheese or vegetables to nuts, cream or jam

SUPPE (ZOO-peh): soup

TAFELSPITZ (TAH-fel-shpitz): cut of beef close to the tail—the top end of the bottom round is the nearest equivalent

TASCHERLN (TAH-sherlin): Viennese jam pockets

TEEGEBÄCK (TAY-geh-beck): small cookies, sweet or salty

TEIG (tyge): paste or dough

TEIL (tile): a cut of meat

TOPFEN (TOHP-fen): a curd cheese like farmer's cheese

TORTE (TOHR-teh): round Viennese cake

VORSPEISE (FOR-shpy-zeh): appetizer; may be sweet or salty

WIENER SCHNITZEL (vee-ner-SHNIT-zel): the most famous and traditional method of preparing the veal cutlet, dipped in flour, egg and bread crumbs and fried in lard

WURST (voorst): sausage

WÜRSTEL (vewrs-tel): frankfurters, usually in pairs

ZUCKERBÄCKEREI (TS'OO-ker-

BEK-keh-rye): confectionery

ZWETSCHKEN (ts'retch-ken): plums

ZWIEBEL (TS'VEE-bel): onion

Hungary

BARACKÍZ (BO-rots-keez): apricot jam

BÉLSZIN (BEHL-sin): filet of beef

BOGRÁCS (BOHG-rach): kettle in which the *gulyás* is traditionally cooked

BORDA (BOHR-dah): chop

BORJU (BOHR-yoo): veal

BORSOS (BOHR-shosh): seasoned with a lot of pepper

BURGONYA (BOOR-goh-n'yah): potato

CSIPETKE (CHEE-pet-keh): pieces of noodle dough nipped off between the finger and thumb and dropped into boiling water. Eaten with stews and soups

CSIRKE (CHEER-keh): chicken

DOBOS TORTA (DOH-bosh TOHR-tah): rich cake of many layers with a chocolate cream filling and topped with a shining caramel glaze

ESZENCIA (EH-sen-s'yah): the rarest of the Tokay wines, like a heavy, sweet cordial with a low alcohol content, often blended with other Tokays

FEHÉR KENYÉR (FEH-hehr-KEH-near): white bread

FOGAS (FOH-gosh): perch-pike from Lake Balaton in Transdanubia traditionally served with the head and tail of the fish standing up from the plate and the back curved

FURMINT (FOOR-mint): the white grape from which Tokay wines are made

FÜSZER (FEW-ser): spice

GULYÁS (GOO-yash): the famous shepherd's stew made traditionally from cubes of beef with onion, potato, caraway seed and paprika

KALARÁBÉ (KO-lo-RAH-beh): kohlrabi

KÁPOSZTA (KAH-poss-toh): cabbage

LEVES (LEH-vesh): soup

LECSÖ (LEH-choh): a thick vegetable stew made from onion, tomato and green pepper cooked together, sometimes with sliced sausage and eaten as a vegetable with the hot paprika dishes or as an appetizer

LIBA (LEE-bah): goose

MÁJ (MY): liver

MÁRTÁS (MAHR-tash): sauce or gravy

MEGGY (medj): sour cherry

PALACSINTA (PO-lo-chin-toh): pancakes like a crêpe, filled with a variety of fillings, cottage cheese and apricot being the most popular; they are served with a sprinkling of nuts on top

PÁLINKA (PAH-lin-ko): brandy—the most famous is the *barack palinka;* apricot brandy

PAPRIKÁS (PO-pree-kash): one of the four great paprika dishes; a stew usually made from veal or chicken with larger pieces of meat than those in *gulyás* and the gravy thickened with sour cream

PONTY (pontj): carp

PUTTONY (POO-tonj): a wooden container in which the sun-ripened Tokay grapes are collected; the number of these vessels added to the wine indicates its strength—and the more there are the more concentrated the wine will be

PÖRKÖLT (PUHR-cult): another of the great paprika stews but more concentrated than the *gulyás* and with a stronger onion flavor; made with larger and fatter chunks of meat. Veal is the most popular, but mutton, beef, pork and poultry may also be used

RÉTES (RAY-tesh): Hungarian for *Strudel;* may be filled with a variety of things both sweet (jam, cream, fruit or nuts) and savory (meat, cheese, vegetables)

RIGÓ JANCSI (REE-go YON-chee): rich chocolate cake filled with a chocolate mousse and topped with chocolate icing; named after a famous gypsy violinist

SALÁTA (SHOH-la-toh): salad

SERTÉS (SHEHR-tech): pork

SZÉKELY (SAY-kay): the inhabitants of Transylvania. Many dishes originated there and bear the name, such as *Székely gulyás,* which is the only *gulyás* made with sauerkraut and a variety of meats and finished with sour cream

TARHONYA (TOR-ho-n'yah): a homemade egg barley used wherever rice might be eaten. One of the most ancient of Hungarian foods, traditionally served with hot paprika dishes

TOKAY (TOH-ko-ee): full-bodied natural white wine from the Furmint grape, which includes sweet and dry varieties; the most well-known is the Tokay Aszu

TOKÁNY (TOH-kahny): the last of the four great paprika stews, in which the meat is cut into long narrow strips. It may be made of beef or veal or a mixture of meats and often contains several vegetables and herbs as well as sour cream, cream or no cream at all

TÖLTÖTT (TUHL-tuht): stuffed

Czechoslovakia

BUBLANINA (BOO-blah-nyee-na): a cherry cake made of a sponge mixture with cherries underneath

DOLKY (DOL-kee): white twisted roll

HUSA (HOO-sah): goose

JATERNICE (YAAH-tehr-n'yee-tseh): a sausage made of liver and lungs, which is boiled and afterwards may be fried

JELITA (YEH-lee-ta): a blood sausage

KLOBÁS (KLO-baahs): twisted sausage with a leathery skin; may have a variety of fillings, the most well-known being smoked pork or veal and wine

KOLÁCE (KOH-laah-che): a finer-textured version of *dolky*

KNEDLÍKY (K'NED-lee-kee): dumplings

LIPTAVSKÝ SÝR (LEEP-tov-skee seer): Liptauer cheese from the town of Liptau. It is a cream cheese made with paprika, sour cream, onions, capers and anchovy

PÁRKY (PAAHR-kee): *Würstel* or frankfurters; sold in pairs

PEČENĚ (PEH-tseh-neh): roast

POVIDLA (POH-veed-la): thick plum jam

ROSTĚNKY (ROSH-tyen-kee): cut of beef like sirloin, pounded before cooking

ŠKUBÁNSKY (SKOO-bahn-kee): mashed potato with flour blended into it

SMETANA (SMEH-tah-na): sour cream

SVÍČKOVÁ (SVEECH-koh-va): fillet of beef

TLAČENKA (TLAH-chen-ka): a large sausage made like head cheese

UZENÉ (OO-zeh-neh): smoked pork

VEPŘOVÁ (VEP-rho-va): pork; usually implies it is roast

VUŘTY (VOOR-stee): sausage like a small knackwurst

Yugoslavia

ČEVAPČIČI (chav-VAP-chee-chee): meatballs made of lamb and beef and grilled on skewers: traditionally made of different cuts of beef

ČORBA (CHOR-ba): a thick soup

DJUVEČ (DJOO-vetch): casserole

DINGAC (deen-ak): full-bodied red wine from Dalmatia

GIBANICA (ghee-ba-NEET-sa): cheese pie

KAČKAVALJ (KAHTCH-ka-val): hard white curd cheese

KADAIF (KA-deef): Turkish sytle pastry made of long thin noodles and nuts covered with a heavy sweet syrup

KAJMAK (KYE-mahk): strong, salty serbian cheese

LONAC (LO-nahts): means "pot" and is a famous Bosnian stew made with many meats and vegetables

MEZE (may-zay): means "nibbles" in Turkish and is used to describe a variety of cold hors d'oeuvres

MUSAKA (moo-SA-ka): minced meat with vegetables roasted in the oven and topped with a sauce made of beaten eggs and milk

PITA (PEE-ta): Yugoslavian word for *Strudel;* made with a variety of fillings, sweet and savory in the layers of paper-thin pastry dough

POGAČA (PO-ga-cha): farmer's bread from Serbia

PLESKAVICA (PLAY-ska-veet-sa): grilled meat patties of pork and veal

RAŽNJIČI (RASN-yee-chee): kabobs of pork and veal

SARAN (ŠA-rahn): carp

ŠIŠ-ČEVAP (SHEESH-cheh-vahp): shish kabob; skewered meat, usually lamb with onions, peppers and tomatoes

SLATKO (SLAHT-ko): thick sweet preserve usually made from plums

ŠUMADIJA (SHOO-ma-DEE-ya): *sumadija* tea is a potent drink made from hot plum brandy with caramelized sugar

Recipe Index: English

NOTE: An R preceding a page refers to the Recipe Booklet. Size, weight and material are specified for pans in the recipes because they affect cooking results. A pan should be just large enough to hold its contents comfortably. Heavy pans heat slowly and cook food at a constant rate. Aluminum and cast iron conduct heat well but may discolor foods containing egg yolks, wine, vinegar or lemon. Enamelware is a fairly poor conductor of heat. Many recipes therefore recommend stainless steel or enameled cast iron, which do not have these faults.

Recipe Index: Foreign

General Index

Numerals in italics indicate a photograph of the subject mentioned.

Credits and Acknowledgments

The sources for the illustrations in this book are shown below. Credits for the pictures from left to right are separated by commas, from top to bottom by dashes.

All photographs in this book by Fred Lyon from Rapho Guillumette except: 4—Bottom (3) Charles Phillips. 11—Map by Lothar Roth. 12, 13—Dr. Grünert. 20—Map by Lothar Roth. 24—Erich Lessing from Magnum. 32—Drawings by Matt Greene—Charles Phillips. 36—Charles Phillips, drawing by Matt Greene. 37—Charles Phillips. 38—Richard Jeffery. 61—Charles Phillips. 62—Richard Jeffery. 74, 75—Dmitri Kessel. 108, 109—Harry Redl. 118, 119—Charles Phillips. 134, 135—Richard Jeffery. 140—Charles Phillips. 180, 181—Photos by Judit Kárász courtesy Corvina Press, Budapest. 185—Charles Phillips. 188, 189—Charles Phillips. 190, 191—Richard Jeffery. 192—Charles Phillips. 194—Ron D'Asaro. 197—Drawings by Matt Greene.

For their help in the production of this book the editors wish to thank the following: *in Hungary,* Emil Turós, Master Chef; József Venesz, head of the National Restaurant Trust; Chefs Emil Eigen and Zoltán Kenderessy; *in New York City,* Paula Arno; Austrian Information Service; Charles Berlitz; The Czechoslovak Store, Inc.; Ginori Fifth Avenue; Hammacher Schlemmer; Hoffritz Cutlery; Jean's Silversmiths, Inc.; The Lys Gallery; Maria Kovács, Tik Tak Restaurant; Paul Kovi, Forum of the Twelve Caesars, Restaurant Associates; Paprikás Weiss Importer, Inc.; Irma Rhode; H. Roth and Son, Importers; Anne Sekely; Tiffany and Company; Nándor Veress, Gay Vienna Restaurant; Yugoslav Information Center; Yugoslav State Tourist Office.

Sources consulted in the production of this book include: *Wiener Küche* by Olga and Adolf Hess; *Gute Wiener Küche* by Albert Kofranek; *The Art of Hungarian Cooking* by Paula Pogany Bennett and Velma R. Clark; *The Art of Viennese Cooking* by Marcia Colman Morton; *The Blue Danube Cookbook* by Maria Kozslik Donovan; *Bohemian-American Cook Book* by Marie Rosický; *The Czechoslovak Cookbook* by Joza Břízová; *Gourmet's Old Vienna Cookbook* by Lillian Langseth-Christensen; *Legujabb Nagy Házi Cukraszat,* by Kugler; *Magyar Francia Szakácskönyv,* by József Dobos; *Regi Magyar,* by Báro Radvánszky; *Hungarian Cookery Book* by Károly Gundel; *Hungarian Cuisine* by Jozsef Venesz; *Vienna* by Ilsa Barea; *Viennese Cookery* by Rosl Philpot; *The Viennese Cookery Book* by Irma Rhode; *Yugoslav Cookbook* published by Lyle Stuart, Inc.

Printed in U.S.A.